I0118374

THE *REAL*
"SATANIC PANIC" STORY

THE *REAL*
"SATANIC PANIC" STORY

Documenting the reality of occult crime and ritual abuse

—An Eye-Witness Account—

GREGORY R. REID

YouthFire Publications

The Real "Satanic Panic" Story
©2025 Gregory R. Reid
Published by
YouthFire Publications
(See back of book for contact information.)

All rights reserved. No part of this book may be reproduced, stored in a retrieval system, or transmitted in any form by any means, whether electronic, mechanical, photocopying, recordings, or otherwise without prior written permission from the publisher. Excerpts and quotes may be used without permission as the US Fair Use Act allows. Scripture quotations are taken from the *King James Version*, with the exception of the verse on page 16, which is taken from NASB. Cover photo from istockphoto.com; used with permission. Cover design and interior formatting by YouthFire Publications.

Publisher's Cataloging-in-Publication Data
Reid, Gregory R. 1954-
   The real "satanic panic" story : documenting the reality of ritual abuse - an eyewitness account / Gregory R. Reid.
   304 p. cm.
   ISBN   978-0-9768045-7-4   (softbound : alk. paper)
   1. Occult Crimes. 2. Ritual Abuse. 3. Sexual Abuse. 4. Devil worship. 5. Biography
   I. Title.

Some of the names in this book have been changed for privacy sake. These are indicated with an asterisk.

For quantity discounts and other ordering questions, call 866-876-3910.

Printed in the United States of America

Contents

Endorsements..9

Why This Book?...12

A Note From the Author....................................13

Preface—Saying Goodbye 15

Introduction...17

1. Preparing for War—1986.............................23

2. The History of Satanism and the Occult..................29

3. Satanic and Occult Crimes.............................35

4. Gathering the Facts 49

5. Media, Midland, and Two Talk Shows..................55

6. The Devil Made Them Do It...........................67

7. The Youth Are the Future 81

8. Grooming the Young and Fatherless 93

9. Discerning Truth From Lies 95

10. Face to Face With the Enemy........................103

11. The Enemy Within.......................................113

12. Bigger Hands at Work..................................123

13. Pinging the Web—Who Is Pursuing Whom? 131

14. Courts, Principals, and Principalities 153

15. Some Don't Survive..163

16. A Tale of Two Towns 177

17. The *Real* "Satanic Panic" Story—Part 1 181

18. The *Real* "Satanic Panic" Story—Part 2 195

19. The *Real* "Satanic Panic" Story—Part 3 203

20. Occult Crimes and Sexual Abuse..........................223

21. The Cries of the Children.....................................239

22. Where David Died..265

23. Down in the Zero 269

24. Light in the Darkness...277

25. Now What? 281

There *Is* a Way Out 284

Appendix: A Note About Deliverance 286

Encouraging Scriptures to Ponder 291

Endnotes..292

Acknowledgements..301

To those who went before—
Officer Dale Griffis, Yvonne Peterson,
Ken Wooden, Gayland Hurst, Russ Dizdar,
Lauren Stratford, and Sue Joyner.
Your labor in the Lord is not in vain.

Nothing spoils a good story
like the arrival of an eyewitness.
Mark Twain

Endorsements

I have known Greg for almost thirty years. I have been involved in several of the "cases" and investigations that are mentioned in this book. I can attest that these are more than just stories and have affected many lives with little or no consequences for the perpetrators. Greg stayed an unwavering course through the years, not backing down from the naysayers and those critical of such investigative work.

Having been involved in several of these cases mentioned in this book, I can tell you they were not for the faint of heart and were handled professionally and, oftentimes, passionately. Not all these cases were prosecuted for various legal reasons, but some of the individuals who commit these types of acts get apprehended for legal concerns at some point.

It takes a very special individual to stand up and fight for those victims of these situations. Greg has been through years of frustration and sometimes torment over the contact that he has had researching, documenting, and investigating these claims. And, of course, dealing with those victims who are understandably shattered and untrusting of anyone.

Again, I will attest that the information in this book is the truth, and we all should give thanks to those like Greg who will stand up for the truth.

Chuck Goode, Detective (Retired)
Edmond, Oklahoma Police Department

In my experience as a former police officer, Drug Enforcement Administration Supervisory Special Agent, international speaker, author, former treasurer of the National Drug Enforcement Officers Association, founding member/speaker of the National Law Enforcement Speakers Bureau and of the National Law Enforcement Training Foundation, I have had the pleasure of working with many of the largest local, state, and federal law enforcement agencies and political leaders in this country and internationally.

Greg Reid stands out as one of the most stalwart defenders and friend of the American street cop. He has offered himself as advisor and mentor to hundreds of cops—local, state, and federal—at all hours of the day and night without hesitation. Greg knows the importance of being there for those who may not have anyone else to call. He has served for many years as the Director for Occult Research and Crime Consultants, Director of YouthFire, ordained minister, and author. His seminars in the field of occultism and sexual and ritual abuse are legendary amongst national law enforcement agencies. His courses stand out as a must for all investigative divisions and the street cop, but he offers so much more. He provides professional expert instruction in his field unequaled at any conference or university.

He ranks among the very best speakers I've encountered. He is nationally recognized and respected as a speaker, lawman's friend, and skilled in his profession. It is my pleasure to offer Greg Reid my highest recommendation.

Tim Sellers
DEA Supervisory Agent (Retired)
US Attorney General's Award for Exceptional Heroism
DEA Award for Valor

———◆———

I am honored to call Dr. Greg Reid my personal friend. I first met Dr. Reid in the late 1980s through a mutual friend. It was on that day I began to understand the dangers of occult and satanic activity in El Paso (Texas) and the surrounding areas.

Dr. Reid and his ministry partner, Tim, took me under their wings, and they held nothing back as they began to teach me and show me the unquestionable evidence of the evil that was taking place in every high school in El Paso at that time. It was happening right under our noses, but we were so ignorant of it even existing. At the same time, many others in authority refused to believe it. This included law enforcement investigators and even clergy who would not accept this evil other than a phase that kids were going through. Yet, young kids by the hundreds were being swept up into the unknown darkness of pure evil.

Dr. Reid's newest book is a phenomenal book, and it is a must-read for everyone, especially law enforcement, first responders, pastors, clergymen (including *your* pastors), school administrators and teachers, psychologists, doctors, and parents.

This is a passionate book that will turn your stomach, mess with your mind, and penetrate your heart. Several times while reviewing this book, I had to push away from my reading as tears flowed from my eyes. This book is also one in which you just don't sit back and read as you would a novel. There is so much information here.

You need to take your time and absorb what is being said and what is being taught. The issues and problems we face in the crimes of the occult and Satanism can be so bizarre, so traumatic, so twisted and evil that it's hard to even imagine that these things really happened and are still happening today.

I highly recommend this book. But you need to understand this: I don't care what you believe about the occult or Satanism. In reality, it doesn't matter. What does matter is that there are those who do believe in it; and some believe in it and take it to the point that they are willing to kill for it.

Detective Tim G. Mehl (retired)
El Paso Police Department

Why This Book?

A Note From the Publisher

"Satanic Panic": A term derived in the late 1980s and early 1990s to convince people that satanic ritual abuse and occult crimes are nothing more than a rare occurrence.

I t has been said that if someone tells a lie big enough and long enough, people will eventually come to believe it.

The dark forces that are behind occult crime and ritual abuse want everyone to believe that what they are doing is not really happening—is not real. But it *is* real, and it *is* happening.

This book is for people who want to know the facts—not the hype. It is for people who don't want fake news but want the real story.

Author Greg Reid has carefully documented what he witnessed regarding occult crimes and ritual abuse. He knows what he is talking about from his roles as an investigative reporter, a law-enforcement trainer, and a survivor of ritual abuse himself.

With a sense of urgency and responsibility to bring to light the reality behind the "Satanic Panic" urban legend, and for the sake of the victims of satanic ritual abuse, this book is for all who seek truth.

Be sober, be vigilant; because your adversary
the devil, as a roaring lion, walketh about,
seeking whom he may devour. (1 Peter 5:8)

A Note From the Author

The first casualty when war comes
is truth.—Hiram Johnson

- This book is as factually accurate as possible. Numerous witnesses were consulted to ensure an accurate telling.

- Much of the actual evidence, both documents and photos, is kept offsite and in reserve, and will only be available to credentialed and vetted individuals with specific need to know.

- This book is not written, primarily, as a "proof book." It is a history, based on my experiences and that of others, about real-world, and real-time interactions with satanic and occultic crimes, and those affected by them.

- The author will not engage in or debate with satanic or occult groups or individuals, or anyone who has persistently tried to silence dissent on these issues. It was not written for or to them, though it is sincerely hoped that this book will bring anyone who reads it into salvation through Jesus Christ.

- The author acknowledges the reality of "fake news"; therefore, when an enquirer sets about attempting to learn the truth, be aware that websites on these subjects have been carefully crafted to eliminate any alternative opinion or view, through the use of mediums such as Snopes and Wikipedia. Learn how Wikipedia *creates* "truth" based on unverified sources. Please do your own diligent research before simply accepting that the first few dozen of interconnected and cross-corroborating websites concerning these matters are the only *truth*. Research the matter thoroughly.[1]

The first to plead his case seems just,
Until another comes and examines him.
Proverbs 18:17

Preface—Saying Goodbye

It was a warm day in April 2012 as we gathered to say goodbye to our friend.

The years had passed quickly. When I first met Sue Joyner, I was just 33, full of fire and determination, energy and passion, and a tad too much arrogance. We had a purpose, and we were ready for anything. Our group was swifter than eagles and stronger than lions. I had been part of a team of fierce spiritual warriors, from coast to coast, called to battle the plague of teen devil worship and occult crime that was sweeping the country like a demonic tidal wave.

And now, here lay one of the pioneers, one of God's most tenacious and resilient spiritual warriors, Sue Ann Joyner, taken from us after a long, brave battle with cancer. It had been her second one. The first had come several years earlier when she had collapsed and had to be airlifted to a hospital to have a lemon-sized tumor excised from her brain.

For over a decade, we had all been knee-deep against the powers of darkness, and had seen it all. Sue had garnered the wrath of a number of individual devil worshippers and organized satanic criminal groups. I knew they wanted her dead. Ritual curses were their prayers.

Sue recovered from that first cancer, and now, several years later, having fought a good fight and kept the faith, she had finally laid down her sword and gone to her reward. I will always miss her infectious laugh, her dead-on Rocky and Bullwinkle "Natasha" accent when I decided to be "Boris" on some boring plane ride, her love for Jesus, her broken heart for ritually and sexually abused children, and her devotion to the truth of Jesus Christ and His Word. She feared little, and the emptiness I felt at her loss was profound on this day as I stood up to honor her in my eulogy.

It has been a long and treacherous battle. Describing war is like trying to describe chaos, confusion, fury, fire, screaming pain, and deafening noise and have it make sense to someone who has no point of reference. You can say, "There was this battle and that skirmish," which can tell someone facts but never defines the experience of battle.

Trying to make sense of it all amid the grief of losing our friend seemed nearly impossible and quite inappropriate at that moment; and yet, during the whole service, I kept feeling like I had to try to chronicle and truthfully convey this battle that we were all fighting. It was a battle others would mockingly call "village folklore" and "satanic panic." But we were there. I was there. I had to tell the truth.

Waging this war has been costly. I've lost friends, family, possessions, finances, reputation, and possible "second careers." I've been cursed, issued death threats, had my family endangered by unscrupulous media people who blew my cover, and been warned by "the other side" to stop or pay the price.

But why should I care what the *champions* of the "satanic panic" storyline think? I don't. Not anymore.

This book would have been much easier *not* to write, to just let it go, just let the other side win.

But I can't.

As I left Sue's memorial that day, I realized that she, and many others, also paid a dear price to oppose the forces of darkness and demonic assault on our kids, our children, and our churches. Only a handful of us remained. May this account honor Sue Joyner and all those who have gone before, those who still fight, and most of all, my God, before whom I attest to the truth of this testament.

Gregory R Reid

Introduction

You have been lied to. You were told that the occult/satanic activities of the 1980s and early 1990s were a hoax, false memories, *satanic panic,* village folklore, and nothing more.

You were told none of it was real.

Those who believed that lie need to be told the truth. Those who were ignorant pawns in the "disappearing act" of satanic crime need to be given the facts. And the lies need to be challenged and confronted with the unvarnished truth.

It is a phenomenon I have often encountered when a person who is unfamiliar with the awful facts behind human trafficking, sexual abuse, ritual abuse, or satanic crime is suddenly awakened to its reality and its horror. It is easier to just shut it off and forget about it because it is too painful to comprehend such evil. The enemy counts on it. I should know . . . I *do* know. Nearly every recall, every story I have written about in this book has taken me back to a truth I could not escape: You see, I am not just a reporter of events. I am a childhood survivor of many of the very events I have written about. I could not write dispassionately about the horrors of child pornography, ritual child abuse and occult bondage because I had been there. Many of the horrific stories of the children I have written about are *my* stories as well. How could I possibly keep from telling the truth?

Since 1986, I have been in the field, uncovering dark occult and trafficking circles, teaching people how to protect their children and raise teens in the Word of God as an antidote to such evils. In this book, I testify and document my nearly ten years (from the 1980s) on the frontlines against occult crimes, the seduction of youth into the occult, and crimes against children. I carried out that work diligently as a youth minister committed to truth, a criminal justice trainer armed with facts, and a private investigator with the blood and mud of actual street work on my boots and on my resume.

I knew, even then, the extreme importance of accuracy, documentation, and details, knowing that if I did not document every detail I could, some things would risk fading. I also knew that people would try to make it all go away and erase the history of what we did. And so they have.

I had no idea what was coming nor how much those details would matter. I am thankful that I kept all the notes, the documents, and the specifics in precise detail and that I have been blessed with a file cabinet brain that recalls it all. Having six gigabytes of information and case files also helped in the writing of this book. I have been troubled, though, to find a great deal of what was once available on various websites—things I had downloaded and printed—has been scrubbed from the Internet. I'm thankful I kept the hard copies.

Today, whenever I bring up ritual abuse and satanic crimes, most of the reactions are the same: "That was proven to be false memories." "It was all a bunch of satanic panic." "Wasn't the McMartin case fake?"[1] "Didn't the FBI prove there was no satanic crime?" And I can only stand back in astonishment and disbelief at these unchallenged and almost always untrue assertions.

Someone or many someones, through unwitting and undoubtedly witting agents, managed to undo in a very short few years most of the work it had taken ten years for us to accomplish. They had rewritten the history of it all and closed the discussion—end of story. And so, it was relegated to the dustbin of history, buried under false narratives, factually flawed opinions, and in some cases, deliberately deceptive information.

But we were there. *I* was there. We witnessed these events. It wasn't village folklore. For over ten years, we fought against some of the most vicious spiritual and criminal phenomena I've seen in my lifetime—I and the men and women who bravely responded to the call to action to engage in this dangerous work, some who are no longer here to tell their own stories. I belong to a small handful who remain in the fight.

I had some hesitancy about republishing this book* and making it available to a larger audience. I decided to take this challenge for four reasons.

One, history *is* history, and we must challenge revisionists who write their own narrative, ignore the facts, and attack any contrary perspective. The *real* history needs telling. And, despite the time that has passed, the spiritual realities contained in these stories remain vital.

Two, these occult manifestations in our world are cyclical. If I've learned one thing in this work, it is that the essentials of the criminal black magick world do not change—the thirst for power, the lawlessness, the bloodlust, and the need to defile innocence. It is the public exposure alone that cycles from prominence to invisibility—that, and the dying of old leaders and the raising up of others—"Uno avulso non deficit alter"—when one is torn away, another succeeds. It is their law. It is their creed. Occult obsession and occult crimes are cyclical.

Three, today in this twenty-first century, occult involvement among western youth is at an all-time high, and there are few safeguards. There are precious few warnings being raised. This book is meant to warn and prepare believers to deal with the new deluge of occultism which, without a doubt, will be hunting for our children and grandchildren.

Four, occultic crimes and the injury of children continue unabated. You may not hear about it. It may not be a talk-show subject. But it's happening. Not long ago, I read of a self-proclaimed Pagan "friar" who opened a school for autistic children and used it to videotape the act of sexually assaulting these defenseless innocents.[2] At the same time, cult "apologists" continue to beat the "satanic panic" drum.

In one case, a high-profile law enforcement agent was taken out of retirement to insinuate himself into a clearly satanic abuse case, one in which the perpetrators admitted to both molesting kids and involving them in satanic rituals. He took the entire case out of the hands of local authorities and ordered the local police working on the case to keep their

---

* The first edition came out in 1997 in a workbook format for classes I was teaching.

mouths shut about anything having to do with the occult related to the case.[3] I just can't let that kind of thing go unchallenged.

After a great deal of agonizing, I decided to update and republish this book as a history, as a preventative, and as a warning. If I am right, I believe we are on the verge of another ugly wave of occult crime and kids in crisis because of unrestrained occult tampering and experimentation.

Those who run the real world of the "dark side," who are resting easy in the mistaken belief that they have caused all the attention on their evil practices to go away, continue to commit crimes against the innocent. As they did in the 1980s, they will likely get arrogant and sloppy again. And when they do, I pray we will be ready for it—for the sake of the victims and the innocent. We've learned from their strategies and our mistakes, and this time, we will not let the truth be silenced.

The original edition of this book (the notebook) was written at the tail end of ten years of our fight against the powers of darkness as they manifested through a modern revival of devil worship and the occult. Even then, the naysayers were lining up to assure everyone there was no occult/devil worship problem in our country. I wrote the truth. I told our side.

Unfortunately, the loud and shrill unending voices of "it's not real" drowned out our attempts of breaking through the bubble of "do not disturb" and allowed those who became "the experts" to be the predominant, highly biased, and *factually* tainted voice of the history in question to be the only "documented" history of this war.

It troubles me because that gap and absence of a louder voice have relegated what was originally written as current fact to—well, history. Devil worship? Ritual child abuse? Human sacrifice? Seriously? That's so thirty years ago; who cares?

Moloch and Baal worship, which required the ritual murder of the firstborn son, became druidism,* which sacrificed children, then black masses in Europe that also slaughtered innocents have mutated into more recent cults, like Santa Muerte-based cartels that revel in decapitation and torture.

---

*A pagan belief system that originated with the ancient Celts in Europe. Druids were the ruling priests.

The victims need to know there are those of us who know they are trapped underground in a world of torture and horror that the world says does not exist.

Those who are and were part of this written history deserve a memorial—something that says, "I was there. This did happen. My work did matter."

I pray that I have honored truth, history, memory, and above all, the God whom I serve in this most crucial account of things as they were and are.

I know this will be a difficult book to read, especially for who are highly sensitive or not familiar with some of the raw evil out there. I ask you to read it prayerfully; and if you are a survivor, please be warned that triggering* is very possible.

As you read this book, may God open your eyes and wake you up to the reality of occult evil—for the sake of our future and the sake of the children.

---

*__Warning: Trigger Alert__—Some of the information in this book is very graphic and disturbing. Please read it with prayer. If you are a survivor, please be cautious in reading it without support. __What is triggering?__ A phrase GenZ has adapted to describe any small offense they might take to someone's opinion is in reality a real phenomenon in the age when survivors of ritual abuse began to come to terms with the awful events and experiences of their childhoods. A smell, a sound, a person, an action, a movie, a song, or other seemingly unconnected things would cause a survivor to be "triggered" and suddenly experience PTSD-like flashbacks and vivid memories of abusive or traumatic childhood events.

I believe Satan to exist for two reasons:
First, the Bible says so; and second,
I've done business with him.

D. L. Moody

Preparing for War—1986

How did it begin? It started on a train.

I was on the Starlight Coastal Express, heading down the California Coast after speaking at my home church that week. I was exhausted, so I went into the lounge car with the big comfortable seats and breathtaking view of the Pacific Ocean, and soon I was sleeping soundly to the clickety-clack of the train and the occasional whistle.

My sleep was disrupted by the entrance of five neatly dressed college-age kids with backpacks. I kept my eyes closed and eavesdropped. (It's a private investigator thing.)

What I overheard stunned me. "Remember when Satan spoke to us out of the fire?" one young man excitedly whispered.

"Yeah!" another exclaimed. "He said he'd own three cities by the end of the year!" On they went, talking about rituals and conjuring demons and instructions from Hell. In whispered words, they went on and on about worshipping Satan and what they were going to do next.

Later I couldn't stop thinking about it. To look at them, they were every parent's dream of perfect college-age kids. But beneath the clean-cut exteriors, they were die-hard devil worshippers.

Raised in Southern California, I understood the reality of the devil and the occult quite well as we were surrounded by cults and their victims and activities. In fact, one of my childhood school friends turned to devil worship and was convicted of a murder when he was a teenager.[1] And here were some more kids who willingly worshipped the devil. This encounter was my first step and wake-up call to prepare me for a coming tsunami of occultism about to strike our country.

I read a book a few months later called *Jay's Journal* by Beatrice Mathews Sparks. It was the diary of a young teen who got into trouble and ended up being recruited into the occult, then white magick, and eventually hard-core devil worship. From a religious home, Jay found himself in a short period of time participating in adult rituals, cattle mutilations, and blood drinking. According to the book, he and his two best friends literally gave their souls to Satan in an adult ritual in exchange for favors, which all three got in a very short time. Within weeks of these favors being granted, both of Jay's friends were violently killed in freak accidents. Jay, increasingly frightened and tormented by demons, could find no way out, wrote a suicide note, took a gun, and ended his life.

A great deal has been posted online to try to discredit this book and its author, Beatrice Mathews Sparks. For us, we had already begun to amass a great deal of information as to the where, who, what, and how of current occult and devil worship activities, and the book confirmed in stark detail what we had begun to uncover.

The book had a powerful impact on me personally. Jay was a boy whose parents knew nothing about what he had been involved in until they found his diary after he killed himself. During the 1980s, his grave was visited by teen devil worshippers who considered it a shrine.

I understood Jay's agony, as my own occult practices had nearly led to my own end at fourteen.[2] Because I got out, I felt I had a mandate to do everything I could to prevent kids from following Jay's tragic path. But the time wasn't yet. It was 1986, and it would be a full year before I began to pursue this calling. I was not ready yet.

In my thinking, I would simply be telling kids about the dangers of the occult. I could never have conceived how much bigger this mission would be. If I had known, I'm not sure I would have felt fit for the task. But God knows us better than we know ourselves, and all the years of prayer, studying Scripture, and understanding spiritual warfare laid a foundation that enabled me to stand through all the upcoming storms we were about to face.

In 1986, I met a lady in El Paso, Texas. Sue Joyner was an ordinary housewife who felt called to raise up an organization called the Watch Network: Watchman's Alert to Cultic Harassment (WATCH), whose original purpose was to expose the occult and bring help and healing to the victims. We met as a result of my searching for answers to my own occult past and seeking a way to minister to those in the occult. I ended up moving to El Paso with the intent of joining Sue's crew and helping with their work.

At the time of my move, I also met a missionary's son, Tim Gamwell, who was working with kids who were involved in the occult, drugs, and other rough lifestyles who told him they wanted to hear more about the God Tim kept telling them about. Tim invited me to come

> I felt I had a mandate to do everything I could to prevent kids from following Jay's tragic path.

to that first meeting that about five kids showed up for. They asked a lot of questions. We did our best to answer them. Then we sang a couple of simple Christian songs, "Jesus Loves Me" and "As the Deer."

One of the kids asked, "Can we meet again?" And we did. We had fifteen the second week, thirty the third, and by the end of the month we were pushing forty—lost kids, kids from terrible and painful backgrounds and broken homes, kids in the occult, Satanism, witchcraft, drugs, gangs, and some who just weren't getting taught the Bible. That simple Bible study began an outreach we called JOEL, (Jesus Our Eternal Lord). Originally, the kids wanted to call themselves "The Misfits" which was vetoed, wanting them to take on a new identity in Jesus. So, JOEL it was.

In time, JOEL touched hundreds of kids, and we were thrust into Bible studies, outings, concerts, and explosive spiritual conflicts and victories. It would be a sometimes difficult but glorious ministry outreach. We learned quickly that not many people wanted to deal with broken, messy kids, especially kids who had been involved with Satanism, witchcraft, and the occult. But God was bringing them in droves.

Unless you were there during that period of time, it is difficult to grasp how major this problem of teen devil worship was, causing one law enforcement official from Florida to call teen occultism "an epidemic." And during that time, he was right.

Once or twice a month, I would help Sue and the others at WATCH pack up the media equipment, books, and things, then head to the church or civic group where we were presenting. I'd help set up the difficult but necessary multimedia presentation on the occult and devil worship Sue had put together. After the presentation, I helped field questions. I listened. I learned. I researched. I began to get ready for a battle I did not know was coming. For the next year, we spoke in churches, youth groups, and public schools. There were always atheist teachers or teachers dabbling in the occult that would threaten us and try to get us kicked out. But by then, many of the schools knew they had a growing problem with teen occultism and devil worship. They often stuck their necks out for us to be there. We found out that many kids were hungry for the truth. Some of them ended up coming to our Bible study.

Unexpectedly, we began to receive requests to speak to emergency workers, police officers, and Army medical personnel who had already begun to witness occult-influenced crimes and medical emergencies. In every setting, we were able to equip them with what we knew. And in every meeting, we heard from other professionals who had had very real, first-hand involvement with cases of satanic cults and individuals involving sexual assaults, arsons, suicides, animal mutilations, and even murders.

1987 was the year I moved to El Paso, the same year that occult crimes first began to be heavily reported in the media, even though they had been taking place for years—sometimes unreported, sometimes unrecognized for what they were. It was the year that "occult metal" became a phenomenon that shocked parents and church people alike, with shock rockers like Motley Crue, soon followed by groups and rock singers like AC/DC, Slayer, and Venom. It was the year, on Halloween, that our local news station aired interviews with older teen devil-worship recruiters who said things like, "If I met Jesus,

I'd cut his throat," and "Your kids are our business. And right now, business is good."[3] I knew we had a long and difficult fight ahead of us for the youth. These teen recruiters meant business. We couldn't walk into this battle unarmored or unprepared for contending with the powers of darkness. We did so unafraid because we knew that Jesus had authority over the power of the enemy—but also with sobriety, knowing that none of this was a game or simple, and kids' lives were literally at stake.

In early 1988, Sue felt the need to begin to pull back from some of the travel to speak for the WATCH work and concentrate more on helping victims. She handed me a letter from a Texas Adult Probation criminal justice agency asking for a speaker and asked me if I would answer them. I did. The West Texas Probation Conference in Alpine, Texas in May 1988 was the launching pad that would take me across the country for the next several years to train law enforcement, probation officers, therapists, and hundreds of others on occult crimes. It was also where I met my counterpart from the probation world, Adult Probation Chief Ben Kennedy, who also had firsthand knowledge of these crimes and came to be a valued friend in the years ahead.

In many ways, this work was not something I was anxious to do. It was dangerous. It was exhausting; and it was emotionally painful and spiritually draining work. But it was necessary, and there was a very real sense that I had been prepared over a lifetime for this.

It is not possible to present the years that followed in a cohesive timeline because, for all of us, it was a 24-hour-a-day, seven-days-a-week task. There was little time to rest, little time for meals, and very little time to keep track of the avalanche of cases we worked on. So, I have attempted, in the chapters to follow, to present these years by the significant, defining issues and people we encountered. Writing it all down has been difficult and at the same time, a relief: difficult because the truth about what we knew and what happened has been systematically erased as untrue; a relief, because I witnessed these things firsthand, and I can tell the truth so people will know what really happened. The "satanic panic" narrative was a lie.

I know. I was there.

Throughout the centuries, Christians generally thought
they were living in a time when Christ's return was
imminent based on natural disasters, wars, upheaval,
and prominent military leaders (e.g., Napoleon).
But never in the history of humanity has occultism
and mysticism been unleashed as it has now.[1]

Ray Yungen

2

The History of Satanism
and the Occult

A little history here might help us understand how modern "Satanism"—at least the sanitized, allegedly non-criminal kind that is put forth as Satanism today—became "normalized." It will also help prepare you for the difficult chapters to follow and help you to see that the practice of sacrifices and child abuse in the name of Satan, the devil, demons, or other gods has not only been going on since the foundation of the world but continues to this day. It is a mistake to believe it does not. And how can we pray for the victims of these horrific crimes if we don't even dare to face the reality of their plight?

A simple reading of Scriptures or of history will show that ancient pagan nations were rife with human sacrifices, especially infant sacrifices, to their gods. Baal, Asherah, Moloch, Chemosh, and Tanit, fertility gods and goddesses required the firstborn male child to be sacrificed. It is nothing new.

Since the sixteenth century, devil worshippers, hiding under the guise of Catholic churches, created "black masses," which were performed at night by renegade Catholic priests who had turned to the Dark Side. Each element of the Mass was perverted and used to mock Jesus. Jesus was the lamb of God, so they chose the goat as their representation of Satan—the "scapegoat," so to speak. I'll leave out for now the more extreme and foul elements of their "religion," which later came to be called Satanism.

Though the black masses continued for years, and according to some experts such as Catholic priest and author Malachi Martin, they are still being practiced, the concept of devil worship itself began to mutate and incorporate other occult and black magick practices, including Egyptian rituals, African rituals, Italian Strega witchcraft, Rosicrucianism, and many others. In the last century, it became a smorgasbord of occult practices, generally becoming a confusing mess and difficult to comb through in order to ascertain which practices were "constitutionally protected" and which were criminally dangerous. In effect, it is not illegal to worship whatever deity you want. It is criminal to break the law in the name of whatever deity you worship. We found some occult groups to be benign and others that spawned and indeed encouraged criminal activity.

In 1875, a Russian woman named Helena Petrovna Blavatsky founded the Theosophical Society. The society's logo was a mix of occult symbols, including the swastika (a widely used symbol in Hinduism as well as some Native American tribes and which Hitler adapted as "the black sun"), an Egyptian Ankh symbol for reincarnation, a Hindu symbol, and the Ouroboros symbol of a snake consuming itself. The Ouroboros symbol is an ancient occult symbol that has been used by gnostics, Kundalini Hindus, and alchemists and is a present-day favorite of modern Luciferians.

Blavatsky was an occult trance-channeler who spent a great deal of time in India and Tibet. She claimed to channel the "ascended Master" Djwal Kuhl from whom she claimed she learned the "root race theory." (According to Theosophy, ascended masters are enlightened beings who, in past incarnations, were ordinary humans but who have undergone a series of spiritual transformations called initiations.) The root race theory is the belief that all of mankind came from root races—the Bhuta, the Polar Race, Hyperborean, Lemurian, Atlantean, and most chillingly, Aryan. You read that right. The Aryan Root Race theory was the idea upon which Hitler began to build his mixture of Nordic god worship, membership in the occult Thule society[2] and other abominable occult beliefs and practices that led to the slaughter of millions of Jews. (Sidenote: For those who believe that Hitler claimed to be a Christian, he did not. From the outset, he talked about "the almighty" and "divine destiny" but was determined to root out and destroy Christianity and Judaism.)

Blavatsky's Theosophy was and is a Luciferian religion, the idea that Lucifer was the real god of light and enlightenment. Blavatsky's movement was passed on to Alice Bailey, who carried on the teachings of Theosophy and Luciferianism through the publication *Lucifer's Trust*, which still exists as *Lucis Trust*.[3] Bailey wrote this:

> The Christian church in its many branches can serve as a St. John the Baptist, as a voice crying in the wilderness, and as a nucleus through which world illumination may be accomplished.[4]

Bailey was well aware of the need to work from *within* the church to teach and preach Luciferian doctrine to prepare people for the "new age." And many of today's "progressive" churches have, indeed, embraced Bailey's New Age religion. In fact, the move within Progressive Christianity has taken a page straight out of satanic philosophy. The call to "deconstruct and rebuild" the Christian faith is simply a rewording of the two words written on the arms of the transsexual Baphomet or Goat of Mendes promoted by the Luciferian Temple: "Solve" and "Coagula"—to dissolve and reconstruct. (In 2020, Harry Potter author JK Rowling had these words tattooed on her arm.[5]) Alice Bailey and her teachings are foundational to the coming one-world religion. Chillingly, Blavatsky and Bailey preached two final root races—the present, which is supposed to be spiritually evolved and made up of many nations, and the final spiritual state in which "great adepts and initiated aesthetics will once more produce Mind-born immaculate sons."[6] A perfect, flawless race. This sounds hauntingly reminiscent of Hitler's "perfect Aryan race" aspirations.

In the 1940s, notorious occult practitioner Aleister Crowley gained an international reputation as a scandalous, perverted monster who openly pursued demons in rituals and created a massive magical system. Born into a wealthy fundamentalist Plymouth Brethren household, he rejected the Christian faith and began a lifelong pursuit of the demonic and occultic. He wrote voluminously, traveled to Cairo, Egypt to do rituals to call up demonic powers, and had the suspicion of murder hanging over him because of a death at his castle in Cefalu, Italy, at the infamous Thelema Abbey. He eventually died penniless of chronic bronchitis, but not before he passed on his dark knowledge to his followers, including Jack Parsons, a scientist in Pasadena, California.

Jack Parsons developed the liquid rocket fuel on which the NASA program was built. He was initiated as the High Priest of the Pasadena Agape Lodge of the OTO. (Ordo Templi Orientis, also called Astrum Argentum or A.A. aka Silver Star, a magical organization that Crowley founded after leaving—or being kicked out of—the Order of the Golden Dawn.)[7] Before Parsons was initiated High Priest by the Agape Lodge founder Wilford Talbot Smith, a grand opening of the Agape Lodge was held in 1935, which was allegedly attended by a Pasadena bank president, the Chief of Police, and featured a poem read by famous actor John Carradine. Parsons died in an explosion in 1952 in what some thought was a black magick experiment gone wrong. But before this occurred, he recruited an assistant High Priest, L. Ron Hubbard, who joined the lodge, had an affair with Parson's girlfriend, allegedly made off with $10,000, and absconded to Florida. While there, Hubbard bought a boat and allegedly told friends he was going to start his own religion and become wealthy, which he apparently did after writing the book *Dianetics* and founding Scientology shortly after that.[8]

Parsons and Hubbard were not the only ones who fell under Crowley's influence; The Beatles included Crowley's picture on *Sergeant Pepper's Lonely Hearts Club Band* album as one of their heroes.

In the sixties, a former circus lion tamer and police photographer Tony LaVey (later known as Anton Szandor LaVey) decided to turn his disdain for the Christian church into the Church of Satan, which he founded on the occult holiday of Walpurgisnacht,[9] April 30th, 1966. He went on to publish *The Satanic Bible* in 1969. *The Satanic Bible* is a blasphemous mockery of Christianity and Christians. Even today, it remains a top seller on Amazon. LaVey also kept intact the classic black magick ritual of reversal of everything, including reciting the Lord's prayer backward. In fact, Crowley taught that writing backward and playing music backward were all part of black magick practices. This partly explains the "backward masking" on records such as Led Zeppelin's song "Stairway to Heaven." And yes, members of that band were involved in the occult, particularly Jimmy Page, who went on to run an occult bookstore in Great Britain and for a while owned Crowley's Boleskine House on the banks of Loch Ness in Scotland, though he only apparently resided there for two weeks. Incidentally, Page had record producer Terry Manning find a way to inscribe words into the lip of their album *Led Zeppelin,*[10] which showed his commitment to Crowley and the dark arts—one side saying, "Do what thou wilt" (the law of the Satanist) and "So mote be it" which was actually a misworded version of the phrase "so mote it be," the satanic, pagan and masonic words for "Amen." As far as I know, this was the first time this had been done on a vinyl record.

LaVey and his San Francisco-based Church of Satan went on to become notorious, even infamous. For a while, it became a Hollywood hipsters club that boasted members like Sammy Davis Jr., Jayne Mansfield, and later, shock rocker Marilyn Manson and King Diamond. Even more sinister, one of the nude dancers for LaVey's San Francisco live ritual shows was Susan Atkins, who went on to become one of the most vicious of the Manson murderers.

The public "Satanists" since LaVey have worked hard to present themselves as law-abiding, "moral" Satanists who simply believe in rebellion and doing whatever they want. "Do what thou wilt shall be the whole of the law" was their law, a "law" that LaVey borrowed from Aleister Crowley for his own "new" religion. They consider themselves the elite and don't care about the poor, the infirm, the handicapped: it is not their business—let evolution eliminate them. As mentioned in one quote from Crowleyan writings that LaVey built his house on, "We have nothing to do with the outcast and the unfit: let them die in their misery. For they feel not. Compassion is the vice of kings: stamp down the wretched and the weak; this is the law of the strong . . ."[11] This is why, during the rash of satanic crimes of the 1980s, they distanced themselves with a simple, *They're not members of our church. We're not responsible for crazy sick kids who probably came from Christian homes.* And just like that, they disavowed any responsibility for the highly incendiary material LaVey produced. In addition, that is when they magically claimed all rights to the term "Satanist" as if they invented it somehow in the 1970s. But human-sacrificing devil worshippers have been around long before LaVey. In fact, there were several fringe groups of Satan worshippers operating at the same time as LaVey's glory days, some of which we were tracking for involvement in gun running, drug dealing, child pornography making and distribution, and even human sacrifice. So, they don't get to claim first rights to that name.

I offer this all too brief history of modern devil worshipping, Satanist, and Luciferian religions so you can understand how a great deal of it came to be part of our culture and even somewhat legitimized.

And frankly, they don't get a seat at this table. Why? Because I actually believe most of them don't commit crimes and don't kill people. So, their protests that, "Hey, we don't do that" will receive a tiny "good for you" from me while I go about addressing those who do and have committed unspeakable crimes in the name of Satan or Lucifer or the Devil. So now that I have given them their "due," we will proceed with the non-sanitized, not politically correct, nor historically altered history of modern criminal devil worship and occultic crimes as we witnessed them, as they really happened. Take a deep breath. The following is going to be a difficult, nauseating, horrific, but critically important look at the satanic crimes they told you did not and do not happen.

3

Satanic and Occult Crimes— The Undeniable Events

gain, the modern narrative is that there is no such thing as satanic ritual crime or ritual child abuse and never has been. Are you willing to look at the truth, even if it appalls you and breaks your heart?

The ritual murder of American college student Mark Kilroy and over twenty other victims in Matamoros, Mexico, on March 14th, 1989, was a brutal and undeniable case of ritual slaughter.[1] The murderer, Adolpho de Jesus Constanzo, was raised as a *brujo* (male witch) practicing the Santeria religion of Central and South America, which originated in Africa known as "Palo Mayombe." He was a professional practitioner of the dark arts of that religion—Brujeria. He was known as El Padrino and The Witch Doctor. Among other things, rituals included placing animal and human body parts in a "nganga" or cauldron to get ritual power. Spines and brains were often removed from Constanzo's victims for ritual purposes.

I was shocked at how easily and quickly many "professionals" downplayed these horrific murders because they happened in Mexico—the thinking being, *what's that got to do with us? We're in America.*

Constanzo's partner in crime, his *bruja* or female witch, Sara Aldrete, was an honor student at Texas Southmost College, which

Mark Kilroy

puts to rest the idea that it was just "a Mexico problem" or that only crazy people do these things.

Constanzo was very well known and respected amongst Mexico's money-eyed elite socialites and was frequently hired by Federales, politicians, and media stars to do magick rituals. He was no stranger to wealth and no small player. Constanzo's slaughterhouse was probably just the tip of the iceberg. You can, in fact, cover up nearly anything in Mexico.

Sara Aldrete was well thought of by both professors and fellow students before her dark alliance with Constanzo led to her downfall. She has been imprisoned in Mexico since 1989 for her role in several murders, serving a 62-year sentence.

Some people, including the then Texas Attorney General Jim Mattox, tried to minimize this crime's threat to the USA because it was thirty miles over the border. We should not have been so smug. It happened here, too.

In the following case regarding a young woman named Carmen, when I first wrote about it, I included horrific details. Here, I have decided to leave out most of those details out of respect for the family and the faint-hearted. I will only say that this murder was one of the most vicious, satanic crimes you could imagine, and the victim suffered through most of it before she died.* The crime scene images are something I can never erase from my mind, and they are

---

*All my original information on this case was given to the WATCH network and other professionals in attendance at a training class at Beaumont Army Medical Center in El Paso, TX, in 1988, given by FBI Special Agent Van McDonald. Some of the details of this case may be debated by those who are recently attempting to discover if the perpetrator(s) of the following crimes were as specified here, but these were the facts as conveyed to us at the time, and I believe them to be accurate.

an ever-present reminder of the reality of satanic crime and why the idea that these things aren't real is demonstrably false.

Carmen Croan was kidnapped from a Country Western bar in Odessa, Texas in August of 1981. She was found sexually assaulted and murdered in an oilfield outside of town.[2]

Time passed. One man was arrested—Murray Galloway—in the Midland-Odessa area following a four-month investigation, and he was indicted for Carmen's murder.

They brought in Galloway's travel-ing companion, Lonnie Lee Crago, for questioning. Crago confessed to being present when the older man kidnapped and murdered 18-year-old Carmen. His partner, he said, was a devil wor-shipper. The murder was done so he could "get his bones" (elevating his High Priest status), and he had to do seven such murders to attain the rank he sought. (These groups operate very much like the mob, in which you have to commit murder to "get your bones" or become a "made man"—a person with

Carmen Croan

power and influence that is to be feared. In retrospect, it makes me wonder who was over him.)

"I told them, Eli!," Crago told Galloway when they brought them back together to try and sort this out. The investigators were confused. Galloway's name was not Eli.

"You shut your mouth and don't say another word!" Galloway shouted. And Crago obeyed. What the investigators didn't know is that "Eli" was probably a coven name, and the younger man was as good as dead now. He broke the oath—a pact each member must sign in blood, swearing them to secrecy on pain of death.

Crago was released and ordered to appear for further questioning. Shortly thereafter, Crago walked into an oilfield, laid his head under a pump jack, and extinguished his own life. Before "they" did.

"Eli" (Galloway) was released and shipped back to New Mexico, without being charged because of lack of evidence and the death of their only witness, where he would face charges there on unrelated crimes. But according to the FBI profiler, the person in charge of the disposition of the case ordered, "Just get him out of town on any charge you can. I'm not dealing with this Satanism crap."

"Eli" eventually was freed. And there were several similar murders in Texas during that time, all fitting "Eli's" profile and method of slaughter.

As far as we know, "Eli" continued "getting his bones" unchallenged.

(Update: "Eli" ran a small jewelry store in Clovis, New Mexico, which had a vast collection of occult/turquoise jewelry. He has since passed away.)

Warren, Michigan: In another case, a young teen girl was dismembered, decapitated, scalped, and her head left in a freezer. All done "for Satan."

Houston, Texas: In still another case, a sixteen-year-old boy was found in a hotel—a bullet in his brain by his own hand. He was still holding a tetragrammaton occult medallion in his hand, perhaps thinking it would protect him. He was deeply involved in fantasy role-playing games that turned him to darkness and addiction to drugs—he saw no other way out. (Again, having seen the horrific crime scene photos, it is impossible to accept the lie that these things didn't happen.)

A nurse at El Paso's Beaumont Army Medical Center talked to us after a class we taught for physicians. "Last year [about 1986]," she told us, "I worked at another hospital here. I was walking to work at 5 a.m., and I saw an ambulance and police cars so I went to assist. There was a woman who had been decapitated, and her body was surrounded by black candles. Why didn't it come out in the papers?" Why, indeed? For one thing—and this speaks to the skeptics' question, "Where is the evidence?"—the police are often very careful not to release details of this kind of crime to avoid public panic as well as revealing details that might tip off the perpetrator. Believe me, there were many cases of ritual murder nationwide that the public never heard about. And there are many, many more that are buried in police files that remained "unsolved" and were never classified as ritual murders simply because the investigators did not know what the earmarks of ritual murder were.

Example—I was approached by the police chief of a small town in the Rio Grande Valley area of Texas during a law enforcement event on occult youth intervention in Laredo, Texas, in October 2003. They had been keeping an eye on a man who moved a trailer to the outside of town, claimed to be a member of a well-known satanic group, and had prostitutes coming in and out of his trailer all the time.

He had completely disappeared the day they got the call that a woman's bloodless and dissected corpse had been found on a street corner, much like the Black Dahlia murder in Los Angeles in 1947.[3] As of that time, they had not been able to locate their chief suspect or make any arrests for the murder.

Unfortunately, because of the massive effort from the occult world, compromised intelligence agency officials, and others, training classes on occult-related crimes were almost completely shut down out of fear of discriminating against someone's religion. By 1992, we had trained most of the police and probation departments in Texas. But after several years of deliberate disinformation, noise-making, and direct attacks on those who were equipped to do such training, we found a new generation of law enforcement that were not trained and often were reluctant to ask too many questions when they encountered occult crimes. It seemed as though we were right back where we started.

El Paso and its twin border city Juarez are deeply steeped in the occult. El Paso had a clinic for years that was literally named after the devil. (I always asked people who had gone there why they felt comfortable going to a medical center named after the devil. They said that nice people worked there.) One terrified man relayed his experience of going in for a small surgery that required anesthesia. The anesthesia wore off too soon. He woke up to see someone in a robe with a candle chanting over him. He bolted from the building and left the city, fearing for his life.[4] One police officer was called to a possible break-in at the house of the doctor who owned the clinic.

No one was home, but the bottom door to the basement was open. The officer went in and saw a scene right out of a House of Horrors movie. The entire floor was painted with a black and red pentagram, with a goat head hanging from the wall. (The goat is the satanic symbol for Satan.)

> The utter lack of discernment in most churches is why devil worshippers were able to infiltrate so many churches during that era without getting caught.

The doctor and his family attended a local Presbyterian church their whole lives and were well-respected members. After their deaths, their son revealed that his parents were Satanists. It was their *real* family religion. (Note: There was no evidence they were involved in any criminal activity.)

This made me wonder, where in the world was the discernment of anyone in that church? The scary answer was there were only two possible answers: either they had no idea that these "outstanding" church people worshipped the devil during the week, which means they had no discernment at all, or worse, they did know. I tend to think that the utter lack of discernment in most churches is why devil worshippers were able to infiltrate so many churches during that era without getting caught. Unnervingly, the level of discernment has not improved over the subsequent decades. In fact, it is weaker than it has ever been. I fear that we were so busy building large churches that we failed to teach people the necessity of true discernment. "But strong meat belongeth to them that are of full age, even those who by reason of use have their senses exercised to discern both good and evil" (Hebrews 5:14). Our discernment muscles have atrophied and have allowed the enemy to slip through our gates virtually undetected.

In the end, all anyone had to do to avoid any scrutiny was to claim that their religion was protected by the Constitution, which it was. It was a brilliant smokescreen that some criminal elements used to cover so many other things. The fear of being sued for persecuting people for exercising their "freedom of religion" kept many people from investigating at all, even when there was legitimate cause for concern.

That is why our classes were so crucial. We were able to move past the political correctness, the superstitions, and the rumors and say, "Here are the facts. Here is how you need to investigate. Here is what you can expect." We rarely had anyone who went through our eight-hour training who left saying, "This is bunk." More often, we got calls from those who, having been trained in what to look for, asked us for assistance.

A major ritual abuse* case in El Paso in one of our daycares contributed to our city being exposed as the occult center of the Southwest. For years, we had a huge occult bookstore owned by the chief of police that was the go-to place for all things occultic, from Wicca to Santeria to Luciferian and everything in between. They had everything from Halloween costumes to robes for satanic rituals for all occasions and ritual holidays which require robes in several colors, from red to black to purple to white. There was the public part of the store and then the hidden part where you could get more sinister things if you knew the code words or had the right connections. Talk about hiding in plain sight!

Stores like this were not uncommon. In fact, one chain occult store in our city sold "spice" (a kind of synthetic marijuana) to teens near high schools but also had more hidden occult items, such as a rare Luciferian Grimoire from England that cost over $750. (A *grimoire* is a book where practitioners wrote their spells, curses, and so on. Many grimoires had the signatures of members written in blood.)

Acting on a tip we had gotten, police investigated these stores and found out they were, indeed, selling something we had heard from others was a big part of satanic rituals—candles made from baby fat. I know that is horrible and inhuman, and it was hard for us to find

---

* Ritual abuse is the systematic sexual abuse of children using occult or religious symbols and rituals to terrify and silence their victims through trauma and fear.

or verify—until they found these being sold at our local chain occult store, available only if you knew who and how to ask.

Was it legal? Unfortunately, yes. Can you believe that? You could get baby fat from medical clinics, universities, and abortion clinics. But in the end, all the officials could do was turn them into the FDA for health violations.

Hard to believe? As of this writing, authorities broke up a body-part selling scheme that was working with people within a major university, bought by a freak shop for things like using a human face for a mask. Sold over PayPal.[5]

It was common knowledge, even in the 1980s, that you could purchase a portable crematorium for a few thousand dollars through occult stores in the big cities.

"Where's the evidence?" the deniers have said for years.

Our fair city of El Paso was built according to Masonic laylines. There are five masonic-built churches. The center of the town is called "Five Points," and a five-pointed star lights up our mountain year-round. The first Masonic lodge was dedicated by American Masonic leader Albert Pike, and it is my understanding that the local lodge still has Pike's "throne." The Masonic order is thoroughly rooted in old occult practices, and in our town, they are the real power in the city.

For several years, our sister city Juarez was host to the annual "Satanas" conference, which had participants from nearly every occult practice around the world. Back then, such events were highly hidden. Today, they are blatant conferences that get national news.

Things here, as in many border towns, are rarely investigated; the occult criminal underbelly is rarely exposed, though it is thoroughly entrenched on both sides of the border. Remember, *occult* means "hidden." The more "occult" it is, the more hidden—and the better the practitioners get at hiding it.

Not Just Local

My second out-of-town assignment was at a National Homicide Convention in Edmond, Oklahoma, in 1988. An investigator had heard of me and called to see if I'd do a workshop. He admitted they were skeptical. "Our guys aren't believers in this stuff. Do you wanna try to make them believers?" I agreed to try. My dad was a cop. I knew skepticism was part of the law enforcement job so my job was going to be a bit of a challenge. But Detective Chuck Goode was willing to take a chance on me. I think I helped make believers out of some of them. Detective Goode already knew from his own cases that occult crimes were a real thing.

A few officers in my class weren't so easily convinced. The first night, when everyone played poker till 3 a.m., one rather lubricated detective swore and ranted that he wouldn't allow any demons in his house—he'd just take his gun and shoot them! After about twenty minutes of trying to calmly explain the improbability of that being an effective strategy against demons, I realized many cops had a hard time accepting that this was a crime issue, not a superstitious or religious one.

Murder in Oklahoma

Detective Goode and I kept in touch. He went on to be the best, most well-researched, and equipped cult investigator in his state. (Or anywhere else, in my opinion.) Sometime after the conference, he consulted with me about a murder. An army reserve captain, who was a male nurse at the Veteran's Hospital psychiatric ward in Oklahoma City and druid to the bone, was arrested. His extramarital girlfriend had been murdered, and their seven-month-old baby girl was shot and killed. First, he paralyzed the mother with a 22-pistol shot. A bottle of "curare" derivative (zombie drug) procured from the hospital was found, fueling speculation that he used that to disable her. The woman had been cut with initials on her stomach and crosses or x's on her breasts.

It was a long, drawn-out trial. By then, investigators and prosecutors knew it was a mistake to bring devil worship into the court, so they prosecuted him the hard way—on bare evidence.

The perpetrator never expected the outcome he got. The self-confident smirk he wore to court the morning he was sentenced disappeared as he was sentenced to death.[6]

As an aside—he may or may not have been a solo practitioner. One tree was mysteriously uprooted and taken from the circle of oak trees in his yard after his arrest. Oak trees are the sacred worship tree of choice in some covens.[7]

The Sins of the Father

Robby was sixteen. I'd been called by his aunt in 1988, who got my name from a friend. Robby, who had moved in with them sometime earlier the year before, had been babysitting their kids. When she and her husband got home, the kids were terrified. Robby, they said, had chased them with a butcher knife. He was dressed in black and threatened to cut their heads off.

I recommended that she call a contact I had in the juvenile division of her local police department. She did. Robby was immediately taken into custody. I made the two-hour drive to New Mexico to talk to him. He was so, so scared. "I don't remember anything. I swear I don't!" I looked into his fear-filled, confused eyes, and I believed him.

But what triggered him? And what was his back story? Sadly, he had gone on a youth retreat that summer with the youth pastor at the Assembly of God church his aunt attended. Robby looked up to and idolized him. But the youth pastor sexually assaulted him, and though he didn't fall apart right away, I believe it was the moment that his own awful history broke his fragile life, and he began to unravel.

Robby's father was a state trooper. The Child Protective Services in Robby's hometown let me look at Robby's file, which carried a long history of parental abuse. A stack of photos showed little 8-year-old Robby, who had been so badly beaten that his back and buttocks were just a mass of welts and black bruises. It broke my heart.

Robby's aunt told me Robby's dad and other relatives were deep into devil worship, perversion, and child pornography.

Robby's former Child Protective caseworker put me in touch with Robby's ex-stepmom as I was trying to find out how to help Robby. She said, "If you tell anyone I said this, I'll deny everything and call you a liar. But when I decided to leave Robby's father, he was at work. He had a padlocked room in the trailer, and he threatened to kill me if I ever went in there. He was always taking Robby in there for hours. Well, I was mad the night I left, so when he was at work, I broke the lock and went in. The whole room was covered with stacks of magazines of naked kids and adults having sex and a ton of film reels, wall to wall."

"Did you report it?"

"No. All his friends are in law enforcement! But I did call Robby's dad and confronted him. He said he was holding it as evidence for the police." Right. She never reported it. Only then did I begin to understand why Robby was so messed up.

Robby's uncle (his father's brother) was an FBI man and was able to get Robby out of juvenile detention, out of therapy, and away from anyone who could help him. All the reports were written up to make it appear that the aunt was the problem and that she had caused Robby's problems. The report said that she was "schizophrenic paranoid." Those were tactics and accusations that would become all too familiar in the coming years: Deny everything; blame the victims and those who help them. So effective. So silencing for the victims. Later on, Robby got out, moved out of state, and tried to forget.

And his father remained a state trooper.

Vicky and Carly

In another case in El Paso, Vicky, thirteen, was sexually seduced by a 37-year-old schoolteacher in 1996. He got her into devil worship. He choked her and raped her, she said. She told us there was a large group of adult devil worshippers involved with rituals and that pornography films were made. She didn't tell anyone because she "loved" him. The press called it a "consensual" relationship, and no word of devil worship was mentioned.[8]

The teacher was arrested on May 24, 1996 after he and the girl disappeared and spent the night in a cheap motel.

We were asked to go pray for her. Fragile, tranced, and fragmented, Vicky only allowed us to pray a little and to comfort and encourage her parents.

The day after Halloween, Vicky tried to kill herself. It may have been the holiday that triggered it. Or it may have been the grueling, heartless, several-hour interrogation by the FBI. They wanted to make sure they could win the case, they said. They were clueless and unconcerned about how this grilling would affect Vicky.

They didn't have to worry about winning. The night before the trial began, the alleged perpetrator tried to hang himself in his jail cell. Surviving the hanging, he clung to life for a few days, dying on the fourth day.

Did he hang himself? My guess was either he was afraid he'd end up breaking the oath in court and preferred to take his own way out rather than wait for theirs, or someone decided not to take any chances and did it for him. (Hints of Jeffrey Epstein, in retrospect.[9])

Carly was a beautiful, vivacious girl from a Christian family who attended New Mexico State University in Las Cruces, New Mexico. She vanished without a trace from her dorm on a satanic ritual calendar date in 1998. I felt from the moment I heard about it that not only was it probably satanic in nature, but that it would not end well. Still, we all prayed desperately for her safe return. I even shared my concerns with local El Paso talk show host Paul Strelzin on his show. Carly was found murdered shortly thereafter, and two alleged perpetrators were arrested. It was Mr. Strelzin who had accessed one of the alleged killer's websites and called me to tell me it had a satanic "cross of confusion" symbol and a spinning pentagram. (A pentagram is a satanic/black magick symbol that is a five-pointed star with two points up and one point down, and it often has a goat symbol in the middle.) On the suspect's "guest list" of people who had gone to his site was young Carly's name. All the while, pundits and skeptics were busy ridiculing stories of satanic crime from their safe, well-protected worlds; this was the kind of real-life, heartbreaking reality we faced day in and day out.

A Dangerous Mission

As many began to decry satanic crime as false, we who fought this evil faced a danger that was ongoing, real, and deadly serious.

I had found a web page that spelled out in no uncertain terms what the real satanic world was about:

A Gift to the Prince—A Guide to Human Sacrifice

- Human sacrifice is powerful magick. The ritual death of an individual does two things: it releases energy (which can be directed or stored—for example, in a crystal), and it draws down dark forces or entities. . . .

- Sacrifice can be voluntary, of an individual; involuntary, of an individual or two . . . voluntary sacrifice usually occurs every seventeen years as part of the Ceremony of Recalling . . .[Author's note: we had heard dozens of testimonies from adult ritual abuse survivors that, at a certain age, usually in their forties, they felt an overwhelming sense that they were being "recalled" and needed to return to their satanic order. This document was the first independent confirmation that this is a real occult working.]

- An involuntary sacrifice is when an individual or individuals are chosen by a group, temple, or Order. Such sacrifices are usually sacrificed on the Spring Equinox . . . there are no restrictions concerning involuntary sacrifices other than the fact they are usually in some way opponents to devil worship or the satanic way of living.

- A Temple or group wishing to conduct such a sacrifice with magickal intent must first obtain permission from the Grand Master or Grand Lady Master . . .

- First, choose the sacrifice(s)—those whose removal will actively benefit the devil worshipper cause. Candidates are zealous, interfering Nazarenes [Author's note: Christians], those (e.g., journalists) attempting to disrupt in some way established devil worshipper groups or orders . . .

- There are three methods of conducting an involuntary sacrifice: (1) By Magickal means (e.g., the Death Ritual), (2) by some person directly killing the sacrifice(s), and (3) by assassination. . . . Those who participate in the Ritual of Sacrifice must revel in the deaths.[10]

This amounts to an Internet order and instruction to eliminate Christians and those who interfere with devil worshippers. It also details how to lure the victim, kill them, and dispose of them to hide the evidence—and a chilling warning that any participant who "breaks the oath" and tells will be hunted down and killed.

I have given you a mere fraction of what I know and have seen. Look, I know how painful these true events are to hear, but any honest person can see that there was much more to this than you've known or been told, real events that the de-bunkers want you to believe never occurred. This is not a fantasy. This is the real, heartbreaking truth of satanic crime.

A Final Word

As I have alluded to, Satanism thrives by inciting fear in people and thereby silencing them. The Holocaust was a perfect example of how a man named Adolph Hitler could rule a whole country through fear. Machiavelli, in his book *The Prince* (1513), gives specific instructions for someone who want to rule a country saying that it must be done by fear—punishing, even executing those who oppose him in any way—which serves the dual purpose of eliminating the opposition *and* creating an example to incite fear. John Calvin[11] and the Catholic popes with their inquisitions[12] both did this very thing. Yet, if we give in to fear, the enemy is given free rein to trample over our lives. So much damage has been done in the name of fear.

> Ye are of God, little children, and have overcome
> them: because greater is he that is in you,
> than he that is in the world. (1 John 4:4)

4

Gathering the Facts

In 1987, when I initially moved to El Paso, Texas to aid in the WATCH network, a lot of my efforts involved tracking down ritual sites, homes where nefarious activities allegedly took place, and interviewing kids and adults who wanted to give us information.

Those interviews could be a bit precarious. Because of the growing involvement of kids who read Anton LaVey's *Satanic Bible*, we got numerous calls from people who claimed to be the first cousin/brother/daughter/lover of infamous Satanists or other occultists of note. Though a few of those stories were true, the overwhelming majority of those stories were not. And that is an important point to make: While skeptics painted us, therapists, and others as those who were gullible and quite willing to support crazy, unprovable stories, most of us were, in fact, scrupulous in interviewing and vetting people with a story or information—especially kids. At the same time, I rarely dismissed a story out of hand, no matter how unlikely or crazy it may have sounded initially.

In fact, I made that mistake one time and never again. Sue Joyner was going with our team to interview someone from California who had run away from a devil worship cult. Sue wanted to know if I wanted to go, and I declined because the man claimed to be a relative of a well-known devil worshipper, and it just sounded like a made-up story to me. The man had a girl's first name and a very strange last name in addition to the name of a well-known devil worshipper. I immediately dismissed it because it sounded like either he was making it up to get attention or he was not mentally well. Sue and our team did the interview and wrote all the details in a file.

It wasn't until after Sue passed away and I began to go through all the files she had turned over to me a few years before that I found that file. When I read it, I realized the man was probably telling the truth. The female first name, it

Sue Joyner

turns out, was the first name of the famous devil worshipper's wife. His middle name was a druid name for a very ugly satanic ritual holiday. I had missed it. And his information included the name of a funeral home where bodies were cremated for the cult, which confirmed several other bits of information we had gathered on the same crematorium and where the high-ranking occult families stayed when they came into town. His information was identical to testimony from several others verifying where these high-ranking people stayed while in El Paso. After that, I vowed never to throw anyone's testimony aside just out of hand. Sometimes the most bizarre, unbelievable stories turned out to be absolutely true. (More on that under chapter 21, "Cries of the Children.")

Ritual Sacrifices

The other thing we did in the course of mapping and uncovering ritual sites was documenting the sites where animals had been sacrificed. There were a lot in our area. Some were obviously done by adolescents. Some were clearly more sophisticated and deliberate, done by adults. We learned that adolescents were sloppy, usually intoxicated or stoned, and the animals were tortured and jaggedly cut. On the other hand, adult groups sacrificed with purpose in ritual. Like several other religions, animal parts were often used to do specific rituals to curse people (e.g. eyes were taken out and sacrificed to blind their enemy, legs were broken to cripple, and mouths sewn up to make mute). Human sacrifices often followed the same pattern.

All over the country at that time (circa 1980s), animals were found in ritual settings or just in the open air out in pastures or desert areas with body parts removed, surgically excised, and often with no blood present.

In fact, as of this writing, these "mutilations" continue, often leaving authorities without an explanation. On April 23rd, 2023, six cows were found mutilated in Madison County, Texas, in a fashion identical to what we found all over the country in the late 1980s and beyond.[1]

Alien abduction stories provided the perfect cover for many of these groups. Sometimes, they left signs that the area had been "sanctified," like red rope to mark off an area, parchment paper with sigils (an occult symbol denoting a god, deity, or desired magical working), and candles. In a ritual homicide, the body would be placed in a north/south position with the head at the north.

We found a number of animal sacrifices, many that were clearly marked with ritual indicators such as red cords tied around their feet. At that time, this was one of the angles that law enforcement was able to pursue: cruelty to animals. That is, until Vodoun, Santerían, and other Afro-Caribbean groups sued on the basis of religious grounds and had the courts rule that animal sacrifice was allowed. I'm sure all the devil worship groups were thrilled to have yet another cover to carry out their cruelties undisturbed and unprosecuted.

In our town, we found an abnormal number of ritual sites, and we investigated and photographed all we could. We knew, in fact, that most criminal sacrificial and abuse activities would be held in private homes or on ranches that were inaccessible and protected by armed guards at the three-mile mark, one-mile mark, and close perimeters. It gave me chills to think about how many of those were taking place. We were contacted by a man who came across a large ritual group in the desert of perhaps fifty people in robes around a large fire, chanting. He was terrified. Our group showed up just as the numerous trucks and vehicles were leaving. The police were alerted but didn't show up. The next morning, our team and a couple of off-duty police officers went out to find that the entire site had been bulldozed before we arrived.

In 1989, we got a call from a sheriff's department right outside our city limits to ask us to come and look at the house of a recently deceased woman in her eighties. When she died, the hospital contacted her only son, and he angrily said, "I don't care. I'm glad she's dead. I don't want her stuff." We went to look at her house. Her entire patio was an intricately inlaid stone pentagram. Inside, all the doorknobs and cabinet knobs were real animal skulls. We don't know exactly what she was into, but it was fairly clear that she was on the dark side.

We investigated another "rumored" ritual site, not knowing if we were just chasing a false lead. We were told there was a mesa far out in the desert where there were several stone altars. We found it, exactly as we were told. Someone later told people they were just picnic tables. Right. All arranged in a circle, on stone pedestals. But "alternate explanations" were—and still are—always quickly forthcoming by "experts" from satanic or other occult groups quick to pooh-pooh it and say, "That's stupid. It's got nothing to do with devil worship or Satanism!" Almost on command, or demand. Predictable. And the harder they tried to downplay something, the closer we wanted to look at it. "Methinks the lady doth protest too much."

Complications

At some point, the waters started to get a bit muddied, and clarification was needed. There were any number of witchcraft (Wiccan) groups that conducted their rituals outside, often "skyclad" (naked). Before we were able to train a lot of law enforcement officers, a few officers got a little overzealous and piled Wiccans in with devil worshippers and thought they needed to be prosecuted somehow. Well, you can't in our legal system. Wicca and Satanism are protected and, in some cases, tax-exempt "religions." It is important to note that, thankfully, most people who practice witchcraft don't kill animals and are as horrified by the ritual slaughter of animals as we are. The First Amendment guarantees us all freedom of religion, and that includes religions we may strongly disagree with. In law enforcement, it was extremely important that they understood the difference between protected religion and those who were hiding behind occult religions to break the law, prey on children, and worse.

After a while, between the Wiccans and the LaVeyan-type follow-ers, they kicked up a lot of dust, accusing us of persecuting them and threatening all kinds of lawsuits against us, making our work all that more difficult.

Not very long after we began training others, nearly every law enforcement, probation, and mental health class had a Wiccan, Satanist, druid, or whatever, disrupting classes and accusing us of spreading lies and persecuting them. I can say for sure none of that was true of myself or my associates in our network. In fact, we were all extraordinarily careful to distinguish between protected religious activities and criminal ones.

I have recently thought back—and especially in the light of what may come as a result of writing this book—and realized what an enormous, time-sucking distraction dealing with "harmless" occultists was—and may yet be. Frankly, they always took up just a tiny corner of our criminal justice classes—enough to show the class that they could cause a lot of noise and deliberate sensationalism designed to mock and make fun of Christians, but not really much of a criminal concern.

But all the while, when people are so taken up with their rantings and circus antics, the real crimes remain deeply hidden. I carry the truth of that as well as the reality of crimes against children, done in the name of black magick, Satan, and other evil gods that I have witnessed for over thirty years, some of which I can never share with anyone, and I can never "unsee."

None calleth for justice, nor any pleadeth for truth:
they trust in vanity, and speak lies; they conceive
mischief, and bring forth iniquity. (Isaiah 59:4)

5

Media, Midland, and Two Talk Shows

From the very get-go, I have not been a media fan. I had been in the public eye and in ministry long enough to see how easy it was for some in the media—if not most—to take a little bit of news and twist it into something that bore little resemblance to the truth. The fundamental truth behind most media stories and those who cover them is simple: "If it bleeds, it leads." In some ways, the absolutely awful reality behind ritual crimes and devil worship activities is that it was made for prime time. That was the danger, as well as some degree of opportunity for those of us who were trying to bring light to this field. We knew we were being used for ratings, but we sometimes took the chance because we were using the media to get intel, leads, and inside information. It was a bit of a dangerous dance. Sometimes, it paid off; sometimes, we made reliable friends, and sometimes—most of the time—we got used, stabbed in the back, or grossly misrepresented, and the story bore no resemblance to the interview or information we gave. We learned to be extremely wary, and we were grateful when they got it right. And occasionally, we made real friends. You know who you are!

While we were just beginning to do out-of-town training and local criminal justice classes, we were also, as I said, photographing and documenting ritual sites. For two years, we were contacted several times a year by local television stations that were doing specials on Satanism, devil worship, and the occult, especially during Halloween. The local channels did a fair and accurate job of exposing this in our community. We took them to show them ritual sites in the desert, ritual sites in tunnels under the city, and other places. For example, in 1989, we found an entire ritual room directly underneath our largest mall in El Paso, apparently accessible only through waterways and tunnels. We let them interview (in silhouette) some of the young people we'd helped extract from the occult. They also interviewed other young devil worshippers whom they had contacted who were recruiters for covens and were proud of it. There was a clear and dangerous problem with our youth in our city, evidenced by a growing number of arsons, church desecrations, grave robbing, rapes, animal mutilations, and even murders. Similar crimes were taking place not only in our city but also around the country.

Soon, every media outlet wanted in. It was the sensational ratings grabber du jour. We knew that. They knew that. But if our participation could help us find and save a victim or a kid, we'd play. But we wouldn't compromise. Just please, tell it as it is, we asked them.

Geraldo

I received a call from *The Geraldo Rivera Show*. They needed someone to fly to New York and be on a show concerning the Matamoros murder, ritual abuse, and Satanism. I quickly packed and flew out at an ungodly hour to make the trip to get to the show on time. In New York, a crazy limousine driver picked me up and drove me at eighty-something miles an hour down to Times Square, showing me where the drug dealers hung out, where the prostitutes worked, laughing in-between and saying, "Welcome to New York, ha, ha, ha!"

Dumped out at the bottom of a narrow set of stairs on a dirty street, I ascended to the *Geraldo* studio where they rushed me in to makeup, and I was given a horrific wig and fake beard. I went on the show in disguise as "David," in order to protect my family.

On the news feed from South Texas were state Attorney General Jim Maddox, Lieutenant George Gavito, who was the chief investigator on the Matamoros case, and Brownsville mayor Nacho Garza, among others.

The show centered around the Matamoros murder of student Mark Kilroy. In the studio were me and former FBI Los Angeles agent Ted

Gundersen, who was fast becoming a legend in our work. We had spoken on the phone before this, and it was good to meet him in person.

Bill Huddleston (Mark Kilroy's best friend) and Bill's mother were also on the panel with us. They had been persuaded—or maybe I should say conned—into doing the show, being told it was a tribute program for Mark.

It wasn't. It was Geraldo's "I told you this stuff was real" show. And even then, I granted him that moment since he was one of the only ones who took satanic crime seriously at that time.

Bill and his mom were allowed to speak briefly, and Ted gave his testimony as to how extensive these things were, I told some of my story, and the gentlemen in South Texas kept insisting this was just a "Mexico" problem. Geraldo saw my agitation and asked me to comment. I came out with both barrels blazing, confronting the Texas State Attorney General with the fact that we were currently working on several cases of ritual crime all across the state of Texas. It was utter nonsense to assert that these crimes only occurred in Mexico. My vehement statements may have helped to explain my less-than-warm reception in some law enforcement circles back home in the months to come!

After the show, we were unceremoniously thrown back into a limo and taken to our hotels. I sat in the back with Bill and his mother, and she explained how betrayed they felt by being lured into doing this show, thinking it was going to be about Mark. And Bill . . . he just shattered into a million pieces on the way back to the hotel as I tried to just put my arm around him and comfort him.

Fast forward to a decade or so later. Geraldo made a huge name for himself, covering the Desert Storm war. And then he tells people he regrets doing all the shows on devil worship since none of it was real. What a sad commentary. Mr. Rivera, it was real, and we went on to pursue it while you climbed the ladder of success on the back of hurting people like Bill Huddleston.

That was my first taste of "big media," and it was a profound disappointment. Thankfully, my next major media involvement would prove more fruitful.

KMID News in Midland, Texas, contacted us. They were doing a five-night segment called "Kids in Satan's Shadow." They, too, were seeing a rash of satanic crimes and youth involved in devil worship and other forms of the occult. They asked if they could come to El Paso and interview us and perhaps get a tour of our local sites and activities. We were glad to accommodate.

I could tell the KMID News crew was a bit spooked by what we said and what we showed them, along with some of the people they interviewed. Who wouldn't be? To your average Midland/Odessa resident (or resident of so many other towns in America when this wave of occultism hit), this was unheard-of, scary, Hollywood-horror-movie-type stuff. We were getting used to it, so taking these folks to ritual sites in the desert and underneath the city's waterways was just business as usual for us. They took it well, though, and they took it seriously. I was pretty confident they were going to cover this issue fairly and thoroughly.

And they did. In fact, they called me a day or two after returning to Midland and said they were going to do a talk show special after the Friday night conclusion of their weeklong series. Could I fly down and be on the panel? "Absolutely," I told them. I flew down at the end of the week for the first of what would be many returns to the Midland/Odessa area, unintentionally stirring up trouble, making some cops angry, and city officials even angrier in our quest to see kids set free from the growing scourge of occultism and devil worship.

The studio audience was packed for the live show, which was broadcast after the last segment of "Kids in Satan's Shadow," which turned out to be the best, most thorough coverage of the satanic scourge up until then, or since, really. The atmosphere was tense and electric.

The panel was cleanly divided. On one side was me and Dr. Hurst (who, early on, was one of the best and only experts on occult crime and activities in the nation). Dr. Hurst was a professor at Odessa College in Odessa, Texas. This was our first time to meet, and I found him to be a congenial and clear-thinking man who could more than make our case and the reasons for our concerns. Dr. Hurst was one of the expert researchers of the horrific serial murders committed by Dean Corll of Houston, Texas, between 1970-1973, who had raped and murdered at least twenty-eight young boys.[1] Dr. Hurst knew his stuff, and he was more than prepared to make a case for concern about the rash of devil-worshipping cults and crimes in their area.

On the other side of the panel were a Catholic youth pastor, a Baptist pastor, and a law enforcement official whose name and position have escaped me. (Unfortunately, all footage of this show has been lost.)

Behind a screen were the parents of a teen daughter whom they feared had been seduced by and taken away from them by a boy who was rumored to be involved in witchcraft or some other form of occultic practice.

Dr. Hurst made the opening case, and I reinforced it with information about what had been unearthed (an unfortunate but accurate analogy) in our city.

From there, all three of the other panelists spent time downplaying our concerns, explaining them away, and denying that it was a threat at all. I was stunned. The law enforcement person I could understand. He didn't want anyone—especially an out-of-towner—to give his fair city a bad name. However, the Catholic youth pastor talked about how his youth played *Dungeons and Dragons* and how they believed the solution to these concerns was to "accentuate the positive." The Baptist pastor simply said nobody should worry about the devil because—Jesus was stronger (which I agree with)—and that we were just glorifying the devil (which was nonsense and was just avoiding a serious issue our kids were facing.)

I was looking at the audience, and squarely in the front row sat the chief of police and the chief deputy of the sheriff's department, neither looking very happy. In fact, they were giving me and Dr. Hurst the Darth Vader death stare. Later, it was explained to me by some local law enforcement that we were dealing with a town that had yet to acknowledge a drug or gang problem in their schools. Especially at a time when they were facing a severe economic downturn, they didn't want a couple of troublemakers like Dr. Hurst and me driving property values down any more than they already were.

At some point, the two law enforcement people were given a chance to deny the problem.

The parents told their story, and questions were taken from the audience and by phone, and the rest went by so fast it was a bit of a blur. The show was interrupted by a young teen who called in to proclaim that he was involved in Wicca but was not a devil worshipper and that he was being falsely accused by the parents and others. Then a young man stood up and told everyone that he had practiced Wicca and worse, and it was a lie to tell people it was harmless. After that, it was *Katy bar the door*. They extended the program to two hours, and it nearly became like a *Jerry Springer* episode. But it didn't, thank God, and I felt that all sides were able to present their cases well. I was very proud of the news team. They handled everything calmly and with great clarity.

After the show ended, Dr. Hurst and I had a good exchange and promised to stay in touch. The rest of the panel avoided any contact with us at all.

When I went backstage, the crew was ecstatic. They hugged each other, hugged me, and laughed and hollered like they had won the lottery. Their ratings went through the roof, higher than any program they had done so far. I was glad for them, and I sincerely hoped we had done some good.

"C'mon, let's go!" the crew said, as they tossed me in the camera-man's car, and we all headed for the local C&W bar to celebrate. I was just going along because they asked, being neither a "boot-scootin" type or a beer lover. I was just honored to have been asked.

So, I hung out for two hours or so until closing, and we headed out to the news truck and found the windows were smashed. There may have been a satanic symbol as well if I recall correctly. The crew was stunned and scared. "There is bound to be some kind of retaliation," I told them on the way to my hotel room. "These people don't joke around." I told them about Jesus and about how His blood alone could protect them from these things. I believe they heard me loud and clear.

After I got home, several calls came in as a result of the show. Two or three were invitations to speak to youth groups. One, in particular, I didn't hesitate to take: A Halloween outreach at Bonham Junior High in Odessa. Although I was clearly being called upon and equipped to speak to a variety of criminal justice groups about occult crimes, my first calling and my first love was to speak my own testimony and proclaim the saving power of the Lord Jesus Christ to a lost world. I would take that opportunity over addressing kings and presidents.

Over the summer, Ben Kennedy (my friend from Andrews, Texas who was chief of the adult probation department) called me to tell me that some local officials had also expressed an interest in having me come up and lead an outdoor youth outreach, which we planned in advance of the Midland/Odessa Halloween one.

We were already walking into a mess. In those early days, we had to contend with a lot of false information, rumors, and outright lies. One that was circulating all through the area was that a satanic group was planning on sacrificing a blond-haired, blue-eyed girl on Halloween night. It was enough of a concern that the police investigated it as much as they were able. Unfortunately, authorities were so busy tracking down false information that if something awful was taking place that night, they missed it.

I later learned that this was what some devil-worshipping groups called "zap action"—spreading false rumors, especially in Christian circles because we were unfortunately quick to believe and spread such stories without verifying if they were true. I had little doubt that while we were busy chasing the wind, real children and real teens were being hurt somewhere

> In those early days, we had to contend with a lot of false information, rumors, and outright lies.

that night. We had already been prepared with a thorough education on ritual dates and what they mean, and which groups practice what on what date, etc. Some were exclusive to satanic groups, some to druid or Odinistic groups, some to Wiccans, and many were mix and match. All these groups recognized the solstices and equinoxes as well. They all practiced something different, with different purposes. Unfortunately, some of them did ritual sacrifices of animals, humans, and even children. And the blond hair, blue-eye template, while seeming odd, is a reality to both black magick groups and human trafficking groups. In black magick groups, they have written that "the perfect sacrifice is that of a male child of perfect innocence, around six years of age."[2]

Other writings—and even some honest practitioners—say that the more the child is forced to suffer at the time of death, the more power the sacrifist receives. We took those realities seriously.

The Andrews event was well-attended but not without incident.

Ben, my friend in the Andrews Probation Department, and I did a training for local law enforcement and other agencies. I managed to touch on Masonry because part of our classes involved teaching them to identify various symbols to determine the nature of the ritual site, if they found one, or decipher the many symbols that might be found in the journals or writings of criminals that might indicate what they were involved in. The pyramid and all-seeing eye always came up in our section on occult symbology, and I explained its occult history, meanings, and purposes. Almost inevitably, especially in Texas, it brings up the question as to why these symbols of the pyramid and all-seeing eye are on our money. I carefully explain the Masonic nature of the symbol and hope to leave it there since membership in the Masonic order in law enforcement in parts of Texas is almost mandatory if you want to move up the ranks in your career. And as it is just a small part of the training, I usually was happy to just move on after that. But in this class, an officer started asking deeper questions, and I answered them with answers that disturbed and angered him, pointing out how thoroughly enmeshed in the occult that Masonic rituals, practices, and symbols were. He, like many others, thought it was compatible with being a good church person. I shattered that illusion, and he got up and left.

During the lunch break at the local Andrews diner, that officer stormed into the place carrying a shopping bag. He headed straight for our table. "Here," he said, depositing the bag at our table. "You were right. I'm getting out. Here's all my stuff. Thanks for telling the truth." He turned and walked out before we could say a word. The bag was full of pins, books, an apron, and a ring, among other paraphernalia he had accrued during his time as a Masonic Lodge member. The people at the table were stunned. I was just thankful he saw the truth as a Christian and got out.

I had met a group of young people in the Dallas-Fort Worth Metroplex who had started a little Christian band, and we had them come and play for our youth outreach in Andrews that night. But just as the outdoor event began and the band started to play, a black cloud descended on the stage and attacked the band. It was a massive swarm of locusts—big ones! It was like some weird scene from a Hollywood horror movie. Everyone was pretty freaked out, but we managed to pray, recover, and we had a great outreach.

The Bonham Junior High Halloween event on the 29th and 30th of October was without incident. We expected trouble. We had heard rumors that there *would* be trouble. But it all went off without a hitch. When we gave an altar call, several kids came up, and one came right up to me, asking to pray to receive Jesus. I grabbed one of the young men who came with us from El Paso, and we led him to Jesus. After he had prayed, he bolted for the door. We followed him out. He was crying hysterically and screaming, "It burns, it burns!" We sat on either side of him. "What burns?" I gently asked. "THIS!" the young man yelled, pulling up his sleeve to reveal a huge pentagram tattoo. He was in agonizing pain. "Make it stop!" he begged us. We prayed and bound and rebuked in Jesus' name until the pain lifted.

We had a long conversation with him. He claimed to have seen the sacrifice of a young boy. The details were hard for him to remember because he had been completely stoned when it happened. Did it happen? We may never know for sure. It is my understanding that he later disavowed any Christian connection and thought the whole "anti-occult" thing was a joke. Not unusual, unfortunately. I don't know how many times we assisted young people and even some adults only to have them return to their old ways—or worse—even denying the nature and seriousness of what they had been involved in. I was shocked to hear that some kids we had ministered to were claiming that we simply made up the whole thing to manipulate them and keep them in our control. I was astonished because they were there when we prayed for a young woman who was cursing Jesus. They watched as her eyes went completely white as she began screaming, "I'm blind, I'm blind!" (We persevered in prayer, and she was set free—at least for the time.) How hard it was to hear that they were later saying it was some kind of a trick. But then, when you witness raw spiritual warfare, you either surrender to the One who has power over the works of darkness, or you just go into denial, which is what some did. It broke my heart, but it would not be an unusual phenomenon in the days to come.

So, whether the young man with the pentagram tattoo from Odessa just couldn't deal with things and turned back to darkness, turning his back on the Lord, I cannot say. Who knows? Perhaps, and hopefully, I will be able to talk to him again someday and remind him of the night Jesus rescued him from great darkness.

As a friend of mine says, *no good deed goes unpunished.* So, on my next trip to the area the following weekend, I had learned that the head of the sheriff's department (a Master Mason) had been spreading some rumors about me. I decided to call him and see if we could straighten things out. I got through to him by phone.

"This is Greg Reid," I said.

"Yeah, I know who you are," he said, cold as ice.

"I hear you're telling people I'm a phony and making over $2,000 a pop talking to people."

"I don't care what you make," he said.

"Well, good," I said. "So, stop lying about me, ok?" I didn't imply any litigious intent, but I think he may have understood that possibility. It was a useless call. I knew I would get blacklisted in that part of Texas because everyone did what this man said, and that was that. Well, almost everyone . . .

My next two meetings were youth-related, and I was happy to meet a local law enforcement officer who sponsored me. He just laughed when I told him about my run-in with his boss. Apparently, he was not a fan.

"I want you to meet a friend of mine," he told me. "He's a youth services investigator with the department. I think it would be good for you guys to meet." I was not particularly anxious to, judging by my less-than-friendly law enforcement reception in the region so far. But I agreed to meet with him anyway.

Jim was a short, stocky man in his mid-sixties with a salt-and-pepper Marine haircut. He was immediately engaging and friendly. We sat down to eat, and he began to talk. "I heard the Sheriff doesn't much care for you," he chuckled, and I nodded.

"Not much."

"Well, anyone he doesn't like is a friend of mine. So, you're in friendly territory tonight," he assured me. I was relieved.

Once we got to know each other a bit, he got down to business. "I want you to know you're right on track with what you're doing." I must have looked surprised. "I've been in law enforcement and the juvenile system for years," he went on. "This town is full of this evil stuff." (He was speaking of Midland/Odessa). "They don't like you talking about it, but believe me, it's all over this place. It's kids, adults. Everything."

"Good to know I'm on the right track. Thank you for that," I replied.

His voice lowered, and he came a little closer. "Look, I want you to think long and hard about what you're doing. I understand why you want to do this, believe me. But I need to let you know that I have an undercover contact in a large coven in San Antonio. They know about you. They know you are looking into the murder case of that girl out here."

I was stunned. "What? How?" I asked incredulously.

"They have known about you and have been keeping an eye on you for quite some time," he concluded.

I felt sick. I suddenly felt unsafe. "How could they know?" I replied. "I haven't talked to hardly anybody about that case." In fact, I could only think of two people I had even mentioned it to.

"Well, they've got a pretty good network," he answered. "Just want you to stay safe and watch your back."

Believe me, I was going to do just that after the meeting.

I would be more than happy to provide a written confirmation of what Jim told me, but I learned that shortly after our meeting, he disappeared. They found him not long after his disappearance. He was found in a veteran's hospital in Fort Worth, his memory nearly gone, and I was told, "He'll never carry a gun again." They chalked it up to a change in blood pressure medication he was given a few days after our meeting. I will never be confident that is what actually took place, neither will I ever know for sure. I am the only one left who can recount the details of that very sobering meeting that night in the Permian Basin.*

Despite that sobering meeting, further doors were about to open in the Permian Basin, doors that I could not allow fear to keep me from entering. The war was real, and I was ready for the battle.

---

* The Permian Basin is a large sedimentary basin spanning parts of Texas and New Mexico.

My son, if sinners entice thee, consent thou not. If they say, Come with us, let us lay wait for blood, let us lurk privily for the innocent without cause: Let us swallow them up alive as the grave; and whole, as those that go down into the pit . . . My son, walk not thou in the way with them; refrain thy foot from their path: For their feet run to evil, and make haste to shed blood. (Proverbs 1:10-12, 15-16)

6

The Devil Made Them Do It

I'm not a cop," I would tell law enforcement classes. "I'm a researcher and a P.I. I can't do your job, and I wouldn't try. I don't have your skills. I respect what you do. By the same token," I continued, "if you get a skinny teenager in your office who is growling, speaking in weird languages, picking up 100-pound desks, and throwing them across the room, call us. I think we can help."

With the advent of occult crimes and a tsunami of youth involvement with Satanism and occultism, it was inevitable that we would have to eventually deal with the ugly demons wherein these kids had opened their lives. When this happened, few people were prepared to handle them. Sometimes, the infestation was easily dealt with, and sometimes, it was brutally difficult. And sometimes, I suspect, no one was able to intervene before the ugly thing that got hold of the young person brought his life to a tragic end.

Kids Dabbling?

In the beginning of the unexpected and truly frightening rash of satanic involvement and crimes done by kids in the 1980s-1990s, the skeptics were always quick to react with a glib, "It's just kids dabbling." And from the very beginning, I contended that a dabbler today could be a murderer or suicide statistic tomorrow, and neither you nor I could know when that line would be irrevocably crossed. And we had plenty of evidence to prove that point. A whole book could be written about the many tragic ends to young lives and those around them who did not understand the incendiary nature of the occult and devil worship. It wasn't just a philosophy. It wasn't just a fad. It was a surrendering of one's will to unknown demonic entities that always required and exacted payment for such foolish "dabbling."

Tommy Sullivan Jr. was a fourteen-year-old boy from a good home with good grades. He began to read and study Satanism and the occult. Within a short period of time, this young soul became so twisted and overcome by evil that he stabbed his mother over two dozen times in their basement, set the sofa on fire in order to kill his sleeping father and brother, ran out into the snow, slit his wrists, and nearly decapitated himself with his little boy scout knife and died.[1]

One of the most horrendous teen satanic-based murders was the murder of seventeen-year-old Gary Lauwers by Ricky Kasso, also seventeen, who was heavily into the occult and devil worship practices. Kasso was acquainted with the members of a loosely organized group of friends who sold marijuana and referred to themselves as the "Knights of the Black Circle." (A perusal of a Facebook page under this name is extremely chilling.) Lauwers was stabbed between seventeen and thirty-six times and was forced to say "I love Satan" by Kasso. Kasso and his other friends James Troiano and Albert Quinones left Lauwers in the woods, where he was covered in leaves and branches. Kasso had a seriously disturbing background, which apparently included digging up graves and attending occult-specific ceremonies on ritual dates like Walpurgisnacht (April 30th).

Kasso committed suicide the day after his arrest by hanging himself in his jail cell.

There were so many suicides, murders, and other horrible crimes committed by kids in that era, and it was always so infuriating to hear the skeptics say that the kids were merely unstable or mentally ill. But many times, they were neither until they started ingesting this dark poison known as the occult and devil worship. Many were just average kids until they opened these doors through occult involvement. That involvement flipped a spiritual switch, and the results almost always ended tragically. Rare and blessed were the ones who, despite opening those doors, managed to escape and leave it behind to grow into somewhat normal adulthoods.

However, I have counseled hundreds who indulged in the occult in their youth. Many are still struggling spiritually, relationally, and socially because of the scars these practices left. One young man who had read *The Necronomicon* by H. P. Lovecraft—a highly dangerous and demonic book presenting itself as fiction—said that it damaged him so badly that he still feels its pull after thirty years.

You can't mess with the occult without it doing damage to your life. It is a spiritual principle and has proven to play itself out in the lives of countless people over the decades.

During that era, there were not enough counselors, pastors, or youth pastors to handle the barrage of young people who were involved in the occult and devil worship, leading to really bad outcomes. For us, kids weren't just a case. Because of Jesus, we knew the pain and the evil that had taken hold of them was real. The Scriptures say that Jesus "was moved with compassion" and would heal and deliver people (Matthew 14:14). We sought to bring that message of healing and deliverance to them. We genuinely hurt for these kids.

One of the most difficult suicides I have known of was that of a sixteen-year-old boy who was heavily involved in *Dungeons and Dragons*. Through the game, he eventually became involved in dark magick practices. One night, he locked himself in a motel room, drank himself into a stupor, and took pills. Then he took a shotgun, put it to his mouth, and pulled the trigger. I will never forget those crime scene photos of that terrible tragedy—nor the photo of a tetragrammaton occult "protection" medallion that he had tightly wrapped around his hand before ending his life. There was no protection—just the end of a tormented young life.

I think of him when I hear the pundits and Monday morning quarterbacks blather about "it's just kids dabbling" or "crazy kids." It's so easy for them to say; what do they care? In fact, honest Satanists have often said they don't care. It's just survival of the fittest and good riddance to the weak and those who aren't strong enough to survive. Yes, folks, that's the heart of most true modern Satanists and Satanism. They really don't care about anyone but themselves and their tiny dark little circle of friends and family.

Opening the Gates

In 1989, I was contracted as an occult intervention specialist to counsel occult-bound kids at Crossroads, a rehab hospital wing for troubled and addicted kids that was part of Sierra Mountain Medical Center in Big Spring, Texas. My contacts there were Mark, a counselor in his forties, and Rita, an adolescent recovery director.

I was a little nervous when Mark picked me up at the Midland airport. This was the first time I had been asked to help kids in a rehab setting. But Mark was a very friendly "good ole boy," easygoing and solid, and he immediately put me at ease.

Mark made one statement that really hit me hard and focused my vision for my time at Crossroads. "God didn't just open the gates of Heaven and let me in. He opened the gates of Hell and let me out." I let those words sink in deeply and breathed a silent prayer that God would somehow help me show these kids through Jesus the way out of the occult hell they were trapped in.

I spoke to all the youth in the unit in a group setting about the dangers of the occult, about twenty kids in all. There were three boys in the unit who were pointed out to me as hard-core devil worshippers. And I watched them carefully. One by one, Rita arranged for me to talk to them privately.

It was a secular hospital, and references to "God" in their twelve-step program had to be vague, of the "he-she" higher power variety. You could call on a rock to help you if that was your "higher power." But they ran into a problem; devil-worshipping kids called on *their* "higher power"—Satan—for help. I told the staff they needed to be more specific about the program's nature of "higher powers," or else these kids would leave the facility stronger in their commitment to the devil than when they first came in. You can see the dilemma. Unfortunately, today, if you told a kid in a program that he couldn't worship the devil as his higher power, the ACLU would be all over you and sue you right proper. The devil knows how to guard his prisoners well.

Why, you might ask, would kids want to call on the devil to help them break their drug addiction and graduate from the AA program at the hospital? In higher occult circles, drugs are just used to control lessers; the highest members avoid drugs altogether—unless for specific ritual purposes—so as not to lose their power and control. One jailed devil worshipper told me that Satan had appeared to him and told him he had to let him get arrested in order to get off of cocaine. Satan said he needed the man to be clean so the man could become a more powerful black magician.

(Note: the reality is, all those who worship the devil—especially kids— are just throwaway trash to Satan. He doesn't care that most of them are destroyed, and if he can deceive a few into "getting clean," thinking they will be a better kind of black magician, that works for Satan, too.)

Rita, the head of rehab, "bent the rules" a little. We both knew that only Jesus Christ could deliver kids from the darkness they had touched. "But I'm under rules," she told me. "So, you go in with them, I'll shut the door, and you do whatever you need to do to get them saved and delivered. I don't know a thing, okay?" She had already cleared it with the parents.

Reaching Their Hearts

My first meeting was with John, who was sixteen. Before I met with him privately, I heard him playing some chords to a song. "I know that!" I said. "That's 'When the Children Cry.'" It was by the metal band White Lion and had become an anthem ballad for many kids in that generation.

"You do?" John said in surprise.

"Yeah! Can you teach me to play it?" He did, and then he sang a few of the lines.

When the children cry
Let them know we tried
And when the children pray
Let's show them the way.[2]

As John sang the song, it was hard to keep the tears back. Kids like John, who were on the surface so "into" the devil, when caught in their vulnerable moments, would rather have you know that this is their real heart. They hurt. They cry. They're afraid.

Later, we talked and prayed. John dedicated his life to Jesus and abandoned his occult practices. When I heard from him six months later, he was staying close to the Lord and putting the nightmare of occult and Satanism addiction behind him.

David was harder. When he was first admitted, he was so demon-ically out of control that no medication would bring him down. He'd been in lockdown for several days before they finally let him into the regular hospital setting. David and I talked, and slowly, he told me of his confused journey to the Dark Side. He used to be a youth leader in a Baptist church. When he began to struggle, he'd begun to doubt.

He had asked his church leaders for help. "I need God's power!" he pleaded. "They did miracles in the Book of Acts, didn't they?"

"Well, son," they told him, "God doesn't do those things anymore. You just have to believe."

It is possible to have a form of godliness and deny the power thereof! (2 Timothy 3:5). It is possible David had a belief in a religion but never met Jesus. He was at a crossroads.

Discouraged, under attack, and hurting, the devil knew how to lure him in. David discovered the Ouija board—fake power—and everything began to snowball until, within a year, he became a bonafide, *Satanic Bible*-reading, animal-sacrificing devil worshipper.

"David, your church friends may have meant well, but they were wrong," I told him as we sat in Rita's office, which was softly decorated with Southwest art and cattails in a vase. "God does have power. He still does miracles."

"He does?" David asked with the eyes of an injured child.

"Yes, He does. And He's strong and powerful enough to set you free."

After a long talk explaining what surrender to Jesus was all about, he wanted to receive Jesus. We prayed. You could feel the demonic clash and struggle, and then David got set free and totally committed his life to Jesus Christ.

Evan was fourteen and had been court-committed to the Crossroads rehabilitation unit. Evan was another kind of kid altogether. He was a self-confident, skinny, dark-haired boy who strutted around the unit like a boss, wearing a felt hat and avoiding me like I was a cop. I'd walk toward him, and he'd take a right hook—to anywhere.

So, I set him up. Any way I could, I was going to try to get into his space and get him to talk to me. On my second to last day there, we were on a collision course. We both headed down the hallway toward each other, and Evan had no right-hook escape. I passed him, turned around, and said, "Hey!" He turned around defensively.

"What?!"

"You better watch that hat."

"Why?"

"Because I like it. I'd hate to see it disappear."

Evan grinned for a split second, then got away from me fast.

I saw him talking to another kid a while later. I passed by. "I want that hat," I said casually. "Better keep an eye on it."

"Right," he said, grinning a little more. He was catching on to me trying to open up a conversation with him. I think he wanted to talk, but he was afraid of the results. I understood. After all, I was just a stranger to him.

At three the next afternoon, the time came. Evan and I sat in Rita's office, which she had made available for me to counsel the kids. He was shaking all over. I tried to keep as calm as I could as he slowly, fearfully, began to tell me where he had been.

He remembered very little of how it started. His parents told me that when he was about eight, he went on a field trip with kids from his school. When they returned later that day, all the kids on the bus were crying. Evan's parents were upset and questioned the bus driver. He told them he had no idea what was wrong with them, and so they let it go. Evan remembered nothing about that trip.

Evan's next memory was when he was about ten. This was real-time—not recovered—memory. He told me he was walking home from school, and a white stretch limousine pulled over to the curb. The door opened, and a man said, "Get in Evan," and he obeyed. He was taken to a ritual.

"When?" I asked. I had gotten pretty good at telling when a young person was lying or just wanting attention. They usually say, "Oh, Halloween. I was the High Priest, and I killed a baby." But the time frames and all the little details he gave me convinced me he was telling the truth.

His parents noticed a radical change in Evan's behavior ever since, but they did not know what to do about it. As he got older, he got more reclusive and rebellious and began hanging out with bad people. They felt helpless and scared of him, and unfortunately, were of that era of parents who never looked in his room or "invaded his privacy." He often stayed over with friends in his early adolescence, his parents not knowing that was how they were able to ensure his participation in the group rituals.

He was frightened and reluctant to go into detail. He said he was forced to have sex with adults. Someone was sacrificed. He had been forced to participate in several rituals. They got him hooked on drugs. The drugs were free at first. Then he had to do what they wanted, or he wouldn't get his fix. He felt totally trapped.

Evan had been committed to Crossroads as a result of his parents finally finding all his satanic paraphernalia in his room. My good friend Ben Kennedy, who was the Andrews, Texas chief adult probation officer, had been called in, and he thoroughly searched Evan's room while Evan was at school. He could tell just by what was in the room that Evan was not just at risk but volatile and a danger to his whole family. "If you don't get him into custody right away, someone might end up dead." The parents, scared and already having lost control of their son, made the arrangements, and Evan was taken into custody after school that very day.

His parents had no idea just how close a call it was. Evan told me he was planning to kill his parents, his brother, and himself, and it could have happened at any time if they had not sought intervention.

Evan prayed with me to surrender his life to Jesus. His words came hard, and the demon presence in the room was dizzying. But he made the breakthrough.

After we prayed, he was shaking and nearly in tears. "Satan's not gonna kill me?" he asked.

"No, Evan," I said. "Satan can't. You belong to Jesus now." He was still shaking. "What's wrong, Evan?" I asked.

"I'm afraid God can't forgive me for the things I've done," he replied softly.

"There's nothing He can't forgive."

Evan then proceeded to go into detail about one of the most grotesque and chilling ritual sacrifices I had ever heard of. Someone died in a terrible, nightmarish murder. They made him help. I was stunned. "Evan . . . you were just a boy. They drugged you. They trapped you. God forgives you. God loves you."

It was hard for him to accept. He was broken, scared, and guilt-ridden. So, we prayed again for forgiveness and cleansing and that God would take away the nightmares Evan had been having ever since. I prayed Evan would make it through the rocky days ahead of him.

Skeptics will say, "Why didn't he go to the police? Why doesn't he go now?" First, thanks in part to the skeptics' work these last years, no one would believe him. Second, with all the drugs he was taking, the details would be so cluttered and confused that nothing could be certain. Third, he loves and is protective of his family. He was considered to be a "satanic traitor" now. Retaliation was a very real possibility. Would *you* tell?

Evan wasn't going home when he got out of the Crossroads program. He'd opted to enter the Exodus program run by Yvonne Peterson, one of the only halfway houses for victims and cult-bound teens.

Before Evan left for San Antonio, we talked heart to heart, looking out through the glass windows at the fading sunlight over the Big Spring foothills. When it was time to go, I prayed for him and hugged him. He was so scared. Evan was one of the first male survivors I had met. He was one of the few who had lived, got out, and was strong enough to tell the truth about what he'd been through and take steps to put his life back together.

What a miracle it was to see Evan at a conference the following year with the Petersons—totally transformed, nearly three inches taller, healthy, and happy. He was free. The year he had spent at the Petersons at the Exodus program had really led him to a miracle of Jesus' healing love.

A Countrywide Problem

These kids were everywhere. There was a boy in Colorado, eighteen, druid by birth. He was so destroyed by sexual abuse that all he could do when he came to the altar at the church I spoke at was convulsively weep while we prayed for him. He hadn't cried since he was three.

I met a young lady I was called to work with at Crossroads during my second year there, who was knee-deep in witchcraft. She directly and verbally challenged the power of Jesus in me in Rita's office. The room transformed in the challenge, and I watched as a desk lamp moved across the desk a half an inch. (I was never impressed with the devil's cheap parlor tricks.) I stood and challenged the demonic powers in her. The "spell" was immediately broken, and the demonic presence backed down and left. Jesus' light immediately filled the office. She was stunned and shaken. She realized God's power was much stronger than anything she knew, and after a few hours of explaining the truth of the Gospel to her, she surrendered to Jesus that afternoon.

I met a young fifteen year old after speaking at a youth group in Euless, Texas who requested a private meeting with me along with the youth pastor. In jagged words, punctuated by sobs and trying to catch his breath, he poured out the nightmare he had experienced—the nightmare of being repeatedly sodomized at the hands of a coven in Marshall, Texas. After praying, he finally broke through his much-undeserved shame and committed his life to Jesus.

But the story that burns the deepest in my heart and memory is the story of one of the young men who came to our youth group, Tommy.*

He had spent most of his childhood under the brutal hands of evil foster care "parents" who were unspeakably cruel and abusive. He was finally adopted, but the damage was severe, and when he was with his adopted parents in Germany, he joined a gang that was heavily involved in drug dealing, drug running, and occult practices. He said he saw a real human sacrifice at the age of fourteen. We met him shortly after he and his family moved back to the USA. He was sixteen now.

He wanted nothing to do with us. But one of our young ladies, Michelle, wasn't going to take no for an answer. She talked Tommy into coming to one of our rock-climbing outings in the desert. He hung back and watched. He was sarcastic, angry, and untouchable.

"Are you coming to Bible Study tonight?" Michelle asked him.

"Hell no!" he replied.

"Whatsamaaater?" she teased. "Afraid of a little Biiible Study?" She sure had a way with people. She literally intimidated Tommy into coming.

And he kept coming—for months and months, saying little. We just loved him, and hugged him, and let him know Jesus loved him. He wanted nothing to do with Jesus.

We had joined forces with a great church in Las Cruces, New Mexico that had taken a genuine loving interest in our youth. We had outings with them—and they with us. Tommy always went. But he would change dramatically whenever we visited them. He would become sullen, angry, and withdrawn.

---

* Not his real name.

Tommy was highly demonized.

Little did we know until later that Tommy was doing curses against us. When we would have an outing, often things just went wrong. A flat tire, followed by overheating, followed by a freak wind dislodging the hood of my car when I was putting in water and slamming on my head. The kids said Tommy would just watch, giggle, and mock.

But it was actually more serious. "I had two bullets," Tommy told me later. "One for you and one for Tim. I was just waiting for the right time." Tim was the head of our youth ministry.

Our friends in Las Cruces were hosting a concert with Dony and Reba McGuire. We were walking in as they were walking outside. Tommy growled at them. "That's Tommy," the pastors said. "We really love him." And they meant it.

Later, Tommy went into a demonic fit of sorts. The pastors and elders took him to the back to pray for him, and Tommy ended up ripping the elder's Sunday coat. I had to hand it to these folks, though—they didn't know what they were getting into, but once they did, they hung in. In fact, their own stand against occultism in Las Cruces and New Mexico had brought them a number of retaliatory actions, including sacrificed animals being placed on the porches of their homes. Still, they were brave enough to have me come and teach an entire night on the dangers of the occult, even while a man sat in the back row carving a bone the whole time I was lecturing.

But Tommy's condition couldn't stay like this forever. And one night during Bible Study, it came to a clash. I was teaching that night, and I admittedly was getting increasingly upset at Tommy's disruptiveness. Tommy had his head bowed and his hands put together in the devil's horn configuration. I stopped, pointed at him, and sternly said, "Tommy! Knock. That. Off!"

He looked up. His eyes were glassy, and he looked startled. "What? he said. "I didn't do anything!" And I realized he had no idea what he did. He had been in a demonic trance.

After the meeting, I was on my way out to take a few kids home, and I was not happy. Suddenly Mike, one of our adults, stopped me. "Greg! Tommy wants to accept Jesus!"

"That's good, Mike," I said, and I am ashamed to say I was skeptical. Then Mike stopped me in my tracks, "But he wants *you* to pray for him." My heart was pierced with conviction and shame. I realized at that moment that Tommy probably didn't believe I cared or that God did either. I think he was testing me. He was saying, "Are you for real, or just like everyone else who's ever rejected me?"

I gathered Mike, my partner Tim, and Tim's brother-in-law. We piled in the back of Tim's van and started to pray. There was only one bench in the back, no seats, and Tommy sat on the bench. I began to explain how to get saved, then began leading him in a prayer for salvation. I knew it wasn't going to be easy.

"Tommy, repeat this prayer after me. 'Jesus, I know You died on the cross for me.'"

"Jesus, I know You died on the cross for me."

"I know that I'm a sinner."

Out of Tommy's mouth came a deep, growling, not-Tommy voice. "I know I'm not a sinner! rrrrrrrrrrrrrrrrrh!!"

All of a sudden, Tommy slumped to the floor and began slithering around the van like a snake, growling. It took all three of us to restrain him. Tim's brother-in-law restrained him from behind, and Tommy bit through his leather glove. We earnestly prayed, but there was no letup. We tried to get him to pray. He wanted to pray, but every time the words started, something took his voice, and he could not confess the name of Jesus, just "Je . . . Je . . . Je . . .," and he would growl again. I searched my spirit desperately for an answer. We were missing something.

Then, it hit me. I knew what we had to do. We prayed that the blood covenant Tommy made with Satan would be broken in the name of Jesus Christ.

"NOOOOOO!" the demon screamed, and Tommy began to choke. We kept rebuking the demon in Jesus'. Suddenly, he was still. We waited in silent prayer. Then, we started the prayer again. Tommy prayed to receive Jesus. In an instant—he was born again. He emerged from that prayer a totally different person!

When we got out of the van, Tommy was glowing. Even at night, his eyes were shining with Jesus. Several of the kids were still there. "I just accepted Jesus!" Tommy grinned, and everybody knew he really had. The change in him was dramatic and permanent. What a victory!

Like all the kids that broke with the occult, Tommy had many struggles ahead. But he never again returned to the occult. It was such an incredible testimony when we returned to the church in Las Cruces. The pastor called Tommy forward, and put an arm around him. Near tears, the pastor said, "Here was a boy some had all but written off. I'm so thankful God didn't. He's taught me a lot about loving kids, no matter what. We're proud of him. We love him." Tommy was grinning from ear to ear.*

Though the struggles were strong, Tommy completed his GED, got married, and had kids—one of whom just graduated from the Air Force Academy. He still loves Jesus and is considering going to seminary. He's a true survivor by the grace and power of Jesus Christ. He was a brand plucked from the fire, an orphan who was caught in the devil's trap and who we were honored to love and bring to Jesus. He's living proof that God's love is stronger than any power the devil may have.

> Who hath delivered us from the power of darkness, and hath translated us into the kingdom of his dear Son. (Colossians 1:13)

Tommy was one of many who made it out. Many others did not. I grieve and mourn for every young person who did not make it out, who did not hear the truth, who was not reached. And all these years later, I still believe that proclaiming the truth about the Gospel and the power of Jesus to save even the most broken and desperate—especially to a generation that has no hope without it—is more important than ever.

---

*IMPORTANT: On page 286 of this book, I have included an appendix that discusses my views on deliverance of demons. Please take the time to read this important message.

A Word About Deliverance

Perhaps more than anything else, the unseen realm of demonic forces creates a great deal of confusion and controversy among Christians. And when it comes to deliverance, many so-called "deliverance ministries" have gone to such unbiblical extremes that in the end the entire concept of delivering someone has been discarded and rejected.

And yet, according to the Bible, there *is* such a thing as demonic oppression or possession. Unfortunately, this can happen when someone has opened himself up to the occult (which may include satanic practices and rituals) or other ungodly activities.

The Bible also recognizes the need for deliverance from such forces. There are many verses that address this spiritual battle that can provide help and understanding. Below are a few:

> For we wrestle not against flesh and blood, but against principalities, against powers, against the rulers of the darkness of this world, against spiritual wickedness in high places. (Ephesians 6:12)

> And they were all amazed, insomuch that they questioned among themselves, saying, What thing is this? what new doctrine is this? for with authority commandeth he even the unclean spirits, and they do obey him. (Mark 1:27)

> The Spirit of the Lord is upon me, because he hath anointed me to preach the gospel to the poor; he hath sent me to heal the brokenhearted, to preach deliverance to the captives, and recovering of sight to the blind, to set at liberty them that are bruised.—Jesus (Luke 4:18)

7

The Youth Are the Future

My heart has always been about helping hurting youth and abused children. For years, I was deeply involved in the blood and mud work of rescuing teen devil worshippers, ritually abused children, and sexually abused adolescents.

Search and Rescue

Our youth group began to see more and more kids who were involved in the occult, witchcraft, and devil worship who were drawn to our youth fellowship and were curious about Jesus or genuinely wanting a way out of their entanglement with dark things. We grew to forty kids in a month, and two years later, we had over 150 or more kids coming to our youth center for concerts and Bible studies. It was an awesome time, and it was a treacherous time. We had been warned, "Do what you want, but if you start getting kids out, we will retaliate." We did—and they did. But that's for another chapter.

Tim, the leader of the youth outreach, did most of the hard discipleship work with newly saved kids coming out of very difficult backgrounds and many of them out of occult practices. I was mostly on the road, traveling, conducting criminal justice classes, and speaking to youth around the country. I tried to be home for as many Monday night Bible studies and weekend outings for things like rock climbing and hiking as I could. I had never expected that I would be on the road nearly all year, speaking to various groups of professionals and churches about the occult. In effect, I was wearing three hats: criminal justice trainer, youth evangelist, and part-time youth pastor back home.

In those tumultuous years, we saw kids of every kind, every level of occult and satanic involvement, every depth of demonic bondage. We dealt with those who were born into occult and satanic families, those who were seduced into the occult by music, rebellion, and drugs, and every level in between. The answer was always the same—Jesus. Some came into the Kingdom easily through prayer and repentance. Some went through grueling demonic extractions. And some observed, became a part of us for a while, and eventually just moved on. A few actually attached themselves to us for the purpose of dealing drugs when we weren't watching or were sent by the other side to try to hurt or destroy us. (Obviously, they did not succeed.)

Dabblers?

I was sometimes at odds with "professionals" who wanted to dismiss teen devil worshippers as mere "dabblers" and, therefore, not worthy of serious concern. As I have said before, a dabbler today can become a murderer or a suicide statistic tomorrow, so we must take them seriously. Neither you nor I can tell where that line might be crossed.

The Sean Sellers Story

Sean Sellers "dabbled" and ended up going on a killing spree. He was tried and sentenced to death as an adult in Oklahoma at age sixteen. His story has been presented elsewhere in various media specials and YouTube videos, but I will add what I know.

Sean killed a store clerk and then killed his mother and stepfather—for Satan. He was introduced to the fantasy role-playing game *Dungeons and Dragons* and then witchcraft and the occult through his babysitter when he was quite young. He got a copy of *The Satanic Bible*, and it lit him up. He was not an "official" member of the Church of Satan (he probably couldn't have afforded their $50 membership fee), but then, there are enough incendiary things in that demonic book, on its own, that he probably didn't need to be a member to fall under its dangerous spell.

He started his own coven and started bringing in a handful of recruits. He told one of them that to be a true devil worshipper, you had to break all ten commandments. He claimed he had broken them all except for one—you shall not murder. So, he and his right-hand recruit set up a convenience store clerk they knew, and while Sean's friend distracted the clerk, Sean killed him in cold blood. He got away with it for a while.

His mother already knew he was in trouble but didn't know what to do. I was told that she had broken into his room and found all the satanic paraphernalia, including black candles, black magick books, bones, etc., and bagged them up and took them all to a local preacher who said, "Give it back. You have no right to violate his privacy. It's a phase. He'll outgrow it." He obviously did not.

Shortly after the first murder, Sean locked himself in his room, drank a vial of his own blood (he was addicted to it by then and kept it hidden in the refrigerator), and conducted a ritual, falling into a demonic trance. Then he proceeded to sneak down with his gun into the bedroom of his sleeping mother and stepfather. He shot each of them in the head, and in his own words, "I laughed. I giggled."

Sean called the authorities and pretended someone else had killed his parents. He'd hidden the weapon, but eventually, he was arrested for all three murders. He woke up in a jail cell, not even really knowing why he was there. The "powers" and their attending demons had vacated him, having gotten what they wanted out of him. Then, it slowly came back to him, the horror and awfulness of his crimes.

His grandfather led Sean to Jesus.

I know, I know—"jailhouse religion." I've certainly seen that many times. Prisoners suddenly get religion before parole hearings. That wasn't the case with Sean. (Nor was it for Charles Tex Watson and Susan Atkins, two of the convicted Manson murderers. In fact, Susan was loved and discipled by one of my own spiritual mothers, Audrey Mieir, composer of the classic hymn, "His Name Is Wonderful.") Sean genuinely turned his life around. He immediately started to reach out to the world to tell his story and try to keep other kids from getting into the occult as he had. There's some debate, still, about him doing that. After all, it could have been seen as a ploy. But in the eleven years to follow, he stayed steady and led a lot of people to Jesus from his cell on death row. We corresponded for a while.

Our WATCH team in El Paso had met the ex-girlfriend of Richard Ramirez—the notorious Nightstalker—at a local conference. She asked us to pray for her as she was going to go to L.A. to see him, hoping to lead him to Christ. I encouraged her to contact Sean and ask him to pray as well. He let me know that he hadn't heard from her yet. "But if we can talk, I am sure we can get Richard saved!" Sean said.

Sean felt for sure he would not be executed, but he said, "If somehow, someway, they execute me, so what, ya know? This world sucks anyway. I'm homeward bound . . ."

In another letter to me, Sean wrote, "The Lord is always, always there for me. Who do I talk to when I hurt? God. There is no one else. I can talk to no one here. I go to the Lord. I cry in His arms. Then I sigh, grit my teeth, and keep going. When God is all you've got, it really isn't so bad. Who better to be alone with? And you learn how to really draw near to God because He is all you have. I could be happy no other way because, you see, I have an abundance of true loving friends like you. People who care, people who hurt when I hurt, laugh when I laugh. And who, above all, pray for me."

I had planned to go to Oklahoma to interview Sean in hopes of making a video that would keep kids from making the same mistakes Sean had made. I'd filled out all the papers requesting visitation. Sean wrote, "Hope to see you soon. Plan on staying all day. There's so much I want to talk to you about."

Unfortunately, it didn't happen. I made the long drive from El Paso to McAlester, Oklahoma. I parked and walked to the first entrance, but I found no one at the desk. I kept walking. I walked down the second hallway and found no one there either, so I just kept walking. It was only when armed guards began yelling at me to stop that I realized I had made it all the way to death row before they stopped me! I told them no one had met me, so I just kept walking. They had me go back to the parking lot and start over again!

Unfortunately, I got through all the stations only to be told that my visit had been canceled. Sean and I were both pretty upset. He had been waiting for me all day before they told him I wasn't coming. I always regretted I didn't get a chance to sit with him face-to-face. Especially since I knew some things about him that I am sure he did not even know.

I know how horrible Sean's crimes were. He never minimized them. But I know for certain that he found redemption in the sacrifice of Jesus Christ on the Cross. Some people struggle with that or say it was probably a jailhouse conversion meant to impress the parole board. But I testify that it was not. Sean was consistent all the way to the end.

The fact is, Sean didn't remember much about significant parts of his life. The murders he remembered. But big chunks of his past were blank, which made me wonder if there was more to Sean's story than just an angry kid from a broken home getting out of control and doing the worst.

And there was more. How much, I don't know. But I do know through my own experience, as well as the many survivors I have spoken with, that gaps in memory are often very much an indication of trauma, abuse, and sometimes more.

I know for sure Sean did not remember the event I learned about in a law enforcement class in Colorado in 1990. An officer approached me after the class to tell me that he had personally taken Sean into custody when Sean was about ten when the officers broke up a large outdoor black mass ritual that took place outside of Greeley, Colorado. I was stunned but not surprised. It was a clear indication that Sean's murderous acts did not happen in a vacuum. He had been groomed. He had been involved since he was a child. And he had no memory of that event at all.

There was so much I wanted to talk to Sean about. There were questions I wanted to ask him, things I wanted to pass on to him to help him heal. But it was not to be. Before we knew it, his time was up, his last appeal had been denied, and Sean was scheduled for execution by lethal injection as the youngest inmate to be put to death in Oklahoma history.

I couldn't contact him, except through his girlfriend, who let me know when it was going to happen. I asked her, if possible, to let him know we loved him and were praying for him.

I was in an online chatroom the night of his execution with a group of believers keeping vigil. We learned that he had given a statement to the family: "All the people that are hating me right now and are here waiting to see me die, when you wake up in the morning, you're not going to feel any different. You're going to hate me just as much tomorrow as tonight.

When you wake up and nothing has changed inside, reach out to God and He will be there for you. Reach out to God, and He will heal you. Let Him touch your hearts. Don't hate all your lives. I love you all."

When it was coming down to the moment of his execution, suddenly, there were a number of Satanist trolls on the online group, some of whom were actually guards at the very prison Sean was at, reveling in his execution, mocking his faith in Jesus, calling him a "satanic traitor" for following Jesus. I was enraged and began to engage in the discussion, challenging them, calling them out, rebuking them, demanding to know who they were. They took the bait and began attacking back, and I was downloading and printing the whole thing.

Within a day, I had reached the warden there, Gary, and faxed him everything. He was furious. "I promise you these people will be fired immediately."

But then, Sean lay on the table. He was singing Christian songs, then loudly said, "Here I come, Father, I'm coming home." He told the warden, "Let's do it, Gary. Let's get it on." And as they injected him, he sang, "Set my spirit free, that I might worship Thee. Set my spirit free, that I might praise Thy name." And he breathed his last.

I loved Sean like a brother. I know I will see him again. That night, I vowed to do all I could to ensure there would never be another Sean Sellers story that ended in tragedy.

Sean was one of so many young people who were targets for the devil's destructive plans. I was disturbed that so many of the kids I talked to said they had been raised in church or went to church but found no power or reality there. One girl said, "How can you expect me to believe your God has power when you don't believe it?" This is a powerful, searing question that demands more than a flippant answer.

Devil-worshipping kids talked to me because they knew I recognized that Satan has power (artificial and temporary though it may be). I had seen what he could do and had felt it firsthand as an occult-bound teen myself. Yes, God's power is infinitely greater, so much so that it makes Satan look like a deadbeat amateur. But I never dismissed kids who had experienced Satan's "power," even if it is a lie and simply the manipulation of demons to deceive and destroy those who give their lives over to it. I didn't disbelieve them when they told me what they had heard and experienced, and I understood what usually drew them into the Dark

Side: A need to belong, a need for unconditional acceptance. And I know very well that many churches were just not giving out those things. At least not to the outcasts and the disenfranchised and "difficult" kids.

We weren't looking for messy kids. Unfortunately, we preferred to mostly babysit church kids or minister to the already-saved. And I, in part, understand the issue: kids coming out of the occult, devil worship, witchcraft, and sexual abuse issues are fragmented and hurting, bound and confused, and need healing. They are tough to deal with. But we are commanded to reach them—the least, the last, the lost—are we not? It is not without cost.

For many of the kids we met, rejection was what caused them to leave the church and fall into Satan's clutches. We don't like long-haired, earring-wearing, smoking, black-clothed, unkempt kids very much, do we?

Our youth group accepted the kids who came to us just the way they were. I think it was one of the things that drew them to us. And we had a heck of a time taking them to church. We were asked to leave once—before we even got the kids in the church door! No wonder it's easier for them to be devil worshippers. Satan doesn't care one bit what you look like.

I heard a story that may help you understand the real issue. A prisoner who was on death row for murder shocked everyone by attending chapel and giving his life to Jesus. A prison volunteer spent a lot of time with him. He told his pastor, "You have to meet this guy! He's really on fire for Jesus!" The pastor agreed to meet him.

As the pastor and the inmate sat across from each other in the visiting room, the pastor asked him, "What do you think about Jesus?" The excited prisoner lit up a smoke, accidentally blowing it in the pastor's direction, and said, "Pastor, this is the best @#$@#$ thing that's ever happened to me, I swear to God!"

On the way home, the pastor was furious. "I don't believe he's a Christian at all!" the pastor yelled at the young prison volunteer. "He sat right there and smoked and cussed in front of me!"

"Well," the young man said meekly, "We figure we need to get these guys to quit murdering people, then kind of go from there."

Do you understand? You don't know just how far down people, especially the "devil's kids," may have sunk. God wants us to not be put off by their appearance and disturbing behavior but see and love their souls and let God change them from there. A young person who has participated in ugly and brutal animal sacrifices, sexual orgies, and drug use, or even worse, can surely be forgiven for struggling with the small things after they come to Jesus.

After speaking to a class for probation officers in Beaumont, Texas, three people from the group approached me to talk. "We agree with you," they said. "And we're ashamed to admit it—but we know the kinds of kids you are trying to reach would not be welcomed into our youth group. Their parents would be too scared that your kids would influence ours in a negative way."

I appreciated their honesty. And I completely understood their fears. After all, teen Satanists were trying to infiltrate and destroy youth groups during that time, and everyone needed to be vigilant and discerning so as not to allow their youth to be hurt or led astray. But a youth group and a church can only be effective when they become strong enough in the Word of God and trained in spiritual warfare that such a deliberate attempt to sabotage a youth group would fail. They would know they were exactly where God wanted them to be when it was actually the devil worshippers, drug dealers, and abusers who were afraid of the influence their youth group was having on the other side! Then, they would know they were walking in God's will and God's power.

As to youth groups, unfortunately, we, as elders, do not teach them how to do spiritual battle. We have been gravely mistaken by teaching that the Christian life is *like* a war. It is not; it *is* a war, and it takes more than rah-rah, flash-and-pop concerts with made-up demons and swords and kids in fake armor to produce warriors. It takes raw spiritual education on the reality of this war. It is life and death. It is not a game. We are not steeling kids and discipling them and raising them up with a solid foundation in the Word of God to raise Heaven on Hell's front porch. Unfortunately, we end up sheltering, entertaining, and protecting them instead when they actually should be on the front lines in our pagan-saturated mess of a country bringing the power of the Gospel.

Dealing With the Demonic

Our newly saved and still somewhat "raw" kids had been going to a "normal" youth group once a week. One night before the meeting, I met with one of our boys, Danny. He was fourteen, a skinny little guy with a lifetime of abuse, misuse, confusion, and pain. He'd just gotten out of a mental hospital that his dad had put him in because he couldn't handle him anymore.

"I'm scared," Danny said. "Something evil's in me. I need help."

"We'll see you through it, Danny," I told him. "No matter what—just keep walking with Jesus. We'll walk you through it."

We went to the youth group. I was sitting behind Danny. One of our girls and the leader of our youth group sat on each side of him.

During worship, I saw Danny put his head in his hands and start to shake. I smiled, mistakenly thinking that God was touching him during worship.

Actually, God *was* touching him—but Danny was *not* worshipping. He was getting taken over by the evil he spoke of that could not stand the presence of the Lord in worship.

"It's strong," the young lady turned around and said to me.

"What's strong?" I asked, clueless.

"He's about to go," Tim, my youth counterpart, said.

"Go where?" I asked.

Backward, it turns out, right into me. Suddenly, an ungodly animal growl ripped out of Danny's throat, and he catapulted backward right into me. I grabbed him around his waist, and we went back five rows of empty folding chairs before we landed on the floor, which, thankfully, was carpeted.

It took five people—three adults and two of our kids—to restrain Danny and carry him to the back room so we could get him set free. All of our kids—long hair, earrings, smoke breath, and all—were there, praying fervently for Danny's deliverance. And he did get delivered.

Kind of scary to think of such a thing happening in your youth group, isn't it? But if you've never had to confront that kind of evil in a person, it can be very scary. And if you have never been taught the authority of the name of Jesus Christ of Nazareth, you *should* be scared. But when you do know His authority, there is no reason to fear!

I prayed that God would begin to help youth pastors teach their kids the tools they would need to help set kids free. Kids like the ones God was bringing to us. It disturbed me. Why weren't we teaching Christian kids to fight in this spiritual war? Was it fear when we should have no fear? Was it ignorance when we should not be ignorant of the devil's devices?

Was it a lack of power when we should know that even the youngest child who knows Jesus can set a thousand devils to running at the sound of Jesus' name being proclaimed? We had so far to go!

Praying for kids who had been demonized became a regular part of our Bible studies—not because we sought it or set it up that way, but it just naturally unfolded as part of teaching the Word and during prayer and worship. It just happened.

One night Yolanda attended the study in my home and sat in my recliner. She was a devil worshipper. (And also, a straight-A student.) Tim was teaching. Yolanda had squirmed and angrily fidgeted through worship. Then Tim opened his Bible to teach. "Shut up!" screamed the male voice coming from Yolanda's mouth. "I hate Jesus Christ!"

Tim, never rattled, pointed at her and said, "Be silent in the name of Jesus. When I'm through, I'll deal with you." And she fell completely silent and still as if angels had her bound and gagged.

The minute that Tim finished, Yolanda went into a full-blown demonic fit. We had two pastor friends there who were well-versed in this kind of thing, and the four of us took Yolanda into the back room and began to pray for her to get set free. Our kids were a little rattled. It was one of the first times they had seen something this real. We told them to worship and pray, and they did—earnestly.

As we prayed for Yolanda, she screamed, "I'm blind, I'm blind!" and we watched as a white film completely covered both of her eyes. We kept praying and demanding in Jesus' name that the evil invader would let go. We could feel the tug of war. When the kids in the living room wearied and stopped singing, the evil presence in Yolanda defiantly dug in its heels, refusing to leave. When the kids would start worshipping again, we could feel the rush of the Holy Spirit's power. The demon began to whimper and beg not to be sent away, and Yolanda was finally set free. Jesus won. Prayer and worship and the victory of Jesus Christ broke Satan's back.

For us, it was just "a day in the life" of spiritual reality—the real war. I began to realize that most Christian kids had no idea there is a spiritual war because they had never learned about it, and it really scared them.

Something had to change.

A lot of teen devil worshippers knew the Bible. They were using it to *convert* nominal Christian kids who barely even knew John 3:16.

Yes, folks, we need to be very concerned about kids dabbling in the occult and devil worship.

But I'm even more concerned with Christian kids "dabbling." They "dabble" in God: a verse or two, a nice Christian club or group, no power, no commitment, and no reality. I'm concerned about kids who only make Jesus a part of their lives instead of Jesus being their whole life; they are of no threat to Satan—or devil worshippers—at all. I have to wonder if kids are just modeling us who claim Jesus but leave Him out of our lives except for a few hours on Sunday or Wednesday.

For many of the kids we met who worshipped the devil, it was all or nothing. Life or death.

Speaking of the Devil

I was actually very comfortable talking to teen devil worshippers. In fact, I preferred it to talking with "Christian" dabblers. I found it easier than talking to New Agers, Wiccans, and lower-level occult dabblers of the adult kind. Why? Because they are, in many ways, even more deceived than devil worshippers because they believe they are okay, that they are "good Christians," "good New Agers," "good witches," or whatever. Devil worshippers, at least the real ones, have a little bit of understanding of spiritual reality and of evil. They know they belong to the Evil One. They know I belong to Jesus. And that makes it easy for me to talk to them.

After one large evangelistic youth meeting, a neatly dressed young man in his twenties with gold jewelry and diamond rings took me aside. "I worship Satan," he said straight out. "I like what you said about Jesus and all. But Satan gives me everything I need. I've got tons of money, all the girls I want, and a nice new car. Why would I need Jesus?"

"Does Satan love you?" I asked, looking right into his eyes. "Do you have love? Do you feel loved at all?"

He was taken off guard. He lowered his eyes. "No. Nobody loves me. The devil doesn't either." I gave him my card and told him to call me if he ever wanted to talk or get out. But I never heard from him again.

No Compromise

In the tiny town of Alpine, Texas, nearly 600 people came to a town hall meeting to hear me speak about the dangers of the occult.

As I began speaking, a group of thirteen hard-core devil worshippers—a full coven—black robes, pentagrams, and all—filled the back row, flashing their pentagrams at me.

During the question-and-answer period, a fifteen-year-old Christian kid with a satanic death metal shirt stood up. "Hey, I love Jesus!" he said arrogantly. "I go to church all the time, and I'm a good Christian! I just happen to like this group, pointing to his shirt! Are you saying I'm a devil worshipper because I wear this?"

"No," I said. "I'm saying you're a hypocrite. There's a coven of devil worshippers here tonight listening to you and laughing at you because you say what a good Christian you are. They know you're a phony. So, either get the guts to take off that shirt and get rid of it, or shut up and sit down!"

He sat down.

Even in Satan's world, there's no in-between. It's all or nothing. You can't be "sort of" a devil worshipper. And you can't be "sort of" a disciple of Jesus Christ.

How come we teach our kids—one of God's choicest weapons to break open the satanic, pagan, occult world and lead out the captives in the power and love of God—that being "sort-of" a Christian—not too fanatical, just a good church-going kid—is acceptable?

Until we begin to preach God's Word, challenge our kids, and raise them up in the spiritual reality of this spiritual battle, we can kiss this generation goodbye as they fall numbly into the arms of the eagerly waiting Evil One.

Kids are the future. Let's wake them up!

Remember not the sins of my youth,
nor my transgressions: according to thy
mercy remember. (Psalm 25:7)

8

Grooming the Young and Fatherless: A Nazi Occult Story

A rizona is one of the hot spots in America for both Nazi-type groups as well as occult groups, and it was not unusual for us to find a mixture of the two. As mentioned before, Nazi philosophies go very well with true occult satanic ones.

One winter night in December 1988, I spoke at a small church to give a basic presentation about guarding the church against occultism. It was a small but receptive group. On the front row was a young man in his early twenties who was writing furiously as I spoke. I was a bit concerned. But during the half-hour break, he approached me with his mother and told me he had been part of a Nazi occult group, and he wanted to show me some of the material they used in their "services." I told him I would talk to him afterward. From a broken home, this young man was taken in by a "mentor" through a school program and began to be recruited slowly by this elderly gentleman into Nazi and occult philosophy. He was sworn to secrecy at one point and made to take an oath of silence.

His mother was there as he was sharing this with me. She had trusted the man after a while, and when he offered to take her son to Germany during the summer of his last year in high school to learn about the customs and language of the land he came from as part of a German language course the boy had taken, the mother agreed. It never occurred to her that her son would be in harm's way. As a single mother, she was just grateful that this father figure for her son had been so willing to help him.

The young man told me that while he was in Germany, he was fully initiated into the group called the Black Order of the 4th Reich, which included witnessing the murder of two people, both Jewish, in a sacrificial offering to the devil. (Sacrificial does not necessarily mean drawing a pentagram and doing rituals—it can merely be a murder offered to Satan for power or to prove one's worthiness to belong to the group.)

The old man had died and left his Nazi SS uniform to the young man and expected him to carry on the group's goals and membership. The younger man had panicked at some point and got out. He had already given all the information to the authorities some time before I came to the church to do my presentation, and they followed up on it, but I did not hear back as to what they uncovered. That is not uncommon, and it is not unusual for rings like this to be broken up and people jailed under different criminal charges, and we never hear about the rest of the details unless it's somehow leaked to the press.

The mom confirmed all of it and said she had seen the uniform herself when her son confessed, and she suddenly realized that the man she trusted her son with was actually a war criminal who had gotten away.

While I was teaching that night, the young man translated into English several pages from their German language "hymn book" that they used in their satanic rituals and gatherings. Some were for preparation before killing or creating mayhem; some were asking for satanic power to enable them to destroy, and many others. What was shocking was that this young man, who had taken one class in German and spent one summer in Germany, was capable of translating several pages back and forth from German to English and from English to German like a born citizen. There was no question as to his credibility.

He wrote at the bottom of one page, "I regret helping to build this destructive racist under-society. And it was a great discredit to my ancestry that I led these Blitz Gruppen for the devil."

A "fringe group?" Perhaps, but dangerous and deadly, and one of many we encountered when we extracted young people from their grip—youth who had no sense of connectedness, no fathering, no solid family. Hitler said, "He alone who owns the youth, gains the future." It grieves me to this day that, even as the issues change, the fatherlessness of a generation leaves the youth as fodder for the devil's minions.

9

Discerning Truth From Lies

I t's always been crucial to take this work extremely seriously. I was always aware that one false step could endanger my family, my friends, or my own life. I was also keenly aware that my ability to discern between the real and the fake in this work could spare—or cost—someone's life. It has been difficult to walk in the two worlds I have lived in—first and always foremost, as a servant of Jesus Christ and secondly, as a private investigator and police consultant whose work necessitated swimming in the cesspool of evil and somehow still maintaining my walk with the Lord. It was never easy investigating the brutal crimes we encountered on a regular basis. It was also difficult to spend eight hours at a time training criminal justice, medical, and educational professionals on occult crimes and not be able to openly share my faith. There was always an opportunity—but it couldn't be my primary forum in law enforcement and criminal justice classes. I wonder if Daniel felt as I did, trying to stand in the mire of Babylonian witchcraft and demonic darkness yet still serve faithfully and without compromise.

What made our work even more difficult was the many non-credible people our work and conferences seemed to attract. Unfortunately, a number of these people were Christians.

I understood the seriousness of the spiritual issues and dynamics around occult crimes and occult workings. I was committed to doing something for the sake of Jesus in an arena where few venture. I knew that Jesus Christ is the only real hope for healing, not only for the victims but for those working with these cases.

Having said that, let me give you another perspective. Let's say your car breaks down. You take it to a mechanic. He may or may not be a Christian. (Being a Christian does not necessarily equate to being a good auto mechanic.) Hopefully, he knows his stuff. He gets working on your failed transmission. Then a Christian comes along and tells the mechanic, "Praise God you're doing that. I'll pray for you. You know, if you were a Christian, you'd be a better mechanic. Hey, I can help you. Let me pray for that transmission. It probably needs demons cast out of it. Move over. I'm going to help." Perhaps the mechanic would be grateful for the prayer, depending on the difficulty of the repairs. But move over and let someone who doesn't know anything about cars do the repairs? I don't think he'd go for that!

There is no doubt that the issues I've written about—devil worship, occult practices, child abuse—all carry weighty spiritual implications. And there always needs to be spiritual healing through Jesus Christ for the victims. Everything else is a Band-Aid. But sometimes, when a person is bleeding out, a Band-Aid is better than nothing at all. So, I am thankful for therapists, law enforcement, probation workers, and others who can stem the blood flow of satanic child abuse and crimes.

But our work was sometimes complicated by Christians who were somehow allowed into the law enforcement seminars, having no criminal investigation background. Rather than coming to learn, they used it as a forum to preach. We each need to know our place. Or, to put it another way, some of us need to get out from under the hood and let the mechanics do their jobs. I am not a cop. I would never dare presume to do a cop's job. My job was different, but that was a good thing. In some ways, I had a whole lot more latitude to investigate than law enforcement did. But I would never have presumed to replace law enforcement with my own limited training and experience. Both approaches, in their proper place, were needed. And what we could contribute was unique and often welcomed.

Knowing our limitations and being willing to cooperate with those who "work under the hood" in the long run gave us an open invitation to speak to them freely about Jesus Christ as well, and many listened with respect.

I hate to even speak of these issues, but it is a sad fact that the Christian community often muddied the investigative waters inadvertently and turned away those who could help. In other instances, preachers and pastors were so ignorant about the real issues that they only served to distract and downplay the profoundly serious issues we were confronting.

At the same time, we were faced with stark and startling new dangers as we began to acquire new information about how the "other side" sought to create confusion and disinformation to keep us from doing our investigative and spiritual work effectively. (See "zap action" in chapter five.) This is how it worked: They would start a rumor about devil worship and inject it into the public somehow, preferably through Christians who have a reputation for spreading rumors readily and gullibly—then the rumors just spread.

As an example: "We heard that a blond-haired, blue-eyed twelve-year-old girl or six-year-old boy would be kidnapped and sacrificed on Halloween." As I said before, one year in Midland, Texas, and in Andrews, Texas, where my friend Ben, the probation officer, worked, those very rumors nearly caused widespread panic. The school kids panicked. The teachers panicked. The parents really panicked. And the cops, the counselors, and law enforcement were so busy quieting fears, putting out fires, and investigating nonexistent ritual sites that it very well could have happened . . . elsewhere . . . with a helpless victim that didn't even fit that description . . . and there was no time or resources to even start looking for it.

Example: "The president of Procter and Gamble is a devil worshipper. We know it is true because look at the thirteen stars and moon on Procter and Gamble products. They were on talk shows telling how they gave their lives to Satan in exchange for making them rich!"

I don't know how many dozens of times we were told this thing, called about that thing, or handed printed information about this or that. These rumors were patently false, untrue lies. We had all the official letters to prove it.

More wasted time. It served to make a lot of Christians look gullible and unreliable. The devil worshippers enjoy the game. It's a great sport and a great cover-up.

One thing we needed to be clear about was the first basic rule of investigation: Supposition is not evidence. Everyone can "suppose." I do it all the time because that's part of putting the pieces of a crime puzzle together. But I would never give weight to such suppositions—or "what if's"—without some proof to back them up. Proper documentation is essential. It is imperative in this weird world of occult shadows and actual occult crimes to base all we do and say on facts as much as possible. No one ever calls me and says, "I heard this . . ." without getting a thorough vetting about where they heard it and how. I'll follow it up. But I can't give weight to it without a substantial reason. This field is so sensitive and dangerous that Christians cannot afford to be part of unfounded allegations, accusations, and rumors. The enemy is watching and laughing when we do—and unfortunately, skeptics are waiting for every slip-up to further "prove" that we are all "flakes" and that there is no satanic crime. We are dealing with real criminals—stealthy, organized, and deadly. We understood all this from the beginning and treated these matters with the utmost caution and diligence they deserved.

Fast forward three decades. We are now in the Internet era where "fake news" is a regular part of our media and social media reality. Anyone with a YouTube channel can make any number of claims, even outrageous ones. And rather than vet it out and "see whether those things were so" (Acts 17:11), we too often spread it, forward it, and believe it.

Even as far back as 1987, at the beginning of our work, we had to contend with "fake news"—false rumors, false accusations, and phony claims. From the beginning, we understood that there were many people from the occult world—pagans, Wiccans, wannabe Satanists, etc.—who were determined to prove that all our claims were false. So, I made a commitment not to present any information as fact in my criminal justice classes unless they were provable facts.

In my criminal justice classes, I covered many issues: ritual crime, ritual crime dates, levels of occult involvement from non-criminal to criminal, crime scene investigations, teen devil worship, generational Satanism, and others. After a year or so, I had amassed enough information to present a trimmed-down and concise eight-hour class. At the start, I would announce, "There will be some things I present today that are speculative. That's a part of what we do to figure out the many facets of a crime of this nature. And I will tell you if it is speculation. Otherwise, everything you will see and hear today is one hundred percent take-it-to-the-bank fact—a verifiable, indisputable fact." This was very important to me. In the early days, even in some of the professional classes, there were those who were teaching totally false and dangerous things. With all eyes on us and potential lives at risk, we could not afford to deviate even a scintilla from the facts. And doing this has served us well.

Greg, teaching a class

After a while, the survivor network—those who claimed to have been victims of satanic upbringing and abuse—was a mixture of credible, real ritual abuse victims as well as some who claimed to be survivors but were so non-credible that I cringed just listening to them. And this was hard for me because I knew real survivors, people whose entire lives had been devastated by sexual abuse and ritual abuse since the earliest age. It was painful to hear people whom I knew were not credible spreading things that would hurt the real survivors. (More on this in chapter thirteen, "Pinging the Web")

This phenomenon has spread into current times as well. More recently, there have been two or three "survivors" with YouTube channels who have made claims that strained any credulity at all. One, in particular, claimed to have been a sex slave to some of the most famous people in the world, from celebrities to politicians to royals. These so-called survivors have amassed large followings, including from many survivors. But as usually happens, their story grew more elaborate as they went on. Then, they began to attack other survivors who had YouTube channels. They began to attack friends of mine. Worse, they asked survivors to send their personal video testimonies. I was appalled. They were painting a huge target on the entire survivor community—all, in my opinion, for their own personal aggrandizement. It personally broke my heart because most survivors I had met were not famous, did not want to be famous, knew no one famous, but were brutally and ritually abused by evil people whose names weren't even known and who struggled daily just to get by. It almost prompted me to create a t-shirt—partially based on my own "abused by no one famous" history—that said, "I was abused by no one famous, and all I got was this lousy t-shirt." Inappropriate, maybe, but I think most survivors would understand the irony of it. All these "celebrity survivors" were sucking all the air out of the room for real survivors. The real survivors' voices were slowly getting buried by those with sensational stories that no one investigated. Or worse, the real survivors looked to these "celebrity" survivors for hope and validation for their own stories—many ending up getting taken for a financial and psychological ride and left with no more answers than they had before.

And let me say this: in the face of all the false accusations coming at us—we didn't believe or disbelieve a survivor's testimony out of hand. Some were very believable but turned out to be false. Some were so horrific as to be almost impossible to accept, but turned out to be true. It took a lot of wisdom and discernment to tell the difference.

And I have come to know that a great many of the outcries against famous celebrities and politicians are, in fact, true. As I said, unbelievable does not mean untrue. It took the Jeffrey Epstein case to wake people up to the level of involvement in evil predatory rings by well-known people, and Epstein is just the tip of the iceberg.

Even before the so-called "satanic panic" era, there were false stories, as I write about concerning John Todd in chapter eleven, who was running an occult bookstore during much of the time he was preaching in churches.

We will never know just how many of the accounts we heard were true. Sometimes, these stories, for a variety of reasons, were a mixture of true and false. I believe that sometimes people were deliberately sent to the church just to create confusion, fear, and division.

For all the confusion and lack of credibility that was brought in by a few Christians, by and large, believers were the backbone of prayer and support that kept us going. Most of the flakiness came from the outside. It never failed: After I would do a talk show or radio broadcast, the stations would get a number of calls. They'd pass them on to me or pass my number along. From that stack of maybe 100 calls, only about ten percent had credible information. The other ninety percent were so exotic and obviously untrue that it was a discipline to keep myself from just hanging up. One lady claimed I was her long-lost brother; I just didn't remember. Another called several times a week incessantly with "information" that was completely and obviously false. He'd already talked to a lot of cops. I was the last one on his list to call.

Lastly, there was the man who called after my appearance on *The Montel Williams Show* to tell me he knew the locations of many of the missing and abducted children. You better believe I called him right away. All went well for about twenty minutes until he told me he got his information by placing a pendulum over a map and letting it show him where they were. What a disappointment. But I had to follow up on every call because out of the ninety percent flakes, maybe just one bit of information might lead to a real missing child. It's a procedure we had to go through. "Trust, but verify," as our former President Reagan said. Don't act until you know what and who you're dealing with. I've had to learn to trust my gut instinct and, more importantly, to hear and trust the Spirit of God in discerning truth from a distracting fantasy. It's saved me a lot of time and wasted energy.

From adults to children and the kids in between, we talked to hundreds of people. And when all of it was sorted through, we obtained a great deal of valuable information. For the record, we never found deliberate falsity with the children that we personally worked with. With teenagers, we learned how to "screen" them. Talking to them and asking specific questions about what they knew could pretty quickly determine whether to help or refer them to a counselor who could give them the attention and help they needed. With adults, it was a mixture and a challenge. It was a constant learning curve.

One final word. We were often told by secularists that Christians had no business being involved in occult crime investigations because we had a Christian "agenda." Of course, we did. We still do, just as Elie Wiesel and Simon Wiesenthal, who committed their lives to making sure the evils of the Nazi Holocaust never happened again, have a Jewish "agenda" which we must all respect and support. We Christians have a clear calling from Scripture to defend the innocent and see that justice prevails over those who, in the name of Satan, would destroy children and youth. Don't fault us for that.

I did find it ironic that while many in law enforcement refused to work with us because we were Christians, a number of them turned to psychics for information. It seemed hypocritical that good Christian investigators were told to "keep their religion to themselves" (which, for the most part, we did) while psychics were considered credible sources when they are more evangelical about their practices than most Christians.

We were prepared to go to the ends of the Earth to track information we felt had even half a chance of saving a child. Along the way, we would have to sort through the whole bowl of shredded mess of lies and truth, rumors and leads, facts and fantasy—because at the very bottom of the bowl there could be the real thing. And the real thing might be the very piece of information we needed to pursue criminals seeking to hurt children.

I trust you will understand the life and death seriousness of what we dealt with and be very thorough in your discernment of what you hear, what you learn, and what you believe about what you are told. Working together with those of various gifts and occupations, we can do a lot of damage to the demonic underworld if we try.

Psychic pseudo-cops need not apply.

10

Face to Face With the Enemy

His name was Michael A. Aquino. He was the founder and head of the Temple of Set, an Egyptian black magick order. Aquino, once on the Council of Nine of Anton LaVey's Church of Satan, broke away from LaVey in the mid-1970s and founded his own order. He was convinced LaVey did not understand the reality of black magick. Aquino believed the Egyptian god Set appeared to him while on a tour of duty in Vietnam and told him LaVey was finished and that he would usher in the next "age," the "Aeon of Set." (This is detailed in Aquino's *The Book of Coming Forth by Night*.)

Aquino had a long military career in the Army and had reached the rank of Lieutenant Colonel. He was deeply involved with the Army's psychological warfare intelligence division known as Psy-Op. He and then Colonel Paul Vallely, who later became a well-known news commentator during the Iraq War, co-authored the paper in 1980 titled "From Psy-Op to Mindwar: The Psychology of Victory" for the military. [1] Aquino helped enhance Psy-Op, advocating, among other things, psychic weaponry, and the use of electromagnetic "sound" weapons. He had a top-secret clearance and was apparently an expert in mind control.

Aquino was investigated—and acquitted—on child sexual abuse charges coming out of the Presidio Army daycare facility in San Francisco, California in 1986. Despite credible and serious oral testimony from the children who saw and identified "Mikie" as one of the ones who hurt them, there was no hard evidence, and the case was closed.

I first saw Aquino on *The Oprah Winfrey Show* in March of 1988. He and his wife Lilith were defending themselves as moral, decent people who were the hapless victims of a witchhunt based on hysteria. They adamantly denied abusing children. They adamantly denied adhering to Nazi philosophies, despite his having written extensively about attempting to recreate Nazi occult rituals at the Nazi Party SS headquarters at the Welwesburg Castle while on a tour of duty in Germany in 1982.[2] Deny, deny, deny. Remember? Deny everything. Blame the victims. That's fine. Nothing could be proven. And in law enforcement, as I said, suspicion and supposition are not evidence. Personally, I believed the children. But in the absence of hard evidence, you can't go after someone just because he's a devil worshipper—or a "Setian." Devil worship is protected by the Constitution of the United States. You can worship anything or anyone you want. Law enforcement's concern, of course, is when someone uses their religion as a cover-up for criminal activities.

Aquino had participated in a police academy debate in Killeen, Texas, in February of 1989. He was, by all accounts, persuasive, convincing, charming, and personable.

In October of 1989, Aquino was coming back to Killeen for another debate. And this time, I would be on the other side of the debate table. I was tired of the denials of the testimonies of the children who claimed to have been ritually abused, and I wanted to face Aquino down—bad.

But that was *my* plan. God had something else in mind.

The three-day cult crime conference was held at the Sheraton Hotel in Killeen, Texas, in the central part of the state. It was being sponsored by the Killeen Police Academy under Chief Walker Veal in conjunction with the Central Texas Council of Governments. They had law enforcement officers attending from all over the nation. I began my journey from El Paso to the conference on an unusually warm day in late October. In addition to being part of the debate team, I would also be teaching a segment on occult crimes.

I always felt a little out of place at these things. After all, until Sue Joyner handed me the letters from people requesting a speaker, I had no idea I would ever be teaching law enforcement. I had been quite comfortable working with Sue and the others from the WATCH Network prior to this. I was willing to step into this new role but uncomfortably aware that I was on my own at events like this.

The "Killeen Conference" came to me by what, at the time, seemed to be a divine appointment. I had been sharing information with Sergeant Ferguson with the Fort Worth gang task force. While visiting him one afternoon, he showed me a brochure for a "cult crime conference" that was to be held the next day in Belton, in Central Texas. I decided I wanted to go, and he asked me to check it out, to see if it was credible, and to get back to him.

I went to the Belton conference the next day. When I walked in, I was surprised to find my anonymous personal story that had been published in the Believe the Children newsletter in the conference's handouts. I met the conference coordinator, Beth Stokes, of the Central Texas Council of Governments. She asked a little about me, and I told her I was the one in the story in the handout. She was very glad I was there, and in a last-minute and unexpected invitation, Beth asked me to address the conference. I did, and my message seemed to be well received.

I was able to report back to Sergeant Ferguson that these were top-of-the-line folks, and he and his partner ended up going to the first Killeen Police Academy training on occult crimes. It was one of the first of its kind in the nation.

A few months before he attended, he and another task force officer came to El Paso to see what we had. We showed them a complete ritual setup that was on loan to us from the Hudspeth County Sheriff's Department. It was found in an abandoned car in the east desert outside of El Paso.

It contained dozens of potions, powders, and different occult objects and amulets. There was a black cloth with a pentagram, black and red candles, an "athame" (ritual knife for bloodletting), and a "Book of Shadows"—a notebook that all black magicians and many Wiccans keep containing all their spells—often in a coded language or alphabet.

It also contained ashes and bone and teeth fragments. Sent for analysis, they turned out to be the cremated remains of an adult and a child. It took a long time to translate this *Book of Shadows*, which contained dozens of evil spells.

After Sergeant Ferguson and his partner took pictures of all we had, I took them on a grand tour of all the known ritual sites in our city. They took dozens of photos.

During the information-sharing class in Killeen, an El Paso officer laughed and said, "This is ridiculous. We don't have one single ritual site in El Paso. We don't have any satanic crime in our town." Sergeant Ferguson and his partner, with a briefcase of El Paso photos, looked at each other in astonishment. They decided it wasn't worth bothering to show proof to someone who was that ignorant of what was going on in his own district. Sergeant Ferguson continued to do major work in apprehending criminal cults, gleaned a warehouse full of confiscated ritual crime scene evidence, and arresting some dangerous people—until his superiors required him to back off and concentrate on the growing gang problem they were facing.

It was 82 degrees that October day as I drove from El Paso to Fort Worth to stay over with friends before heading south to Killeen. The temperature dropped steadily all the way there until it was almost like winter—cold, windy, rainy. A perfect spooky weather condition for what was bound to be a spooky conference just a few days before Halloween. It was unusual for a non-law enforcement person to be invited to speak at these conferences, and I was honored to be asked. Beth, the co-coordinator at the Belton conference who was also helping with this event, convinced Walker Veal, the academy chief, to include me in the conference. He was skeptical about my ability to come through. I had to prove myself here. I was determined to do so.

While I was staying with my old college buddy and his family, we went out to eat, and I expressed what was, in fact, my over-enthusiastic zeal regarding Aquino. But my friend stopped me in mid-rant as we were talking the day before the debate. "Look," he told me, "Stop thinking about going after Aquino. He needs Jesus just like everyone else." I didn't like that at all. I *wanted* to go after Aquino, just like Peter, who chopped off the servant's ear on the night Jesus was betrayed. But I knew my friend was absolutely right. I asked God to forgive me for my arrogant attitude. I asked for a heart of mercy for Aquino, the same way He had mercy on me when I was a die-hard occult-practicing teen.

As if things weren't spooky enough, as I headed south to Killeen, I happened to tune in to *The Bob Larson Show*. Bob had a live radio talk show out of Colorado. Highly criticized by many for his money-raising during commercials, I was not so critical, as I had heard him reach out to many people—especially kids in the occult—that many churches would have nothing to do with. Whatever his flaws, at least he was trying to do something.

That day's program had a caller who was desperate for help. She was from a generational occult family, which included her parents, grandparents, and herself.

Right in the middle of the call, the woman was completely taken over by a demon. It was so terrifyingly real that I nearly pulled my car off the road to stop and listen. I had already dealt with many, many demonized people to a greater or lesser degree. This one was real, and it was bad. I had tears coming down my face as I listened to Bob trying to get her free, her pleas for help, and then hearing the demon take over again. (I still have a recording of that program. I take it out occasionally to play for skeptics.)

"This—this is what it is all about!" I said out loud. "This is what I am working for!" How many thousands of victims were out there, just like this young lady? It steeled my determination to go to the Ritual Crime Conference and get my points across to everyone there and right in Aquino's face too. (So much for my friend's godly advice!) I was sick to death of people like Aquino and other occult apologists promoting occult practices as being innocent and harmless.

I checked into the Killeen Sheraton late that afternoon. I asked at the front desk where Chief Walker Veal was, and they directed me to the "courtesy room" upstairs. A courtesy room, for those who may not be familiar with police conferences, is a polite term for a fully stocked blow-out bar.

"I'm trying to find Walker Veal," I said to the man who was bartending.

"Who's asking?!" the man said with an intimidating leer. I nearly jumped back.

"I, uh, I'm Greg Reid."

"Oh man, I'm sorry!" the man laughed, extending his hand. "I'm Walker Veal! Sorry, bud. We've had some threats. I thought you were this ya-hoo we got calls from today. Make yourself at home!"

The sweat on my forehead dried, and I looked around for Beth. I found her sitting at a table with a green visor poker hat, taking everyone's money in five-card stud. She greeted me warmly and explained to me that a preacher had called that day demanding free admittance so he could come down and cast demons out of everyone. *Oh, brother,* I thought. *Why do these conferences always attract these people?* For those of us who were believers trying to do a professional job, it made it all that much more difficult to be heard.

I retired to my room. An hour later, I got a call from my cop friend from Ft. Worth. "Hey bud, hear about the incident up here?" I'd heard on the news driving down: A jet had taken off at Carswell Air Force Base, went straight up, then straight down, plunging the pilot and passenger to their deaths.

"Yeah, I heard. What about it?"

"Guess who was in the basement near the crash doing his wicky-wacky stuff when it happened?"

"Aquino?"

"Yes sir! Think he had anything to do with it?"

"C'mon," I joked. "You're a cop. You going superstitious on me?"

"Nah, come on," he continued. "Do you?"

"I won't rule it out."

"Well, better watch your back."

Greg with Detective Alan Peterson, one of the pioneers of ritual abuse investigations

"I'm not too worried," I said. "But I'll be careful." I couldn't prove Aquino was really at Carswell, but my friend wouldn't have called me if it wasn't a verified fact.

I barely slept that night, tossing and turning, praying about the opposition that had already appeared at the Sheraton creating an oppressive atmosphere and disrupting my sleep.

Beth called me at 6:30 that morning. "Guess what? Aquino bailed out! Lilith called and said he had back trouble, and he was going to stay in St. Louis so she could take care of him."

"That's not what I heard," I replied. "My sources tell me he was three hours north of here at Carswell last night! Now what?"

"He's sending his associate up from Austin to fill in for him."

"Well, we'll make the best of their game. See you in a few."

After breakfast, I saw Aquino's replacement sitting in the hallway—a black-clothed, pentagram-wearing young man in his thirties. Within a moment, my heart filled with compassion. "Hi, Don," I said, extending my hand. He reluctantly shook it. "I'm Greg Reid, and I'll be on the debate team this morning. I'm looking forward to it." He said nothing.

I was late getting to the debate due to a last-minute schedule change someone failed to advise me about. Much to my dismay, the debate had already started. I stood at the back wall and waited for the first break so I could join them. It shook me up when I heard the tall, burly cop in black boots standing next to me mutter, "Somebody oughta take him out to the back forty and shoot him," referring to Aquino's young stand-in for the debate. This wasn't what I wanted at all. I had to try and turn all this around.

It's Texas, so there were a good number of Christian cops there. But I knew I might not be able to count on them to support the direction I was going to try to take the debate.

After the break, I sat on the stage and gave my introduction. What came out of my mouth shocked everyone, even me. "Don, if anyone has a right to hate you, it's me," I started. "Devil worshippers nearly destroyed my family and destroyed me. But I don't hate you." I continued, "I came here to tell you Jesus loves you. He died for you just like He died for me." No applause—just stunned silence from the audience.

"I didn't ask him to," Don replied.

Well, that went well, I thought to myself. But now, it was time to cut to the chase. "Having said that, I need to read several quotes from Michael Aquino's *Crystal Tablet of Set* and ask you some questions." He looked surprised that I even had that document. *The Crystal Tablet of Set* was the initial temple manual you were given after becoming a member of the Temple of Set. It was hard to get. Full of ammunition. I'd already loaded the gun.

I read from one of Aquino's essays on black magick where he quoted from Aleister Crowley: "Sacrifice cattle, little and big after a child," and then I read a longer quote:

> For perfume mix meal and honey and thick leavings of red wine; then oil of Abramelin and olive oil, and afterwards soften and smooth down with rich fresh blood. The best blood is of the moon, monthly; then the fresh blood of a child . . . then of enemies . . . then of the priest or of the worshippers; last, of some beast, no matter what.[3]

"Sir," I asked, "Why does Dr. Aquino quote this when he claims not to believe in human sacrifice? How do you explain this?"

Don was completely taken off guard. "You would have to ask him what his intentions were. I have not read that myself."

I quoted from the manual again:

> We have nothing to do with the outcast and the unfit: let them die in their misery. For they feel not. Compassion is the vice of kings: stamp down the wretched and the weak; this is the law of the strong.[4]

"Sir," I began. "This sounds pretty Nazi to me. And what does it mean 'stamp down the wretched and the weak'?"

Don didn't contest this. He said the poor, handicapped, and suffering were none of his business. On it went. He kept denying knowing about the things I was quoting.

"Who is Satan to you?" I finally asked.

"Well, we don't believe in a literal Satan like that. Satan, to me, is a principle."

"Oh," I mused. "I understand. You're the devil-worshipper version of a Sunday Christian. You don't have a personal relationship with the devil." He didn't get it. Actually, neither did most of the audience. (If you don't understand either, write, and I'll explain.)

I told him he may not know his Magus Aquino very well if he didn't know what he had written, and he might find himself involved in something more dangerous than he realizes.

During the question period, one Christian cop was mean spirited and venomous. I literally had to confront him to make him stop. I knew I lost most of the Christians right there, but I also knew I had to stand where Jesus would. And Jesus would not have been so abusive to someone who didn't even know Him.

During the break, I approached Don and shook his hand. "Don, I meant what I said. I know I'm not your intellectual equal. But Jesus really does love you."

"You're the first Christian that's ever shown me any Christian charity," he said. I was dumbstruck. Don was not my enemy. Don was reachable.

I don't remember the rest of the debate. Afterward, I was embarrassed by people coming up to me and "congratulating" me for "kicking his butt." I didn't. And I hadn't intended to, though I had intended to expose the dangerous nature of this kind of occultism, and I think we succeeded in that. But equally important to me, I wanted to let Don know how much God loved him. It wasn't about "winning."

By contrast, Don stood in a corner, alone. I broke away and spoke to him as he was leaving. "Don, here's my card. If you ever decide Aquino isn't where you want to be, please call me, and I'll be there for you."

"Well, maybe in a few years, I'll figure out it wasn't what I wanted," Don responded. "You never know. Thanks." He gave me his card too. That encounter in those brief moments let me know there was a real person in there, just like all of us. I prayed for God to set him free.

He sent me a Halloween card. It was a good-natured irritation.

I sent him a Christmas card, good-naturedly doing the same.

I haven't heard from him since.

If you happen to read this, Don, Jesus still loves you.

And I'm still praying for you.

But evil men and seducers shall wax worse and worse,
deceiving, and being deceived. (2 Timothy 3:13)

11

The Enemy Within

Everyone I know who worked with ritual abuse survivors or investigated occult crimes had to deal with people who attempted to infiltrate their work or ministries. These people sometimes succeeded in getting on the inside of churches or ministries, finding out what they knew about the workings of the occult world, and disrupting, dismantling, and sometimes destroying the work before disappearing into the shadows, never to be seen or found again.

They sometimes worked within churches. Some adult members of the occult world would move into a community and begin attending a church. They would start giving large sums of money in the Sunday offerings. Then, these usually well-to-do, sophisticated but hidden devil worshippers got to know the pastor and elders. Able to impress leaders with their "loving concern," enthusiasm, willingness to help, and generous giving, they soon became trusted members of the church hierarchy. The best starting place for them to work was the church prayer meeting or "care group." From there, they would begin expressing "prayer concerns" about certain people, carefully planting seeds of doubt about the integrity of certain leaders or strong Christians in the church. Those seeds were carried and grew into rumors, then gossip, then dissension, until they accomplished their goal—a church split, the prayer group divided, legitimate people and ministry reputations ruined, and sometimes, the pastor's marriage and ministry ended up in shambles.

Why did they do this? To mock God. For sport. But more than anything, to gut the power of prayer, evangelism, and discernment in the church. The true church and committed believers are the only ones who are a true threat to the demonic agenda of the satanic occult world.

I personally watched them shred two churches this way. A friend was actually able to see a "prayer book" from the other side that was a 24/7 calendar/manual on how and when to pray against churches and Christians: who to do workings against, when, and who to target: pastors, ministries, churches, families, and evangelists.

Acid Test?

Many Christians were made aware of these schemes as a result of a couple of books on spiritual warfare written by former occultists. However, two big problems resulted.

First, we were wrongly told that the only way to know if people were devil worshippers was to ask them, "Who is your Lord and Master?" This idea was no doubt based on the Scripture that says,

> Hereby know ye the Spirit of God: Every spirit that confesseth that Jesus Christ is come in the flesh is of God: And every spirit that confesseth not that Jesus Christ is come in the flesh is not of God. (1 John 4:2)

Unfortunately, we've misapplied this verse. It is speaking about those who taught that Jesus was just a spirit and never man, which was a Gnostic doctrine. The Gnostics were the first church heretics, and John addressed that issue in this verse. To use this verse as a test to see if someone is a devil worshipper infiltrator is ineffective. How do I know? Because I've had hard-core devil worshippers tell me that learning to say, "Jesus is my Lord and Master" is part of their training, and they are considered rather accomplished when they can withstand worship, prayer, Scripture teaching, and reading, and say, with an appearance of utter sincerity, "Jesus is my Lord and Master." It is not easy for them to resist the presence of God and worship—but it is possible, and it is one of their goals. To prove it, one devil worshipper mouthed these words to me as plainly—and seemingly sincerely—as I could. So, this "acid test" doesn't work. We know from the

Book of Job even Satan can stand in God's presence (Job 1:6). One group called this ritual being "Christed in Lucifer."

The Litmus Test

So how can we know? Not by good works alone. Anyone, Christian or devil worshipper, can do good works. A person's fruits—the fruit of the Spirit—love, joy, peace, longsuffering, gentleness, meekness, goodness, faithfulness, and especially by true godly character—is a good initial indication that a person is truly of God. But even the "fruits" can be imitated, so we need much deeper discernment. Discovery of sedition, gossip, false teaching, secretiveness, exclusivity, pride, and arrogance may be much better indicators of undercover devil worshippers than merely uttered words. And discernment, yes, is a gift of the Spirit that we need to be armed with, but there is a very necessary understanding of discernment we learn about in Hebrews 5:14:

> But strong meat belongeth to them that are of full age, even those who by reason of use have their senses exercised to discern both good and evil.

It is a muscle needing exercise and a tool needing sharpening, and the way we do that is to be immersed in the Word of God. A true Word-based church that is solid in doctrine has a much smaller chance of being infiltrated.

One method of unraveling churches they used was to gain good standing, then using the information many already had learned and dispersed about infiltration, turned it around. They began subtly planting suspicion about truly godly, prayer-filled people, suggesting that they may be closet devil worshippers. It was very effective. We need more true discernment than ever.

> And no marvel; for Satan himself is transformed into an angel of light. Therefore it is no great thing if his ministers also be transformed as the ministers of righteousness. (2 Corinthians 11:14-15)

Accusations

A nd we must not give in to paranoia of unfounded suspicions that some of these "infiltrator" teachings have surely led to. In fact, lately, I have been less concerned with outside interference than I am with all the modern teachings that have led to people accusing people in the church of having a "Jezebel spirit" or an "Ahab spirit." It has created just the confusion and division the enemy counts on to disable us and keep us from being a united force to reach the lost and contend for the lost. Let us not unknowingly do the other side's work for them.

A Cautionary Example

I t was in the 1970s that the churches began opening their hearts and pocketbooks to a young man named John Todd, who claimed to be a former druid high priest. Within a few short years, he was literally scaring churches into arming themselves against "them": The devil worshippers. Only later did we learn he had been running an occult bookstore when he was not out spreading paranoia and fear. Todd later was incarcerated in South Carolina for a conviction of rape. After being released from prison, he was sent to a psychiatric facility where he died at the age of 58. While the whole truth will likely never be known, it did serve early on as a warning about anyone we bring in to talk about these things. We need to discern, check out, and verify. Too much is at stake if we back the wrong person.

It is vital we learn to discern by the Spirit of the Lord. Yes, there are infiltrators. Know also that it is imperative they be discovered, not by human means or suspicions, but by the Spirit of God. Paul said "to know them which labour among you" (1 Thessalonians 5:12).

Recruiting from Youth Groups

I nfiltration and teen recruitment were highly effective during that time through teen devil worshippers. Part of their job and training was to appear as good Christian kids, attend youth groups, and recruit out of there. Part of their training was to know the Bible much better than most church kids, then one by one, use the Scriptures to change their thinking, doubt what they've been raised to believe, and slowly introduce them into the occult—and eventually, the Dark Side. All this was done, not in a group setting, but separately—in friendship, one on one.

The only way to keep kids from being indoctrinated by demonic lies is to teach kids to know God's Word well, walk in His power, and learn to discern. It is such a great burden to me that most Christian kids can't even quote John 3:16. Having come out of great occult darkness myself, I can assure you that the Word was my greatest weapon, protection, and deliverance. What chance do Wordless Christian kids have against devil worshippers, atheists, and occultists who can tie them in knots with the same Bible they are supposed to love?

We didn't try to figure out who the infiltrators were, but it almost always came out in time. As John said,

> They went out from us, but they were not of us; for if they had been of us, they would no doubt have continued with us: but they went out, that they might be made manifest [that it might be shown] that they were not all of us. (1 John 2:19)

Our prayer should be that God would bring to light the hidden things of darkness so that the enemy will have no cover. A Word-solid, humble, repentant, loving, and Jesus-seeking church has less of a chance to be hit this way than will a program-oriented, fellowship-busy, social church that has no passion for God and no genuine Word-based and Spirit-led pulpit. A status quo church has a big target painted on its corporate chest.

A Wider Problem

I discovered early on that there were more kinds of infiltrators than the ones I've discussed here. And they have different goals.

Wiccans—the practitioners of "white magick"—did a great deal of infiltrating in our ranks and our public presentations during those first ten years. But they were fairly upfront about it most of the time.

Wiccans are a loosely bound worldwide group of "nature-loving" people who lay claim to ancient mysteries, deny making human and animal sacrifices, decry the Salem persecutions, and have few rules except "harm none." "Do what thou wilt and harm ye none" is the "Wiccan Rede" or law. Very close, obviously, to Crowley's "Do what thou wilt shall be the whole of the law."[1] Spiritual repercussions from such practices are the subject of another discussion at another time, but the fact is, devil worship and Wiccan religion have very little in common in a philosophic or practical sense. Devil worshippers worship Satan. (Modern or LaVeyan-type devil worshippers worship "self.") Wiccans worship a pantheon of pagan deities, including Diana, Hecate, Isis, and so on. I found it interesting that during a Salt Lake City talk show, a Wiccan called to protest the idea that they believed in the devil. "Don't you worship a horned god?"

"Yes," she replied, "But he's not called Satan."

"Don't you call him the Lord of the Underworld?"

"Yes, but that's not Satan!"

"Excuse me, but don't you call him Lucifer?"

Crickets . . . Well, call it what you want, but whether they know it or not, in their blindness, they don't realize they are actually in bondage to Satan.

Wicca is deeply enmeshed not just in the New Age movement but also in the educational system and the media. Perhaps the most famous of the modern witches is Laurie Cabot, the "Official Witch of Salem," so crowned by former presidential contender Governor Michael Dukakis. She is also the founder of the Witches League for Public Awareness (WLPA). Another well-known Wiccan is Hollywood luminary, Cybill Shepherd.

In the beginning, one of my law enforcement friends published a very informative, vital periodical called *File 18*, which detailed and tracked various aspects of cult-related crime. It didn't take long for someone from the Wiccan community to somehow infiltrate our ranks, get a copy of *File 18*'s mailing list, and notify the editor and the readership of their intentions to monitor everything our groups said and did.

As things progressed, other groups made us aware that they intended to monitor our public meetings and use any number of methods to make it tough for us and to stop us, including lawsuits and hexes if necessary.

The hexes didn't bother me. But the people who performed them greatly succeeded in muddying the waters, becoming a major distraction at every conference and workshop open to the public (and some not) for years.

Not a Witch Hunt

We did not investigate witches, as it is their legal right to do what they do. Unfortunately, Christians often confused the issue by insisting witches and devil worshippers are one and the same. Not practically and not in activities. After a while, it became a painstaking task, both for the benefit of misinformed Christians and for extremely defensive Wiccans, to say upfront that our work did not investigate protected religions. This was about investigating crimes by those who hid behind occultism, devil worship, black magick, and other destructive practices.

As a believer, I have a very clear position on the dangers of any form of the occult. But we live in a secular world. When we taught law enforcement, they were not there to hear our theology. In fact, people who came out of the gate with that approach lost nearly every person in the room, Christian or not, because these officers were there to learn criminology. We did our level best to do just that—and if someone brought up the spiritual components, then we absolutely would address that, and freely. We had certainly seen trainers of other persuasions do the same and even recruit from those classes. I learned how to stay on the right side of those parameters.

Yet even with all the precautions and care we took, we found ourselves constantly interrupted or disrupted by occultists, druids, and Wiccans at our meetings.

They would sign up for classes or workshops, then publicly challenge our information and try to use the question-and-answer forum to accuse us of persecuting them and proselytizing others for our own religion. (I found it interesting that many pagans told people that Christians should "keep their faith to themselves," but they freely tried to recruit at every opportunity.)

A number of occultists, psychics, and Wiccan/pagans would contact law enforcement officers and offer their services as "informants" about the "dark side" as well as offer to be psychic crime-busters. An alarming number of cops—many who wouldn't even get near a Christian—actually used those services.

Within a short time, we saw those inroads with law enforcement and other professionals used to call into question the character and trustworthiness of good investigators and victim advocates. (Nine times out of ten—they targeted Christians.)

They ran a successful campaign. There were precious few meetings we taught where occultists, pagans, and others weren't present, disruptive, and evangelistic. They were the bane of our work—accusatory, difficult to reason with, and a genuine crippling agent in our quest to expose real criminal activity.

Weathering Personal Attacks

I was a bit of an easy target because I was trusting and naïve in the beginning. I thought if you did a good job with credible information, you'd be applauded and thanked for being helpful. I was wrong. Within a year of my public presentations, a friend from Alamogordo, New Mexico told me a local police officer she knew had been informed by a New Mexico Wiccan that "Greg Reid was a black witch, a devil worshipper, and a high priest of a coven of over 100 people" and warned him to stay away from me. It was really more amusing than annoying. I've been accused of many things—disorganization, overzealousness, and a quick-trigger temper—guilty as charged. But a devil worshipper of a large coven? I couldn't even organize a small cookout and would be lucky if three people came to it. It was easy to sluff it off. Ridiculous rumors, regardless of whether they were from Christians or pagans, were just what you had to deal with.

The problem was that if enough things like that were said "behind the scenes" and you weren't even aware of it, it really hurt your credibility. And it certainly did mine at first. You couldn't fight it. By the time those rumors got to me, it was second or third-hand gossip.

In 1989, I was busy preparing for my next presentation on cult crimes at the Killeen, Texas police academy. My good friend, Beth Stokes, who opened the way for me to speak at several conferences to professionals in Central Texas, booked me to address the Ritual Crime Conference for the Killeen Academy.

Weeks before the conference, Beth called me. "I've got to tell you something about Alex Ross."

Alex and I had met at a conference in Big Spring, Texas, a year before. He was a local officer and a cult crime "expert." His presentation, I remember, was good—but I was a little put off that the minute I began to present, he left. We were getting used to some of that. There were a lot of showboat experts in the beginning who were unwilling to learn from anyone else.

During the break, Alex, Chief Ben Kennedy (whom I'd met at the Alpine conference), and I were talking with some folks at the back table. "What do you think of Mike Warnke?" one of the attendees asked. Mike Warnke was a former devil worshipper who was then a Christian comedian who had recently been asked to consult with several police departments about satanic activities. I was about to say that I really appreciated that he was willing to help victims and children who were cult victims. I began by saying, "He's led a lot of kids to Jesus," when Alex cut me off.

"He's a black witch, and I can prove it!" Alex spat out, shocking all of us.

"Really?" I said, genuinely interested, as I didn't know everything. "What proof?"

"I can't tell you," he said coldly. "It's confidential information." Well, then. Even this early in my career, I was getting put off by people who dangled information in front of me and then withdrew it because it made them feel powerful and like they were the real experts, but this business was too serious for that kind of arrogant one-upmanship.

Killeeen TX Police officers
(Greg and Chief Walker Veal in back row)

"What about Alex?" I asked my friend Beth who had called prior to the conference.

"He found out you were speaking and said if you're there, he's dropping out."

"Why?" I asked.

"He says you're a phony, and he's got proof that . . ." (I'll leave out the other slanderous things he said.) He was doing the same thing to me as he was doing to Mike Warnke!

Again, I had to laugh. "What did you tell him?" I enquired.

"I told him we trusted you, and if he had a problem, then we'd rather he not come anyway." And he didn't.

We were definitely better off without him there; we already had enough "one-course experts" out there who took other people's material and started teaching it as their own, making it difficult for good people to do their jobs. I was grateful for people like Beth in the professional world who knew the difference, and I was thankful for her going to bat for me.

I fired off a letter to Alex to confront him, man to man, about what he was concerned about with me. I knew he was very involved in his church. I appealed to him on the basis of Scripture, which says we are to take matters to each other first. We needed to handle it as Christians, and if he had a problem with me, he needed to let me know. I received a cold reply, quoting the Scripture about "judge not lest you be judged," as if, somehow, I had judged him. "I have nothing against you personally," he continued, "but those I trust say you are not who you say you are and not to be trusted."

I decided to let it drop because I happened to know who these "trusted" people were—they were witches. I began to see the big picture and saw the first hint of a deliberate disinformation campaign meant to disable our work. I was one of dozens of good people who found themselves victims of smear campaigns that were meant to keep them from doing their work. The best defense was a good resume, good written recommendations, a proven track record, and a really thick skin. The attacks did not stop, but persistence was the key to doing good work in the face of deliberate smear campaigns by those whose credo was supposed to be "harm none."

12

Bigger Hands at Work

At a deeper and much more wicked level, we began to discover that there were those who claimed to be survivors of satanic ritual abuse—adult survivors—who also got close to law enforcement and professionals in our field but were, in fact, still into the occult, or had been "programmed" to play both sides. They would go for help or to offer their assistance, then report back to their coven or group what they had learned.

We encountered one "survivor" who managed to gain a great deal of influence over a number of professionals and law enforcement groups. Because of this "survivor," they determined that I was a bad guy and spread that to local folks. Sue Joyner called me and warned me that, as a result, there was a cop who was "after me." I set up an appointment to confront the situation, and the officer, Manny Cabrera,* was cold and told me if I was a phony or a devil worshipper, he was going to expose me. I told him if he was, I would do the same thing. I handed him my credentials and resume, hoping to come to a place of accommodation. After all, we were both allegedly fighting bigger enemies. He said he had already checked me out, and I had him affirm that he hadn't even found a traffic ticket. He threatened to call my parents and have them confirm "my little story" about having been in the occult, at which time

---

* Not his real name

123

I believe I brought the word *lawsuit* up. My parents were both not well. I told him if he even thought about calling, I would bring legal action for harassment. The meeting ended.

Sue called me a day later. "He's not going to let it go, G," she told me. "He's really determined to smear you."

We called a meeting at Sue's house to resolve things. It was Cabrera and another cop he knew, Sue, my co-worker partner Tim, and another friend who was in a significant position both as a DEA agent and someone who rode shotgun with Cabrera early in their law enforcement careers. "I know you, Manny," he said, subtly suggesting there might be things Cabrera didn't want brought up. "You're barking up the wrong tree. I've known Greg for over twenty-five years, and I'm backing him up one-hundred percent." Cabrera finally left, making a parting shot at my integrity which was vile and evil. I restrained myself from responding as much as it made my blood boil.

This is one of many similar incidents where people claiming to be survivors or experts got into the mix and tried to discredit or ruin good people. Were they "infiltrators?" Undercover devil worshippers? That may be going too far. But these incidents definitely made us wonder who was who in the zoo.

Perhaps it was not a surprise that Cabrera, who had become a right-hand man to our chief of police, was investigated years later for attempted cover-up of drug dealing. So, we really had no idea who he was working for, but it probably wasn't for the home team.

Another survivor was very involved in the survivor community as well as with one particular therapist who was treating survivors in a high-profile ritual abuse case (children who were accusing a military official of ritually abusing them). This survivor called the therapist in a panic late one night. She begged the therapist to meet her at a grocery store. When the therapist arrived, the survivor was nowhere to be found; the therapist was suddenly kidnapped at gunpoint and driven around the town in the dark, during which time she was shown a picture of a baby that had been sacrificed and was forced to listen to a tape of children crying at a satanic ritual. She was released after an hour with a direct threat to drop the case.[1] There is no way to ever know if this survivor set the therapist up deliberately and knowingly or was triggered to do so. But it was one of many examples of survivors who have been "triggered" or sent a programming cue to do what they were told to do. More on that later.

Two other incidents I believe will make my point about the difficulty of knowing who was who and what their intentions were and the possibility that some had a darker purpose in their involvement in our network:

In October 1989, after the training conference in Killeen, Texas, I was asked to speak at a hospital in Glen Oaks, Texas, just north of Fort Worth. The staff decided to sponsor a workshop for the local community and professionals on occult crimes, teen occult addiction, and ritual child abuse. I co-taught the class with a friend of mine who was also an advocate for victims. We began to field questions. All went well until a woman in her thirties stood up. She was a Wiccan. Rather than ask a question, she literally began crying and telling everyone how awful we were for assaulting their religion that was "older than Christianity," and so on. This was becoming a familiar interruption. Thankfully, I didn't have to say a word, as my co-teacher just interrupted her and said, "We're not persecuting you. We're not even talking about you. Next question." That very effectively ended the discussion. I was kind of sorry it did because I wanted to answer one bit of disinformation witches always bring up. They always point to the horrible persecution of "their people" at the Salem witch trials as an example of the terrible treatment they suffered under Christians. And the answer was so plain. Anyone who has even read a little about the trials would figure out that wasn't how it went. Yes, innocent people were accused of witchcraft and executed. Perhaps a few real witches died. What we do know is a lot of decent, God-fearing Christians were also accused falsely and executed. But who accused them? Two teenage girls, who had practiced magick and fell sway to the slave woman Tituba, who practiced the occult.[2] So, Christians were persecuted at Salem, not just witches, and the original accusations came from kids who messed with the occult, not from believers.

But the moment passed. I was happy that it did, really, because these trainings were not debate forums.

The class was successfully completed, I returned to the home I was staying at. There was a call waiting for me from a small police department in the Metroplex area. I called and spoke with an officer who said they had found a lot of weird writings in the water tunnels underneath their town. Would I be willing to come down and check it out? Always willing to help, I agreed. He told me to show up at 5 p.m. the next day.

If I'd thought about it, I would have realized something wasn't quite right. The town was so small that, typical of many smaller Texas police departments at that time, they went down to a skeleton crew at night. In the back of my mind, I wondered why they wanted to go check out these tunnels just as it was nearing dusk. That seemed a little iffy to me. Why not do it in the daytime? The light would be better.

But I wasn't fully thinking about those things. I just showed up late the next afternoon. I walked in and extended my hand to the captain, which he did not return. "Sit down," he said coldly. "So what makes you think you're an expert?"

"I don't claim to be," I said. "I am suspicious of people who do claim to be." I wanted to remind him that he called me. I didn't ask to meet with him, but I just let it go, already feeling uncomfortable and on the defensive.

"What do you think of these?" he asked, tossing a photo album in front of me. I was a little reluctant to open it up. During the previous three years, at almost every conference, someone from the local police department or an out-of-state law enforcement officer would ask to see me privately to look at a set of murder or autopsy photos to see if I could identify any ritual tags. It was never easy, but if I knew it was coming, I could manage to keep nausea at a minimum and work out the trauma of seeing such vicious butchery later on when I got back to my hotel room. As if you can ever get the images out of your head. You can't.

Not knowing what I was going to see, I took a deep breath and opened it up. There were pictures of what appeared to be deceased, mutilated teenagers covered in blood. I immediately began to fight nausea. "These are real?" I asked quietly.

"Nah, they were evidence we got at a pedophile's house. He liked to molest kids. He also liked to dress them up like this for fun."

What kind of sick game is this?, I thought to myself. Why would this cop pull such a bizarre stunt? I have some cop friends who have pretty offbeat senses of humor. When you work this stuff long enough, you almost have to have an "unusual" sense of humor. It's a defense mechanism against the horror you see. It's survival. Strange humor is almost part of the work. I don't mind joking and kidding if it's coming from friends or trusted associates.

But here I was, in a small, strange town with a very cold cop, and he's throwing fake photos of mutilated kids in front of me for no reason. This wasn't funny. This was sick. This felt like . . . something more sinister. If it was a game to see how I'd react, it was pretty twisted, and he didn't get whatever reaction he was looking for.

"Have you read this?" he said, taking a book off his shelf and holding it up for me to see. It was *The Necronomicon*, one of the most wicked and destructive books ever written on the occult.

"Yeah, I've seen it," I replied warily.

"I've been reading it a lot lately," he said. "It's really changing my life."

I'll bet it is, I thought to myself. *Who was this guy, anyway? If he was playing games, he was a great actor. If not . . .*

"I've got some friends coming in to go down with us in the tunnels. They're witches. You got a problem with that?" he said sarcastically.

"Nope, I don't have a problem with it," I said warily, hoping he was joking. I was tired of this questioning.

Then, in walks the woman who stood up at our conference the day before with her Wiccan husband! I couldn't believe this was happening. I was sandwiched between two Wiccans and a cop who was reading the *Necronomicon*. I was starting to think I was in trouble.

We all got in the squad cars and went down to the tunnels. It was the Wiccan couple, me, the captain, and two other cops. We walked down and entered the dank-smelling tunnel. We walked for a long time, maybe an eighth of a mile. There were lots of bizarre symbols on the walls. Some of it was identifiable, and some of it was very cryptic. I tried to take notes.

The Wiccan woman just got weird. "Oh, I can feel really bad vibes!" she said. "Can you feel them?"

"Not really," I said honestly. Then suddenly, something did change, but it wasn't "vibes." It was the cops who stood a few yards away from us, talking in whispers.

"How well do you know this guy?" the Wiccan asked me in a half-panic.

"Me?" I said, taken aback. "I thought you knew him!"

"No, we just got called yesterday. We don't know him at all. We thought you did!" Silence.

"I think we may be in trouble," I whispered. "Let's try and get out of here." I never thought I would be teamed up with Wiccans, but at this moment, we seemed to have little choice, and a lot in common—a desire to get out of there in one piece!

Then, we heard the officers talking—loud enough for us to hear—wondering aloud about how long it would take to find someone if somebody shot a person and left him down there in the tunnels. Now I was really, really scared. In fact, they could do it, and it would take weeks for anyone to find us. They started staring at us.

"Hey, you guys alright in there?" a voice yelled from the top entrance of the tunnel. "You need backup?" The cops looked startled.

"No, we're good," the captain yelled back. They walked toward the tunnel entrance quickly, and we gratefully followed them out. At the end of the tunnel were two officers from the next town. They had seen the two squad cars and thought there was a crime situation so they stopped to assist. They small-talked then took us back to the station and dropped us off without a word, without thanks, without any explanation at all.

I can't say for sure if the captain was a devil worshipper. He may have been playing games with me. But I don't think so. His eyes were dark and evil when he explained how reading *The Necronomicon* was "changing his life." He was definitely not on our side. I never saw the Wiccan couple again. I never had any further contact with the police officer who called me.

The situation left me badly shaken. I had already encountered people within law enforcement circles and military police who were deeply into black magick and had even committed crimes as a result. I realized I had been foolish to go alone. Maybe it was just a sick cop having fun with naïve non-law enforcement people, which is scary in itself. But it could have been a close call with something worse. I made a commitment after that to either take someone with me or be sure I was tracked every moment I was out and would check back when I returned. I never do anything unless someone knows where I am at all times. I also learned to check people out before I ever put myself in such a dangerous position.

Another incident occurred in El Paso that let me know that devil worshippers don't just disguise themselves as good community members, cops, and churchgoers. Sometimes, they take it a step further.

I was speaking with the manager of King's Hill Apartments, an exclusive complex on the West Hills of El Paso in 1989. She mentioned one of their recent tenants was a richly dressed man who showed his Christian minister's credentials and signed a year's lease. He was very nice, she said, and very quiet. He came and went and always paid his rent right on time until the ninth month. They finally served him eviction notices, which he did not respond to. He had already vacated the premises.

When they entered the apartment, they found the entire living room carpet had been removed, the floor painted black, a huge red and black pentagram had been neatly painted from one end of the room to the other, and red and black candle wax everywhere.

Is it hard for you to believe that occultists are interested in, and have been active about, getting inside the churches? It's not conspiratorial for me to think so when I know so. The conspiracy is what is happening, but hidden, even in seemingly good places. I have seen it happen many times. One particular intercepted document really spelled out the "behind the scenes" reality of occultists in our midst, even in our churches.

A paper was intercepted in the early 1980s, accidentally left behind by a member of a Wiccan coven. It was going out to over 8,000 local members of various covens. Among other things, the newsletter lauded a twofold membership increase over the previous year, including over 500 children in their summer youth programs. It rejoiced in the multi-million-dollar renovation of their mansion headquarters in Pasadena, the soon-coming high-quality newsletter paid for by "wonderful supporters" who "provide for the growth of the new age and those who will inherit the new world."[3] The high priestess rejoiced in meeting and making first stage initiates of two Christians who had come to install new office equipment.

She also rejoiced in having four ministers in that area who belonged to them, as well as members of several local churches. (And no, they weren't Universalist or liberal churches; they were fundamentalist churches.) She said they were pretty well covered in the area and were "gathering converts from these groups."

The document also warned the readership that while attending a church, it was best to look like the people who attended, pointing out that they all carry Bibles and "have sickly smiles." (That's how many people view us.) And as an added recommendation, "Don't forget to say, 'praise the Lord' frequently."

The high priestess warned them not to wear their jewelry so they would not be obvious to some who knew about their symbols.

She thanked a great group of bankers from New York who provided for some of their promotional activities without charge.

The priestess ended by thanking two of their deities, Cerunnos and Cerridwen.

For Christian believers reading this book, I hope this chapter shows what a real problem this is for the church today. Devil worshippers and occultists come in all disguises—and guises. In the hidden world of the occult, nothing is ever as it seems. Forewarned is forearmed. Paranoia is a dangerous thing, but a good dose of caution and lots of good solid contacts and intelligence sources have been extremely helpful in keeping us safe and alive.

> My son, if thou wilt receive my words, and hide
> my commandments with thee; So that thou
> incline thine ear unto wisdom, and apply thine
> heart to understanding. (Proverbs 2:1-2)

13

Pinging the Web—Who
Is Pursuing Whom?

The Mind-Control Nightmare

Y ou must understand—all I ever wanted to do was help kids and victims of satanic crime. I don't pretend to be an "expert."

Regardless, in the mid-nineties, my co-workers and I got pulled into a world of sophisticated, dangerous, high-tech investigations so unbelievable I hesitate to even write about it. I hadn't bargained for it, and I wish I'd never gotten into it. It cost me dearly. I decided to go ahead and write this chapter for three reasons: One, we had come across a case so severe, so extensive, and so credible that it had the potential to blow the lid off an entire national, organized criminal satanic empire that reached into the highest levels of society. Two, I became deluged with documents concerning intelligence community involvement in mind control experiments mixed with satanic ritual abuse. That was difficult to digest because accepting that adults wanted to ritually abuse children was already monstrous enough. And three, before long, nearly the entire community of survivors, therapists, and investigators became caught up in a world of "conspiracy theories" based on some facts and a lot of non-credible, unprovable information, and that has to be addressed.

We are in an age when the term "conspiracy theory" is being used to dismiss anything that goes against the radical social changes we are being subjected to so as to deflect and disarm those who contend that these changes are being orchestrated from a *higher* level. Then—as now—it was vital to comb through all the information we had and make sure we were not supporting or validating information or people who were clearly part of the problem of muddying the water through untrue and sometimes deliberately deceiving stories.

It would take a whole book to outline the entire issue, but for now, I will simply risk telling you what happened at our end and give you my own perspective on it.

It was about mid-February in 1993. Our network of cops, counselors, and consultants was getting thoroughly battered, but we were still intact.

A Houston cop associate named Dave called me.

"When are you coming to Houston?" he asked me.

"Not sure. Why? What's up?"

"John [another law enforcement associate] and I did a presentation yesterday. Two cops asked for a private meeting afterward. They showed up late with some boxes of documents. They said, 'You wanna work this case? Work it. We wanna live.' This is a bad one. The officers were getting death threats and dead animals on their porches. This case has names of oil company executives, what number to call to trade a child at the library, codes, where they make child porn movies, locations all the way from here to Colorado, everything. Interested?"

"Me? You better believe it," I answered.

"We're meeting with Jack from Wisconsin on Saturday. Can you get here?"

"You can count on it."

"Bring your truck. I'm gonna load you up with some of these documents."

I traveled to Houston, checked into the La Quinta Inn in The Woodlands, then drove over to the meeting, which lasted about three hours.

This was the crux of the case: A family had gone into therapy—a mother, two teenage daughters, and a ten-year-old boy. At the beginning of the therapy sessions, the boy had a mental breakdown and was hospitalized. His condition quickly deteriorated until he had to be sent to another hospital out of state.

The boy was nearly comatose, curled in a fetal position, moaning, crying, and shaking. He was administered some medicine, and once it started to kick in, he began to talk.

Trigger Warning

What he said stunned the doctors. He told them that when he had been hospitalized in Texas, his dad and a nurse came into his hospital room after midnight. They had a machine with a dial and wires. They attached the wires to his chest, head, and genitals. He said everything went "black" when they turned the dial, and when he woke up, his father was sodomizing him. He said his family belonged to Satan.

His physical exams showed severe sexual injury. In addition, his body was covered with marks from cattle prods and electroshocks. (For the record, it has long been documented that Mexican drug cartels used cattle prods to torture and control their victims.)

The hospital faxed Texas authorities with the information. The police showed up at the father's office and showed him what his boy had said. "Arrest me," he said. "If my son said it, then it's true. Arrest me. We're in a satanic order. We can't get out." An immediate arrest was made, a large bail set, and the following day, someone put up the money to get him out.

As I explained, the two officers who were originally investigating the case quit because their families were being threatened. Dead animals, phone death threats, the whole thing.

Dave loaded some of the boxes of documents into my truck. I went back to my hotel room and settled in late at night to start reading. At 1 a.m., I took my pistol out of my briefcase, loaded it, and set it on my nightstand. According to these documents, they had raped and filmed children at the very hotel I was staying in. The documents I had were written disclosures of three family members, including a ten-year-old who had drawn horrific and detailed drawings of his abuse. They all had little contact with each other during their disclosures and different therapists. Yet, there were thousands of handwritten and typed pages of information that were so detailed and intricate that they were jarring and mind-boggling. There were pages and pages of numbers and codes, names, and locations. The codes were a combination of colors/numbers/Greek letters, which they claim they were forced to memorize via electroshock, drugs, and abuse. Their minds were purposely fragmented, and the codes were used to trigger them to act at a future time to make a call, kill, transport a child, report, and another code to wipe out the memory of what they did. All three adult victims—who were separated 99 percent of the time—gave the exact same codes and information without one single contradiction. It was simply impossible that this was a conjured-up scheme. It would have taken a computer to pull this off.

The disclosures of the ten-year-old boy were non-verbal. They were a child's drawings. They were depictions of his own horrific abuse. And they not only paralleled the abuse the others had described, but they were nearly identical to drawings done by two children in a completely separate case in Oklahoma.

The documents told of a cave outside Fort Collins, Colorado, where they claimed their group buried the remains of humans slaughtered either for betrayal or sacrifice, from babies to adults. I was no stranger to Fort Collins; nearly all our leads on satanic crime and child trading at that time led through or back to Fort Collins.

Another detail spoke of caves in New Mexico and Arizona and claimed that children who were destined for sex trade or ritual purposes were hidden, held, and transported to other states like Nevada, California, and Nebraska. These children were allegedly part of the international human slave trade industry. This information—which at the time was called unbelievable and pure fantasy—was in our hands before the recent cry on human trafficking verified that much of this horrible reality was and is still actually happening.

Three of the victims described a mysterious Dr. Green, who they claimed strapped them into chairs, made them ingest urine or raw animal flesh, and set a screen before them that flashed numbers, codes, and colors. The punishment for not memorizing the codes fast enough was severe electroshock to the point of passing out. The reward for doing good was to be assaulted by "Dr. Green." "Pleasure is pain. Pain is pleasure. Obedience brings reward. Failure means death," he would tell them as they reeled under the effects of injected drugs, electroshock, sleep and food deprivation. All three adult victims told the exact same story without variation.

Caves. Child trading. Electroshock. Dr. Green. I'd heard all this before from several separate victims. I was genuinely alarmed. These documents were not a fantasy. And we had no reason to doubt that they were valid; by just having these documents, my life might be forfeit.

Validating, Researching, and Repositioning

When I got back home, I started to research to see if any of this new information had a factual basis. I began with an excellent book, *Journey Into Madness: The True Story of CIA Mind Control and Medical Abuse* by Gordon Thomas. The book documented the CIA's entrance into the evil, cruel world of mind control experiments in the late forties and fifties under Director Allen Dulles via Dr. Ewen Cameron, an out-of-control psychiatrist with top credentials whose hospital in Canada was secretly funded by CIA "black budget" funds to conduct mind-control experiments.

The CIA's motives looked noble enough on the surface. Some of our captured P.O.W. boys were showing up in Communist China denouncing the USA and proclaiming loyalty to Communism. The government wanted to know why and how they were being "brainwashed." (This was apparently the original use of that term.) Dr. Cameron was given carte blanche and total financing to find the answers.[1]

Government Sanctioned Atrocities

So, Dr. Cameron arranged to commit patients to his hospital, often based on a minor mental difficulty, and kept them for years as virtual prisoners in the hospital basement, experimenting with them.

He gave them electroshock, psychotropic drugs, and incessant repeated messages—"psychic driving"—on headphones, which the patients, because of drugging and/or being strapped down in their beds, were powerless to remove. He called it "depatterning." It was an attempt to reduce a patient to an infantile state and then remake him in his own "healthy" psychological image and likeness.

All funded by our tax dollars.

In the mid-1970s, surviving victims came forward and sued the U.S. and Canadian governments. They won. The CIA paid—but admitted nothing.

President Jimmy Carter banned the project.

But, according to our sources who were in a position to know, it was merely moved from the CIA to a military agency, where it more than likely fell into the hands of certain mind-control experts there.

The military now potentially had the tools necessary to attempt to create the "perfect soldiers," able to obey any order without question, withstand incredible pain, and forget what they did. Could the military resist this temptation just because the President said, "Don't do it"? I believe, and have many reasons to believe, that this program survived and thrived. Could someone who was involved with the psychological warfare department of the military resist such an opportunity, especially someone who is on the Dark Side? No one can prove it, of course.

But the documents I now had in my possession made it staggeringly clear that mind-control experts and satanic child-trading groups, with ties to people in the CIA and military, were a reality and, in fact, working together.

One would benefit greatly from researching "The Finders Case"[2] to see how some of these nefarious groups were funded by high-level government agencies.

The Nazi Connection

Again, much of the information I had brought home from Houston was not entirely new to me. Several victims whom I had debriefed before hearing of the case in Houston had given vivid details of a Dr. Green who spoke with a German accent.

I couldn't help but wonder about this Dr. Green. I knew that documents on public record clearly showed our intelligence community had brought in a great number of Nazi war criminals after the war—doctors, experimenters, and scientists. Our government gave them new identities under the name Operation Paperclip and put them to work for the American government.[3] I wondered if Dr. Green was one of them.

It is known that one of the surviving criminals of World War II was Josef Mengele, the "angel of death," who tortured and experimented on children. He escaped and died years later, apparently—allegedly in Argentina. Over the years, it has been chilling to see case after case of ritual child abuse victims who drew pictures of Dr. Green, "Mr. Green Jeans," or "Dr. Allbusiness," which were much like the available photographs of Mengele. We can't prove he was in the United States, but I found myself wondering if he might indeed have been part of the post-Nazi recruitment effort that saw such luminaries as Dr. Werner Von Braun, who became the hero of the NASA space program. There is an intriguing photo I have of the original "Operation Paperclip" group at White Sands army base, with one man trying to hide himself—someone that bears a suspicious likeness to Josef Mengele. We can't know for sure.

Hard to believe? Of course it is! Who wants to believe that our government would not only exonerate Nazi war criminals but put them to work for us?

It is no secret that the Nazi elite were knee-deep in the black arts. In fact, I had been given access to the testimony of a twenty-one-year-old man in prison in another state who had given an investigator who was helping him some of the exact codes, names, locations, and other information that were in the documents we had obtained. This young man and the family from Houston had never met, and barring the idea of psychic transference (unlikely), the only real conclusion was that this man in prison and this family two thousand miles away who had never met each other, had likely been put under the same torture and were part of the same group network—only in different locations.

Publicly Threatened

I slowly began to publicly dispense the knowledge I was gaining—very carefully, of course, making sure I could provide the documents necessary to prove what I was saying. And now I had thousands of documents at my disposal that pointed to this proof, documents that could end up endangering my life, for real.

Still, I didn't expect the reaction I got. Perhaps I should have.

"Since the late 1940s," I said to a training class for El Paso federal probation officers in early 1994, "the intelligence community has invested millions of dollars into mind-control experiments. By coincidence—or not—a high-level military officer with top-secret clearance is a mind-control expert. He also happens to be a black magician."

A hand went up. "Ever heard of the Delta Project?" asked the neatly dressed middle-aged gentlemen in a business suit on the front row.

"Yes, sir," I responded.

"I worked on that project," The man continued. "I have some of the original documents. Would you like them?"

"Yes, sir, I definitely would. Please talk with me after the class."

The "Delta Project" was one of the first experimental army projects that used New Age methods and ideas, also known as the "Earth Battalion." I definitely wanted those documents!

A large, burly military officer in the very back stood up.

"What do you know about Cyclops?"

"You mean Psy-Op? Mikey's project? I know some."

The burly officer bristled with anger. "This is classified information!" he nearly yelled, the veins in his neck bulging. "No one is to speak about this after this class, do you understand?"

Well, where could I go from there? I don't know who was more stunned, me or the close to thirty federal probation officers in attendance. I simply tried to segue out of it, wishing there was one of those hook things they used to pull bad acts off the stage, and I could just quietly disappear. Instead, I had to conclude the last ten minutes of the class while this intimidating military man kept putting his finger to his lips in a threat to keep my mouth shut. It was the weirdest, most unnerving experience I had ever had publicly so far.

The military man disappeared just as the class ended. No one knew who he was. No one had ever seen him before.

That's when everything began to escalate. Every time I picked up the phone, I heard weird screeching sounds. I had dozens of hang-up calls a day. Often, I picked up the phone, and it was clear there was someone on the line, but they just said nothing. When caller I.D. became available, I tried to track some of those numbers. One was the same government number over and over. Each time I tried calling it back, I would get a disconnected phone number.

Our network already knew there was extensive experimentation with high-tech sound and communications. And we already knew that psychic "remote viewing" was being conducted by the military and intelligence communities. The book *Men Who Stare at Goats* by Jon Ronson, written in 2004, detailed some of these exotic military programs. We also knew the number of devil worshippers in the military had increased significantly during Lt. Col. Michael Aquino's military career.

A Military Connection and Case

In fact, we had just investigated a case in El Paso regarding black magicians in the military. A military police devil worshipper stationed at Fort Bliss in El Paso (one of the largest army bases in the world) had a house full of teenagers, several of whom were underage. Some were there voluntarily. Some, under lock and key. He took some of them to satanic rituals. All the teenagers were videotaped for porn movies with one another, sex with the military policeman, and sex with strangers.

One girl managed to escape to the El Paso Runaway Center. According to the director of the center, in the few months that she had been at the shelter, she had received hundreds of letters from the MP. Some were sickeningly "romantic," but most were vile, explicit, and threatening. He would beg, then demand she come back to him. We investigated this guy; we found out his coven "name." He wasn't a kid. He was a full-blown adult and well known to teen devil-worshipping groups and kids involved in the party scene in the city. He was not a "dabbler." He was hard-core, and he was ruining kids' lives.

When the young lady left the runaway center and moved back to her mother's home, she started coming to our Bible study. As we counseled this girl, she began to open up about the details of what she had been through. She had been lured into the group and seduced by the MP. She told us that the MP's group she had been a part of usually sacrificed rabbits during their rituals, but on that Easter, the MP told her they had cut the heart out of a sixteen-year-old girl in the next state over. I was stunned when she told us this. I had already learned that authorities had found a sixteen-year-old female with her heart missing in that very area this young lady spoke of. It had not come out in the news. The information had not been made public. She would have had no way of knowing about it without this man telling her about it.

The MP was never investigated, even after we had turned our files over to the military authorities. Of course, in El Paso, whose neighboring city is Juarez, Mexico—a city well-known for drug smuggling, child porn, and child trafficking—you never know who is on their payroll. Money talks, people walk. We had heard it all, from the availability of an aborted fetus in Mexico for five US dollars for use in rituals, or a living child, which in those days went for a mere ten US dollars. It was all available if you knew who to ask. That includes buying the services of cops who guard outdoor rituals. Things of this nature rarely got investigated here, and if they did, the investigation never went very far.

So now, fresh off this and another investigation and with thousands of pages of information on mind-control cults and a threat to keep my mouth shut brazenly issued in public by a military officer, I didn't know what to expect and already felt I was in way over my head.

One fall night in 1993, the same year Dave gave me the case files in Houston and I was publicly threatened, I was working on my computer when it seized up. Then, the cursor on the screen kept moving all on its own. I began to panic as I watched it draw large concentric circles across the screen all by itself, and I could not regain control of the computer. I knew that someone was remotely accessing my system. I immediately hit the shut-down switch on the computer. The following day, I rebooted the computer. I noticed that many files and programs began to disappear as I watched, and the computer itself was locking up.

I took it to a friend of mine who was a top-notch computer expert. He called just a few hours later. "It isn't good," he told me. "I don't understand. Everything I'm doing to fix it is making it worse. I'll keep trying. I'll call you back."

He called an hour later. "It's gone. Sorry, Greg."

"What's gone?" I asked.

"Your whole system. It's completely wiped out—files, programs, and everything. I've never seen anything like this. I'm really sorry."

Unfortunately, I had nothing backed up on disk. It would be the first of two computer wipe-outs that happened in three years. But this was just the beginning.

Caught in the Web

Over the next few years, some very unnerving and menacing events took place when I traveled. I was scheduled to speak at the Victims of Violent Crime Conference in Oklahoma in 1996, a year after a terrorist attack brought down the Murrow Federal Building in Oklahoma City. The morning of my departure to Oklahoma, I was about to load my luggage into the car when I heard my fax machine go off. Two cartoons had been faxed over. Both were about death. I immediately called the number that sent the fax, and the phone was answered by an elderly lady who did not even own a fax machine.

Detective Chuck Goode met me at the Oklahoma City airport and helped me check in at the Omni Hotel. He was scheduled to teach at the conference in the morning before my presentation.

That night, I woke up at about three in the morning, hearing a disturbance in the adjoining room. I heard a man begging for his life as he was being viciously beaten. I heard the terror in his voice, and I felt it, too. I quietly called the front desk. "Please send security to the room right next to me. I think they're going to kill someone." He said he would. I continued to listen for another twenty minutes as the sobbing and pleading continued intermittently, then went silent.

Finally, someone knocked on their door. "Security. Everything alright?"

"Yes, everything's ok."

"OK, Have a good night."

Ten minutes later, I heard the door open and close. I waited and called the front desk to see what had happened. I was told that they just checked out of the hotel. I hardly slept for the rest of the night. Between the death faxes and this, I was feeling very uneasy.

The conference was a success, and I thought my part went well. After my talk, I was about to join Detective Goode for lunch when a woman in a black chiffon dress with jet-black hair and heavy makeup glided up and started a conversation with me; after a while, I was just trying to end the conversation so I could get to lunch. Finally, she left, and I caught up with Chuck. "What was all that about?" he asked.

"All what?" I said.

"Dude, you talked to her for nearly twenty minutes." I suddenly realized I didn't remember one single thing that the woman had said. Was I getting so worn out that I was becoming suggestible? It was a scary thought.

In November of 1993, my law enforcement contacts and I convened for our first network conference of the NCIN—The National Cult Intervention Network. The officer, named Dave, who had given me all the documents was getting rocked badly. His superior was giving him a lot of flak for the investigations he was conducting.

Dave didn't understand why until one day he entered an occult bookstore in hopes of expanding his understanding of the occult to aid his investigations. He began examining their athames. (An athame is a curved ritual knife, often used for Wiccan rituals but sometimes for bloodletting in criminal occult groups.) "These are new," he said to the man behind the counter.

"You should know," the man said. "Your captain made them for us."

Occult hands reach far. And Dave was understandably concerned. He had a baby daughter to protect.

Nevertheless, we went ahead and held the conference. John, a law enforcement officer we often worked with and did workshops on occult crimes with, and Dave both spoke, and I did a short session as well. Detective Goode from Oklahoma was also there. Another investigator whom I knew came too; he had experienced his own troubles since beginning to investigate occult crimes. He'd gotten a lot of pressure to back off from his captain. His shifts were changed, and he began to find himself on the receiving end of a lot of ridicule and harassment. One day, his captain called him in to reprimand him. He glanced down at the captain's desk to see a copy of a pamphlet titled "Managing Your Subordinates" written by a confirmed black magician. Only then did he understand; all the in-department pressure suddenly made sense.

There were also two other speakers at this conference. One was recommended to us as the premier expert on a child porn/pedophile ring in Nebraska that we'd followed closely. (For more information on this case that exposed an organized national pedophile network, See *The Franklin Cover-Up* by John de Camp, a book I highly recommend.)[4]

Disinformation

Dave had invited the second of the two speakers, Rick.* He claimed to be an expert in mind control deprogramming and had former ties with the CIA. I had spoken to him a few times by phone, as he was recommended for me to talk to by former FBI Special Agent Ted Gunderson.

During Rick's talk, he scared the fire out of everyone there, even the cops. He accused many people, from congressmen to former presidents, of being pedophiles, programmers, and devil worshippers. He had several cops ready to bail out of the conference, afraid the Feds might burst in any minute to arrest everyone for treason! Rick's girlfriend gave a talk as a "government mind control" victim. But she didn't appear to be deprogrammed at all—more reprogrammed. Empty eyes. Empty expressions.

---

*Not his real name.

She seemed to me to be more like a person who had not had any healing at all and who might still be under severe programming.

And yet, I liked Rick. As seriously naïve as I was back then, I actually thought I could lead him to Jesus.

Rick called me shortly after the NCIN conference. "We're going to Phoenix. There's a victim in a church there. You know I don't really like Christians, except for you. We want to help her, but we've got to talk to the pastors first."

"I'll come down if you want," I volunteered.

"Bless your heart," Rick said. "That would be wonderful. We'd really like that. It's so good to hear your voice. Call us and tell us when you'll be there."

I'd taken the bait, big-time. After all the personal attacks of the last few years, someone was being kind and appreciative, and I fell into trusting this guy, not even considering it could be a trap.

I drove to Phoenix. Because the hotels were packed, I ended up staying in the only available room in nearby Chandler.

When Rick found out, he seemed irritated, even angry. "I had it all arranged for you to stay at this survivor's house!" he said. "I wish that you had called me first."

"Well, you know how it is," I told him, "I don't like to discuss travel plans on the phone."

We met with the survivor and the pastors at the church. I shared a little of my background and how I came to the Lord. "What about you, Rick?" the pastor asked.

Rick's response took me completely by surprise. "I walked down to the altar of my church when I was eight and gave my life to Jesus," he said tearfully. "I love Him. Jesus set me free."

Rick had told me he hated Christians. He told me he was

Greg with First Lady of Texas, Laura Bush, at the Governor's Conference in 1996

not a Christian and that I was the only Christian he liked. He was bald-faced lying, and I knew it. I was shocked that he could lie so easily, and I was in a most uncomfortable position now that I had given him my endorsement.

After the meeting, Rick and I stood outside waiting for his girlfriend to come and pick us up. It was dark. Suddenly, Rick took out a handheld Taser and turned it on.

I jumped back. "What the heck, Rick?" I said, my heart racing.

"Oh, just wanted to check to make sure it's working," he grinned slightly.

I didn't get it. Yet.

The next day, before my return home, I went to Rick and his girlfriend's hotel room to discuss some important matters about deprogramming. They were staying on the sixth floor. A young woman, a news reporter for a small paper from California, was staying with them in their room. As we got to their room, Rick said, "I hear Aquino stays here when he's in town. Suite 666, right down the hall."

"That's interesting," I responded to his comment warily, not knowing if it was true or not. I had heard a rumor that Aquino was doing some work at the University of Arizona during that time.

Rick began to ask me some questions about my own history of occult involvement as his girlfriend watched. Rather than taking notes, the reporter was lying on her bed, intensely reading her Bible.

Rick launched into a tutorial about ritual marks and scars, how to recognize electroshock scarring, what different scars meant, and what had caused them.

He stopped and pulled up his shirt, revealing a scar that went from his ribcage to his stomach. He looked tranced and got tears in his eyes. He said, "They shot me and left me for dead in a Memphis field. I don't know what happened or how I survived." His shirt went back down, and he came out of his trance state, just like it never happened. He wiped a tear away, almost as if he didn't know why it was there on his cheek.

Suddenly, he grabbed the back of my neck and pressed his thumb right below my right eye. He pressed hard, staring intently into my eyes, his face less than a half inch away from my own.

"What're you doing, Rick?" I asked, chuckling nervously. "You can't program me. I'm not hypnotizable."

"I know," he said smiling, as though it were just a big joke. "I was just checking."

I knew it was time to extricate myself from this situation. Nothing about it felt right. I said my goodbyes and left for the seven-hour drive back home.

Halfway home, I realized I had left my briefcase with my most critical and confidential documents in it. I had never forgotten my briefcase before. I never leave it behind when I'm traveling. It stays with me at all times.

I called Rick when I got home. "You forget something?" Rick chuckled.

"You have it then?" I asked. "Oh, thank God. I was hoping I'd left it there."

"Don't worry, friend," he said, still chuckling. "We sent it Fed-Ex. With a packet of coke in it, of course, so you'll probably get arrested when they deliver it."

"Funny, Rick," I said. Not funny at all.

The briefcase arrived the next day. They had thoroughly rifled through it. All the papers were taken out of their binders and were in complete disarray. They undoubtedly had made copies of everything.

I became extremely ill the day after I received the package. I contracted a rare form of influenza, Valley Fever, which, within days, had turned into pneumonia. I was up night after night for at least three days, only breathing a quarter breath at a time. I had to beg my doctor not to hospitalize me.

Over the next two weeks, I recovered slowly. Then, Dave, my law enforcement friend, called me.

"Got news on your buddy from the Nebraska case," he said casually, referring to the "insurance agent" that had been recommended to me as a potential speaker to invite to the NCIN conference.

"What have you got?" I asked.

"He's CIA."

"So, I assume he was at the conference just to find out how much we knew?" I guessed.

"Probably didn't get much," Dave responded. "Good thing he was late and missed our 'private meeting' with Rick. Speaking of which, got some info on your buddy Rick, too."

"*Your* buddy," I countered jokingly. "You invited him, remember?"

Dave laughed, and then he got serious. "He isn't who he says he is. We've got documents from a trial where he was claiming to be a Mafia hitman in Memphis, and he was called to testify in the slaying of a socialite in 1976. And he doesn't have the degrees he claims to have."

"Well, I can believe that now," I said and relayed the details about the creepy Phoenix meeting to him.

"Well, guess who we think was in Phoenix when you were there?"

"A certain military person involved in black magick?" I asked. (Aquino.)

"You got it, bud. We can't prove it, but it's looking that way."

"Dave, what's all this about? I'm getting spooked," I said, a cold chill going down my spine.

"Just be careful. This is some serious stuff. If you need a safe house, let me know. We'll put you up down here."

Rick began to realize that Dave was investigating him and responded by sending threatening letters and a weird joke greeting card with veiled threats and typical intelligence community double speak.

I had to cut off all communication with Rick. The truth is, I didn't necessarily want to. I genuinely cared about him and his girlfriend. But I had to break contact completely with them. I had no idea who he really was. He might have been a programmed victim himself, acting on his own programming. He seemed dissociated, empty, and lost. I believe he was very dangerous—but still, he needed Jesus Christ to heal his heart and mind. I prayed for him and was very sad when I learned of his illness and death.

Opening the Pandora's Box

Almost overnight, the survivor network and the therapists who worked with them were talking about mind control victimization, government programming, and high-tech harassment of victims. It was the newest and most disturbing twist in this long journey I took into the dark world of occult crimes. This was a long time before the Internet and Google became the Censoring Fount of All Wisdom and Knowledge. We already knew about government and military operations such as Operation Paperclip, the Monarch Project, MK Ultra, and high-tech intelligence games and weaponry. In fact, I had been in contact with a former intelligence worker who was lobbying Congress in 1989 to put an end to all government electronic sound weaponry and "microwave harassment." In the years since, once the Internet exploded in popularity, a whole new generation of self-appointed YouTube experts have risen and thrown their own jambalaya mix of truth, unverified information, rumors, and outright falsehoods out there into cyberspace about these issues. It has made discerning the truth from error (even discovering deliberately planted fake information) a daunting—and frustrating—task. But back before everyone claimed to be an expert, before at least a half-true version of all this became public, these things were already being labeled "conspiracy theories." What we learned was true back then, is now verifiable and documented. Ironic now. But at the time, we had to learn as we went along. We had victims of mind control experiments coming to us. We were compiling the documents. We were gathering inside contacts and had been contaminated by bad ones. We were starting to get lost in the confusion and contradictory information.

Disinformation Campaign

I sensed from the very beginning that this aspect was being thoroughly contaminated with false information and completely non-credible conspiracy theories.

During the next year, I watched as many of my associates fell prey to the intrigue, suspicion, and "conspiracy" mentality of the mind control "games." This was no surprise to me: "disinformation campaigns" are an intelligence community specialty. At the same time, on a more personal note, the "games" coming against me continued to escalate. I had known about "ELF weapons" (extremely low-frequency weapons—energy weapons). Aquino had written about them in army papers, and documents detailed way back in the mid-1980s showed our capability—even then—of using directed-energy weapons from over a mile away—targeting (and cooking the internal organs of) a battalion of soldiers.[5] I knew these weapons could create extreme pain and nausea. I knew the military was refining and perfecting them, making them capable of targeting individuals even from a distance. Some of my associates who researched it said they could even cause cancer and brain tumors, as well as project "voices" from afar (known as "voice-to-skull technology.") None of this was speculation. We had the facts. In fact, I had a catalog for low-end "crowd control" energy weapons that you could purchase through the mail for just a few hundred dollars, capable of causing an entire crowd to become nauseated and begin vomiting at the flip of a switch.

And then, of course, there were the government experiments with psychic "remote viewing."

Talk of such things was used by the "other side" to accuse us of being X-files wackos. How ironic to watch news reports about Cuban embassies and even the White House being targeted with some kind of "energy" source that caused disorientation and illness. How ironic to hear an intelligence agency spokesman speak about it with feigned shock and surprise, saying this was not something they knew about. It was laughable. They had been using these weapons for years!

Up Close and Personal

I never expected to be personally targeted. The first time it happened, I was standing outside a restaurant with a friend, someone whom I had come to trust with the details of some of the more dangerous work I was doing, just in case something happened to me. I trusted him to watch my back.

Suddenly, a blinding "starburst" of white light hit my right eye and rendered me blind, while an excruciating pain in my head felt like I'd been struck with a sledgehammer. My hand went to my eye, and I yelped in pain. Less than a split second later, my friend, who was standing facing me, also yelped, and his hand flew to his left eye!

"What's happening?" he said, scared.

"Let's get in the car, quick!" I yelled. The worst of it passed after about ten minutes. I let him know that I was wading in some dangerous waters and why this might be happening. I recovered after the evening, but my friend was sick and vomited the whole next day.

The second time I was hit, I was alone, on vacation, in a hotel in Corpus Christi, Texas. I had just begun to eat my dinner in the hotel restaurant when I was struck nearly blind in my right eye. I went to my room. The pain in my head was so bad I cried. I was moments from calling an ambulance. Gratefully, it passed after about three hours. I had never suffered from headaches, and I was in perfect health at the time. I had a pretty good idea where this was coming from. And I knew, except for God's help, I was powerless to stop it.

After that, things got ridiculous. One of the kids from our youth group was visiting me at home. We were talking at the kitchen table when a phone rang—in the middle of the living room floor—where there was no phone. In fact, the ring itself didn't match any phone I had. My visitor knew it and asked, "Wanna tell me what's going on?"

"Nope," I said, "you didn't hear it. Didn't happen."

"Alright with me," he replied, changing the subject, and we stepped out for some coffee. I was glad to have a witness, or no one would ever have believed this.

Two days later, while having dinner with a friend, we both raised our eyebrows as a phone clearly rang—right next to our table—on the floor! We both looked at each other like, "Did you hear that?" At the same time, the man at the table behind us exclaimed to his girlfriend, "I swear, I heard it! There's a phone ringing right there on the floor! But there's no phone!"

For the next several months, there were a series of unmarked black vans parked at odd times on my block—all with no license plates. At this point, I felt it imperative to retreat and just observe. The weird calls increased, and the noises and incidents grew stranger. There was a period of time when I was deluged with phone calls from those claiming to be "survivors of mind control" who were also calling other investigators and therapists, creating suspicion by telling each of us that the other person they had just spoken with was "the enemy." I was able to trace one of the people who caused this confusion. He claimed to be a "deprogrammer," and I received a large packet of information about him sent to me by his ex-wife. He had dozens of fake IDs: fake driver's licenses, fake social security numbers, fake passports, and several different aliases! It was clear to me that we had a "mole" in our network—probably an intelligence community member on a "disinformation campaign" to undermine our work and create division and confusion in our ranks. Their strategy worked very well. Unfortunately, this man gained a reputation among naïve Christians as someone who was an "expert." He did a lot of damage to survivors and hurt the credibility of the work we were trying to do.

My concerns reached a peak shortly after my mother passed away in 1995, leaving my father alone. My parents had been living several states away. I was in touch with my dad by phone every day and visited every month when I could. One night at 3 a.m., my phone rang. It was my father. "Hey, Pop, are you ok?"

"I'm fine; what's wrong, son?"

"Nothing, what do you mean?"

"You just called me."

"No, I didn't," I said.

"Yes, you did!" he answered, getting agitated. "You said, 'Hi Pop, how are you doing?' and I asked you what was wrong, and you hung up! What's this about?"

"Yeah, Pop, we have to talk," I told him. It was obvious to me that someone had somehow gotten my voiceprint, using it to call my father and play it at 3 a.m.—perhaps just to spook me and let me know they could get to my father any time they wanted. I shared my concern. He, the ex-cop that he was, was nonplussed. He tried to convince me to move back home at the age of forty-five, so he could protect me. I assured him I was okay—but he was my first concern.

"Don't worry about me, son. They come in here, and I'll blow them away. What's the worst that can happen? I only have another year to live, and that way, I'd get three hot meals a day and a nice place to stay." Pop had a terminal illness. He figured if he had to go to jail, at least he would get "three hots and a cot" for his duration on Earth! That was my dad! Somehow, that set my heart at ease. But I did conclude after this incident that I needed to get off the radar.

I did the best, wisest thing I could think of at the time. I put out the word that I was no longer working with mind-control survivors. And after a while, thankfully, almost all the activity stopped.

I continued to watch in horror as many formerly credible people got totally wrapped up in conspiracies and fear to the point of obsession. If the goal was to make us sound absurd, it worked.

Do I believe devil worshippers and mind control government experimenters are working together? Absolutely. It's perfect alchemy—science, soldiers, and the black arts. After all, what else do you expect when we imported Nazi scientists to continue their work right here in the United States after World War II? Did anyone really think it would stop? Well, it didn't. It hasn't to this day.

But I knew we couldn't beat them, and proving anything would be next to impossible. So, I escaped their snare. I knew it was real, but it was useless to fight them on their own terms, with their own games. We win by prayer. We win by extracting victims from their clutches. We win when we expose their lies.

Several of my contacts had gotten so deep into the conspiracy "network" that they began to act and sound certifiably crazy. They carried protection crystals, "detox" spray to clear away death rays, and even weirder things. I knew this was precisely what the endgame was—to make us look utterly ridiculous. I did not want to fall into their trap. I realized that the body targeting and invisible phone ringing that I had experienced was probably nothing more than an attempt to either make me go off the deep end or make me go to the media or authorities so it would be on record that I was "nuts." I simply refused to take the bait and distanced myself from those who had taken it.

Yes, they could fry an entire troop, long-distance, invisibly, via sound.

Yes, they were fragmenting, torturing, and programming children and adults. In fact, even though the Texas case had finally been shut down due to threats, lawsuits, and official harassment, there are to this day still enough leads to eventually pursue this and hopefully use this to stop a lot of their criminal abuse of the innocent, if we can ever find the resources to do so.

I knew ultimately, if they really wanted to, they could probably destroy me physically in a quick hurry and destroy each of us who had touched a nerve in this area without even being traced.

But they had not. And I began to understand why.

They didn't have to. All they had to do was to get everyone acting paranoid and so suspicious that we didn't even trust one another anymore. Then, we would be no threat at all. We'd all be written off and thrown in the stereotype pile with the "alien abduction wackos" while all the real crimes continued unabated, uninvestigated. It was a real trap.

The final straw for me was getting a call from a man who was giving me volumes of what seemed to be good, credible, pre-verified information about some significant cases we were looking into. I wrote everything down as fast as I could. Then I stopped when he said, "Well, I better tell you how I know all this stuff."

"Why?" I asked.

"I'm Jesus of Nazareth."

Oh, of course. Here it comes. I should've known, I thought to myself. I could almost imagine the background snickering. I almost fell for it.

"Well, Jesus, I gotta go. Be careful."

"I don't have to. I told you! I'm Jesus!"

And with that call, the game was over for me.

The next day, I began to disconnect from the people I knew who fell into the "conspiracy network," though it thrives still. The fake deprogrammers are still out there, charging big bucks to deprogram you, as well as sell you snake oil products to protect you from "death rays."

What I knew, but that many of my well-meaning associates did not, is that there really is no protection except by the blood of the *real* Jesus Christ from their weapons if they decided to use them. We'd be dead in a moment if they wanted that. If any of us survived these dangerous waters, it wouldn't be because we carried spray water but because Jesus Himself stepped in to shield us. I knew now we could never completely stop this horrible criminal cabal. But why help them? Why be pawns on their own pathetic chessboard of mind games?

I took myself off the chessboard and went back to basics—doing the most important thing I could, the thing that always bypasses the lies and goes for Satan's jugular—helping rescue and heal the victims, the children, the teens. And leading them to Jesus!

"They" had to find another mouse to play with. I got out of the cage and went back to where I first began—helping the little ones who do not stand a chance unless some of us get out of the "net" and get back to the real, verifiable, prosecutable criminals who are preying on our children.

EndGame.

[F]or he hath said, I will never leave thee, nor forsake thee. So that we may boldly say, The Lord is my helper, and I will not fear what man shall do unto me. (Hebrews 13:5-6)

14

Courts, Principals, and Principalities: Inside the "System"

B y 1995, after a few failed prosecutions against predators who abused kids and brutally hurt innocent children, I found myself jaded and untrusting of the justice system. The False Memory Syndrome Foundation had done so much damage and provided defense attorneys with such a perfect nuclear weapon against children who claimed abuse that I had lost all confidence in our system. (More on the False Memory Syndrome Foundation in chapter fifteen.) I had watched several good attorneys become discouraged enough to move to another district or just retire. I knew we were going to have an uphill battle from then on. The "other side" and their both witting and unwitting mouthpieces had done such a stellar job of convincing the public that "satanic panic" was behind all ritual abuse cases, I sincerely doubted that children had a chance at all in court anymore.

In addition, many child protective agencies were being compromised, infiltrated, or so overworked that they could hardly function. Plus, we were getting growing intel that there were numerous foster homes and child protective agencies that were being used to traffick children. What chance did the kids have?

Still, I kept my hope alive. I decided, shortly after obtaining my private investigator's license, to attend a prosecutors' conference in Tucson, Arizona. I had always viewed prosecutors as the good guys. It did not take me long to begin to question that notion. It just took one presentation to shake my previous view. I remember the words clearly from the experienced prosecutor: "We are living in an *Oprah* talk show society. When you get to court, the truth does not matter. What matters is how good you can make your client look on the stand."

Suddenly, it all became clear. The courts were becoming more and more like great theater, where many attorneys presented their cases grandly, emotionally, and antagonistically in order to win their cases. The victims of sexual assault and ritual abuse were caught in the middle of these often-brutal proceedings. This was especially to the advantage of pedophiles who had made a lifetime career of looking like the most wonderful, caring person imaginable—a volunteer, loving spouse, church elder, youth pastor, trusted doctor, scout leader, and so on. They knew how to present themselves in court.

In contrast, many of the victims of these horrific crimes were broken, ravaged people: teens or children who could be easily manipulated, humiliated, and discredited on the stand. Many victims of organized pedophile groups became street kids, prostitutes, hustlers, and drug addicts as a result of their abuse and exploitation. In court, their testimony was overshadowed by those facts and because they didn't look good. The truth took a backstage to appearances.

I walked away from that conference with my eyes wide open.

Around that time, I received a call from a prosecutor who wanted to consult with me about a prison inmate who was up for parole. He was apparently doing some nasty ritual stuff in prison. I agreed to meet with her to try and answer her questions.

It went well, until it didn't. After about fifteen minutes, her co-counsel walked in and sat uncomfortably close to me. "So, what makes you think you are some kind of an expert on this stuff?"

"Excuse me?" I answered, "I didn't claim to be an expert."

"So why do you think you could be some kind of 'expert witness' in court?" he demanded.

I immediately stood up. "I'm not playing this game. I didn't come down here to get grilled by you to see how I would do in court. Sorry. Not going to do it." And I walked out.

The only time I wanted to see the inside of a courtroom again was if I had to do jury duty. Otherwise, I was done. I'd seen too many of the children who had been abused returned to their abusers. I'd seen too many defense attorneys for pedophiles where they were allowed to humiliate little children while on the stand. I didn't want any part of it.

But then came a phone call. "Mr. Reid, I am a District Attorney with the city. I am trying a case dealing with the occult. I don't know anything about the occult. A friend at Juvenile Probation recommended I call you. Can we meet?" Reluctantly, I met with Gerald and allowed him to ask me questions where I might be able to help him.

He was trying a case of attempted murder of a fifteen-year-old girl by two other teen girls. The incident began at an unsupervised party on Halloween night. This has become the norm in our times; there were numerous parties going on without any parental supervision. At one particular party, kids testified that there was an abundance of drugs and alcohol. One kid who was playing with an Ouija board suddenly began to contort and growl. He was speaking in a low guttural voice like a demon, and he was speaking in another language. The fifteen-year-old girl decided she wanted to go home. It was very late. The two sixteen-year-old girls caught up with her and offered to walk her home.

Halfway there, the three of them went down into a storm drain to sit and talk. One girl said to the younger girl, "Hey, I want to show you something. Lie back, relax, close your eyes, and imagine you're someplace really nice. It will be cool; it's a cool trick." The younger girl reluctantly lay back, closed her eyes, and followed the other girl's guided relaxation words. Suddenly, the younger girl felt alarmed and opened her eyes just as one of the girls was coming down on her with a knife. She held up her arm to defend herself as the girl sliced into her hand, screaming, "Die, B.!"

Just before the second stab, they heard the voice of one of their male friends at the top of the ditch saying, "Hey, you guys alright down there?"

"Yeah, we're fine," the other girl shouted back.

When the coast was clear, they scaled the storm drain and quickly walked away from the scene of the crime, leaving the younger girl bleeding in the ditch. She lay still in the ditch for a while until she was sure her attackers were gone, then climbed out and managed to find help. Her assailants were taken into custody and were going to be tried for attempted murder.

It was a case of two kids "dabbling" who almost ended another's life, and the case was rife with occultism from top to bottom. I explained all the nuances of the occult to Gerald, from symbols to occult games and music, as he listened intently.

"Do you think you would be able to testify in court?" he asked.

I took a deep breath and explained to him that I'd had a couple of bad experiences in the system. But I told him that if he thought it would help his case, I would be willing.

"After hearing what you've told me, yes, I think it would help," he said. So, I agreed.

I showed up on day one of the trial in July of 1996. I wanted to get a sense of things. Youth ministry was my life's work, and it broke my heart to see a parade of thirteen-to eighteen-year-old kids taking the stand to testify to the events of that Halloween night. Out of maybe seven of them, only one of them was accompanied by a parent. These children were "throwaways." No wonder they gravitated toward destructive things. What else did they have?

The first girl being tried and her mom were dressed impeccably, of course. Remember? "The truth doesn't matter. What matters is how good you can make your client look on the stand." They nailed it.

On day two of the trial, they were about to bring in the second girl being tried. When she was called in, the most hideous, blood-curdling demonic scream you can imagine came out of her, and you could hear it throughout the entire courthouse. It was a piercing, overwhelming, banshee-like wailing that continued until it finally faded away and stopped only when the girl was removed from the courthouse altogether before she ever made it to the stand for questioning.

The whole courtroom of people was stunned and frightened. I could tell they'd never heard anything like that before. Personally, this just sounded like a typical demonic manifestation of someone who had given themselves over to the occult world. *This is going to get interesting*, I thought to myself.

A recess was called, and I was next on the stand to be questioned and qualified to testify. Gerald had forewarned me that the defense attorney was going to try to tear me to pieces by attacking my credibility. I took a deep breath. "Try to relax," Gerald told me. "I'm just going to read your resume and credentials out loud first. Then he will probably try to attack those. Just answer the defense attorney's questions simply and directly."

As I took the stand and swore the oath, I glanced over and noticed that the mom and daughter had changed clothes during recess. But now, Mom was very clearly wearing a mojo bag around her neck. *Oh*, I thought, *This occultism must be a family affair.* (A mojo bag is a leather pouch that usually contains things to give protection or to do a spell.)

Gerald read my credentials and referred to some of the training courses I had conducted for various criminal justice agencies. "Dr. Reid, did you do a training for Killeen Police Academy on occult crimes in 1989?"

"Yes, sir."

"Did you do a workshop on occult crimes for the Texas Narcotics Officers Association Convention in 1994?"

"Yes, sir." On it went down the list.

"Your witness," Gerald said and handed the questioning over to the defense attorney.

Then the high drama began, which means that he took my resume, flipped through the pages, sighed loudly, looked bewildered, paused, and sighed loudly again. Finally, he turned to the judge. "Your Honor, I ask that this witness not be allowed. This information is sensational and prejudicial!" That's all he said. He did not ask me a single question.

"I agree," the judge said. "I won't allow this witness."

"Your honor," Gerald protested, "This is the only man in the city that can give motive to this crime!"

"I don't care, counselor," the judge cut him off. "I've made my ruling. The witness is dismissed."

The teenage girl who was being charged for the assault was acquitted on all charges days later. I am fairly sure she and her mother attributed the acquittal to whatever "juju" they had been practicing. And with that, the trial was over.

I sent the judge a long letter with a stack of information about occult crimes, politely asking her to educate herself on the nature of these kinds of crimes. I never heard back from her.

Unfortunately, there is a huge number of those in our local court systems who do not understand the nature and seriousness of occult activities. And that system is filled with people who we discovered were practicing one form or another of the occult, from Wicca to darker things. Some were just curious about the world of the occult, which can be a dangerous thing.

One man named Joe, who worked for pretrial services, had attended a few of my trainings and was fascinated by them. He apparently saw me as the Fox Mulder (from the *X-Files*) of occult investigators. I genuinely liked the guy, though I admit it was sometimes unnerving when he would call me frequently and say things like, "Hey, I just heard about this horrible murder, and I thought of you . . . what do you think?" I thought, *Maybe I needed a less "specialized" job.*

Joe called one morning at about 7 a.m. Anyone who knows me knows that calling me before about ten in the morning is at the least going to yield nearly incomprehensible babbling. (I am a night owl!) "What's up, Joe?" I mumbled.

"Hey, we got a dead fish on the courthouse steps!" he said brightly. I took a deep breath. "And?"

"You need to come down and look at it. It's got weird stuff on it."

"Okay," I agreed. "I'll be down in about an hour."

A small crowd of court employees gathered in the prosecutor's office around the fish, which was all nicely wrapped in butcher paper. "Can you get me a knife and fork from the kitchen?" I asked, and someone ran off to get them. They returned, and with a plastic knife and fork in hand, I gently unwrapped the fish and then cut it open. I found what I suspected might be there: several red and black push pins piercing a piece of parchment paper into the fish. A name on the two-inch parchment paper was faded by the oils from the fish.

"It's more than likely Santeria," I told them. "It looks like someone was paid to either do a ritual to get someone out of jail or to curse and kill a presiding judge over a case."

My job for the day was done. The unusual and unexpected was never a surprise!

Over the years, I learned to be very careful when navigating law enforcement and the judicial system in any town. I was always willing to help, but I learned to be cautious and made sure I knew who I was dealing with by asking people who were in the know. Occultists, everyone from curious dabblers to real devil worshippers, were at every level of society, including those professionals most people looked up to: doctors, lawyers, judges, school teachers, politicians, and even ministers.

I don't now and never have believed that there are "devil worshippers under every rock." But I learned through many years that they could be found in almost every area of society. You never quite knew who might be on the other side. I never gave in to paranoia. Though, as one friend jokingly said, sometimes paranoia can just be a heightened state of awareness!

———◆———

Lilly was sixteen, and she was in trouble. I had gotten a phone call from one of the local high school's Communities In Schools (CIS) counselors asking me to come in to see if I could help them.

Lilly was extreme Goth: she was deeply enmeshed in witchcraft and satanic practices. The mother had called the CIS counselor. She was scared. Lilly had told her one night that she had a bad dream that she killed her mom and sister with a butcher knife.

That next day, while Lilly was in school, the mother searched Lilly's room and found a huge knife under her mattress.

Lilly had already been put on psych meds but wasn't getting any better. I agreed to meet with Lilly. The counselors warned me she was "very scary and dark."

And she showed up, scary-looking and dark, all in black, with an eyebrow ring, nose ring, and occult jewelry around her neck. Glowering and withdrawn, she came in and sat down. I asked a few questions, like what kind of music she liked and how she liked school. She responded with short answers. I then told her about my own involvement in the occult as a young teen. Lilly's eyes began to brighten. Pretty soon, she was opening up about herself. She felt lost and hopeless. She was on seven different psych medications, and nothing was helping. She didn't even know what she was taking or what it was for. Compassion for her filled my heart, even as anger at the system made me furious. This was becoming a trend in the mental health industry: Pumping kids full of experimental and unpredictable drugs because psychiatrists didn't know how to control their behavior. They were essentially babysitting drugs.

We talked for about an hour. I made some lame jokes, and she laughed. She had such a beautiful smile.

When our time was up, we walked out of the room smiling and laughing. The look on the counselors' faces was unforgettable.

"What happened in there?" one asked when we returned to the office. "She never smiles."

"I just treated her like a human being," I replied. "She didn't scare me. I think she figured out I was safe."

Lilly did well after that, and her life got one-hundred percent turned around. I was grateful to have been able to be a small part of that.

I was encouraged when I found out that the vice principal of Lilly's school heard about the meeting and told the CIS counselors that he wanted to meet me and see about the possibility of having me do in-service training for the school.

There's an expression in Texas: Once burned, twice learned. I hadn't quite been burned enough to sense a setup before I walked right into it, so I arranged to meet with the vice principal along with the CIS counselors.

He was late. Very late. And when he finally arrived, he breezed in abruptly. I literally felt the room spinning as he did, and I had to pray to keep from feeling like I would pass out. Something was really not right. He gruffly shook my hand, sat down across from me, and said, "So, what makes you an expert? Have you done any training before?" It wasn't inquisitive. It was accusatory, meant to catch me off guard.

"I don't claim to be an expert. I've done training for several CIS groups from Killeen to Temple to El Paso."

He just stared at me. I couldn't help but notice his big silver cross ring, which was right-side up to me but upside-down to him. "Well, I don't think you need to be 'training' on this for our students."

I felt my anger rising. "I never intended to," I answered. "It's your staff that needs the training. And besides, you called me down here. I didn't ask to meet you. You asked to meet me. I didn't come down here trying to get myself a speaking engagement."

"Well, I don't think we need your training. Thanks for coming down," he said, shaking my hand again and walking briskly out.

The CIS counselors just stared at each other. "We are so sorry, Dr. Reid. We have no idea what just happened here. He's never acted like that before."

"That's alright," I said, carefully choosing my words. "Not everyone is what or who they appear to be." I left it at that, and they didn't ask any more questions.

They gave me a brief tour of the school, including part of the basement, which had been surrounded by rumors for years. You see, this particular high school had a reputation of being a "who's who" kind of school: Almost everyone who actually became a person of "power" in the city graduated from there. It was odd. Even more odd was the existence of secret rooms and tunnels in the basement. No one could ever get too close. The CIS counselors showed me the padlocked gate entrance to the tunnels in the basement. Apparently, only one person had the key. This area was only opened once a year—for a special, invitation-only Halloween party.

Hmm . . .

As they walked me to my car, I noticed that the basement was downhill from a house far up on the hill. I knew there were kids who had testified of being videotaped at drug and sex parties in that house on the hill, then being ushered into the tunnel located behind the house, just in case someone had called the police.

I shared all this information about the school, the tunnels, and the house on the hill with a friend of mine whom I had gotten to know when I taught my classes on occult crimes. He worked undercover narcotics for the city.

"Hey, I can get you into those tunnels," he told me. "Some people owe me some favors. Let me get back to you."

He got back to me a week later. It was a no-go. To his surprise and concern, no one was allowed to go into that place, regardless of what kind of favors they were owed.

The word "occult" means hidden. The hardcore devil worshippers like to keep it that way. Except for the Satanist-wannabe history revisionists, who are open about their non-worship of their non-god known as Satan, most occultists, especially those in the deepest and darkest parts of the occult, hide their involvement. There's usually no public membership roster, although many groups keep the blood-scrawled oaths of their members in their coven Grimoire. Being hidden is crucial. Or, as one of the high-level occult group's credo states, "The guarantee of our tomorrow is today's perception that we do not exist."

I cannot prove that the vice principal was on the dark side. I cannot prove the tunnels at the school led to a predator pedophile devil worshipper's mansion up the hill. However, tunnels did lead out of the westside predator's house, and other tunnels have been discovered with evidence of ritual activity. The whole city is riddled with tunnels. In fact, we had crawled down into a hidden water tunnel that led to a huge room underneath one of our major malls. We found occult symbols, candles, and a ritual firepit in the center of the room. Rumors also ran rampant about an underground group called "The Macabre" that met and conducted rituals in tunnels under the Sunset Heights area of El Paso, even perhaps under the University of Texas at El Paso—a university that is well-known for its New Age, atheistic, occult, and even satanic leanings in some departments. It made sense: there are old Chinese smuggling tunnels[1] recently discovered in that area. We've yet to know the full extent of all the tunnels that honeycomb the city.

After a couple of brushes with people in power and discovering that several judges and business people were apparently part of the "good old boys" club that seemed to cover for criminals (and let the innocent rot in jail if they crossed them), I said goodbye to the local court system. I only show my face once a year for jury duty. I won't ever rule out trying to help if it is possible, but in my experience, the courts have never been friendly in the cases we have worked with concerning ritual crime and crimes against children. We have had to fight tooth and nail on behalf of the child victims. But we keep fighting, and maybe somehow, we can still make a difference for the few who have no choice but to avail themselves of this often-corrupt institution with often-corrupt people running it.

God bless each and every legitimate attorney, judge, and caseworker who does their level best on behalf of abused kids and other victims. You have our gratitude, our thanks, our prayers, and, whenever it might be needed, our help.

And if you have a dead fish on the county courthouse steps, feel free to give me a call.

15

Some Don't Survive

"It's just kids dabbling." How I grew to hate that glib dismissal of kids who were into devil worship. It was so inaccurate. Kids rarely "dabbled" in it. They were obsessed with it, consumed by it, and sometimes, they died from it.

From 1985 to about 1992, teen devil worship was growing to epidemic proportions. In one New Mexico prison for teens who had committed murder, the majority of them worshipped the devil. It's important to understand why. It's important to understand how.

We cannot deny the spiritual void kids face. It is deep. The church has not answered the call well. Nature abhors a void. The same holds true for the human soul; something must fill it.

As explained in an earlier chapter, the late Anton LaVey, former police photographer, church organist, and lion tamer, was the founder of the Church of Satan, which was established on April 30, 1966. He couldn't have imagined in his fondest dreams that his antichrist treatise, *The Satanic Bible*, would become a runaway bestseller nearly two decades after it was first published. Few could imagine that kids would be the biggest readers.

LaVey's book is basically a slam against Christian truths and values. It contains "The Nine Satanic Statements" that mock the Ten Commandments and extol selfishness, lust, and unrestrained indulgence in the sins of the flesh. Adults can read it all they want; they do so at their own spiritual peril. It's a cynical, ugly book written to make fun of the church and establish a new religion of man as his own god.

But in the hands of kids, it can be deadly. Adolescence is a volatile time. I've always contended if a kid isn't screwed up and confused a bit, that's when you need to get him into therapy because then you can be sure something's wrong with him! Confusion and turmoil are part of the nature of adolescence.

However, when you have a teenager who is lonely and alienated, a latchkey kid, perhaps from a broken home who is experimenting with drugs and sex, occult literature like *The Satanic Bible* can be incendiary. How do you think he or she feels when they read, "The Satanist realizes that man, and the action and reaction of the universe, is responsible for everything, and doesn't mislead himself into thinking that someone cares"?[1] Lonelier. More alienated.

Or, an angry kid reads, "If a man smite thee on the cheek, smash him on the other. Be as a lion in the path! Be dangerous, even in defeat."[2] His rage is now justified and encouraged.

Perhaps the most dangerous thing LaVey said is this:

> Do as thou wilt shall be the whole of the law; harm none unless they wish or deserve to be harmed.[3]

Or, as LaVey explained on the ABC *20/20* program on May 16th, 1985:

> We feel a person should be free to indulge all his so-called fetishes that they will desire, as long as they don't hurt anyone that does not deserve or wish to be hurt.[4]

What if a kid decides someone deserves to be harmed or to die? Didn't he just find permission to do it? Or what if he feels someone is bothering him, getting in his space? To that, LaVey said, "If someone bothers you, ask him to stop. If he does not stop, destroy him."[5] More than one satanic youth killer killed because someone "got in their way."

I already mentioned the murder of Sean Sellers' parents and the murder/suicide of Tommy Sullivan Jr. and his mother. They were only two incidents of many people who died, committed suicide, or killed for Satan during the "satanic panic" era, which produced an epidemic of senseless, meaningless carnage. There were multiple murders, suicides, arsons, child molestations, and human sacrifices committed by kids. LaVey denied responsibility for any of it. Not a surprise. I didn't expect him to have Christian values. But how about just some basic ones? If I thought something I'd written had been misunderstood, and someone had been hurt, killed, or committed suicide because of it, I would move Heaven and Earth to make sure it never happened again. But you can see the end result of serving Satan: Utter callous selfishness and disregard for anyone outside of your own sphere of existence. Devil worshippers of the LaVeyan strain and their offshoots have been very clear that they take no responsibility for the negative influence of their words on others.

But kids rarely, if ever, start with *The Satanic Bible*. They usually begin with an Ouija board, death metal music, fantasy role-playing games like *Dungeons and Dragons,* or books on witchcraft that you can now find in nearly every school library, even at grade-school level.

No, not every kid that plays the Ouija board becomes a devil worshipper. But I have met dozens of teen devil worshippers, and all of them began with lesser things. The occult is, at its root, an addiction, and for a number of kids, it culminated in devil worship. Occult tools are the "gateway drugs," as it were, the starting point. Not everyone who smokes marijuana will use crack. But every single crack user I know of started with a joint. It has been the same with the occult and devil worship.

We learned a lot through investigating and debriefing a number of adults and adolescents, and we got a pretty clear picture of how Satanists/occultists were recruiting young people in our area during the time of this youth occult epidemic. The following is a composite of several of those reports.

We discovered that adult devil worshippers were behind the big push to recruit youth during the "satanic panic" era. This is how they often worked: They would raise or train young twenty to thirty-year-olds, usually males, and set them up in cities to start "canvassing" for recruits. They would hang out wherever the kids were. They gave away drugs. Sometimes, they would put flyers on kids' cars at high schools to invite them to a free keg party. We still have some of those flyers. (Note: Thirty years later, they are still holding these all-night parties for youth in our city, in upscale million-dollar mansions.)

A young person would take the bait. He or she would show up at the party. A few dozen other kids would attend. There would be plenty of drugs and lots of alcohol and sex going on in every room of the house. Every skillful fisherman knows how to prepare an alluring lure.

After a while, the recruiter would bring out a Ouija board, Tarot cards, or some other interesting occult game like *Dungeons and Dragons*. Kids would start playing it. The recruiter would just watch to see who had the "touch," the extra interest, and the possibility of going further.

A kid would get tagged, but he wouldn't realize it. The recruiter would now invite him to the next party. The kid likes the recruiter because he's fun-loving and full of energy. But at the next party, there would be just a handful of kids. The recruiter would start talking about "taking control of your life" and tell them that "there's another way." Drugs were everywhere, and the haze of deception was thick. The kid half-heard the recruiter telling them that their group had been specially selected. They were a group without laws and rules, except to have fun and do whatever made them happy. That's what Satan really is about, he told them. Christianity had it wrong. The devil was misunderstood. He's the good guy. He's a party animal. He's your friend. He'll give you whatever you want.

This all sounded good to the kid. In spite of some reservations, he's starting to take the bait. The drugs help tear down his reluctance.

At the next meeting, there were stronger drugs and more mind-bending ones. The teen would wake up the next morning with a terrible hangover, remembering signing something and an animal being killed before he blacked out. It was all coming back to him. But it was way too late.

"I don't want to do this," he told the recruiter as he stumbled out of one of the bedrooms the next morning. "I want out!"

"Sure," the recruiter said as he pulled pictures out of an envelope. "Where do you think we should send these? Your parents, or your school, or both?"

His life has been forever altered as he looks in horror at pornographic pictures of himself in degrading sexual acts with people whose faces aren't even shown. Do you think he would tell his parents or the police, or just give up and stay with them out of fear of those pictures ever becoming known? If you think he would tell, you know absolutely nothing about adolescents.

From that point of no return, recruits were required to prove their worthiness in various forms, from vandalizing and desecrating churches, sexual assault, burning Bibles, and worse. One boy in South Texas had to dig up a corpse and sexually violate it. That boy will never recover from that without Jesus.

Females often ended up being the satanic altar, used by each coven member for sex in a one-night ritual. One girl told us that the first time they killed a baby on top of her, it devastated her. But it got easier, she said. She had started to like it.

Where did they get the infants? The girl told us they bought them in Juarez, Mexico, for a small fee. Sometimes, she said, members who worked at the county hospital maternity ward on the graveyard shift were able to take a pregnant illegal immigrant mother into delivery, put her out with drugs, do a C-section, and take the baby to a waiting car to immediately be taken to a ritual. (As long as the heart was still beating, it was considered an acceptable sacrifice.) The mother would wake up later to be told she had lost her child. Illegal immigrants were not in a position to protest or ask questions back then.

As a member moved up in the coven, the sexual assault and even sacrifice of children would almost always be an expected part of the deal—the cost of power.

Are there kids who devil worship solo? Certainly, there are, but very few that we have ever encountered. We rarely investigated a youth coven that didn't have an adult hand involved somewhere along the line.

Unfortunately, kids who had become serious about moving up the ranks failed to understand that maybe only one in ten thousand had the "adeptness" to even move up one more rung on the ladder of satanic power. All the rest of them are mere gum under the shoes of the real power players—intended to be used and then discarded.

We heard dozens of testimonies like these coming from virtually every state in the 1980s. It was obvious that a mass recruitment of youth was taking place. So, what was this apparent mass recruitment of youth for? It's simple. Satanic recruiters are like Amway. They recruit one, one recruits thirteen more, and on it goes. It's multi-level marketing of evil. And like so many multi-level marketing groups, it's usually only the ones at the top that benefit. You see, in a devil worshipper's mind, if they kill someone, they get "power." If ten others do it for him, he still gets the power. So, it doesn't matter to them if the kid who commits the crime goes to jail, dies, or kills himself. (Some devil worshippers believe suicide is the ultimate sacrifice to honor Satan.) They still believe *they* get the power. In other words, the whole epidemic was a power push for the adults. The kids were just low-level "worker bees" to be used and disposed of.

The adults would explain the deal to them, usually signed in a blood contract: "If you break the oath and reveal our secrets, then you will die by our hand or your own. We've ID'd all your family and friends. They'll die, too." No wonder so many kids killed themselves during that era.

We knew all this was coming. A document that had been intercepted by an undercover law enforcement agent at a major worldwide occult summit spoke clearly of their intentions and purposes for that generation of youth. We weren't surprised at all.

The document was called "The W.I.C.C.A. Letters." It apparently stood for "Witches International Coven Council Association." It was a gathering of black, white, and gray magicians and other occultists from around the world.

Wiccans, of course, were offended by this document, which used the name W.I.C.C.A. They went on the attack when we first published this information. "There is no such organization!" they protested. "This document is just a phony rewording of the racist Protocols of the Elders of Zion." But our source stood by his information. And do you really think these groups are in the phone book? You need to realize that whatever you think witchcraft is, there is a sinister, dark, and evil elemental group worldwide, organized and determined, that considers Wiccans and New Age people "pets"—amusing, deluded, and useful to their own ends.

I sometimes need to remind people that whatever they think witchcraft is in the Western world—communing with nature, pastel-colored magical thinking, and hurting no one—if they want to know what real witchcraft is, spend some time in Mexico. Witchcraft is not benevolent there. It is absolutely deadly.

Occult apologists said the document was fake. Of course, they would say that; it was expected by now. But putting aside the debate about the specifics of the conference, the conference did, in fact, take place. I knew about the conference years before I ever got into this work or saw this document. I was living in El Paso in 1981. A friend had been watching Juarez TV and called to tell me the nightly news station was covering the event—at least from the outside. It took place in Juarez on the summer solstice, June 21, 1981. According to the report, over one thousand people from all over the world attended.

El Paso television didn't even mention it. The Mexican media is much more forthright—and often more graphic—than American media.

Apparently, the W.I.C.C.A. conference organizers attempted to have their gathering in El Paso and were refused by the mayor. Juarez said, "No problem."

Several years had passed since we first received this document, and all the critics and skeptics had their say in ridiculing it.

Then, in Big Spring, Texas, in 1993, I was training teachers and educators for the local schools. I mentioned there had been a major occult conference in Mexico, not going into too many details to avoid any potential argument from someone in the audience.

At the break, a teacher approached me. "My best friend went to that," he said quietly. He had my complete attention. "It was in Juarez. It was called 'Satanas 1.' Almost a thousand people were there."

"Does your friend know where the next one was held?" I asked.

"Juarez, too," he said. "June 21, 1986." Bingo. Only a few people knew that fact.

"What about Satanas 3?" I asked.

"It was supposed to be in Las Vegas, I think, but I'm not sure. My friend didn't go. He killed himself on June 20th that year."

Real event versus satanic panic narrative.

A Dangerously Close Call

We had so many life-and-death close calls with kids during that time. I'm thankful we were able to get some out alive.

Donnie was sixteen. His mother beat him, and his father abused him and discarded him. He ended up with his grandma in Fort Stockton, Texas.

My probation officer friend Ben Kennedy and I were in Fort Stockton speaking to over one hundred cops, probationers, educators, therapists, ministers, and judges. Ben and I made a good tag teaching team. I preferred it when Ben spoke first, and that's how we taught that day.

As always, we got just as educated as they all did. During lunch, an officer confirmed Ben's information that rich Texas ranchers' properties were used for rituals. Guards posted at different parameters to radio up any intrusions would shoot to kill if someone got too close and got through the third parameter. (Now we know that drug cartels do the same thing.) The off-duty officer had gone out on a tip because someone reportedly saw a strange bunch of people driving up to a ranch after midnight. The officer got too close; he was by himself and outgunned. They began shooting, and he fled for his life. When he returned with backup, they were all gone.

West Texas cops and judges made me a little nervous. They could be skeptical, and they were always no-nonsense guys. You were either accepted or not. You were good people or not. Things are black and white. Don't mess with Texas.

So, during lunch, I was squirming a little as a West Texas judge in his sixties eyeballed me across the table in silence. Finally, he motioned across the table for me to lean over so he could tell me something. "Son, they've been sending me butchered corpses down the river here for years. I had no idea why they were cut up and marked like they were till I saw y'all's class this morning. Now I know it was satanic. Thought you'd like to know." Thank you, sir. Indeed, I did.

Ben went over to speak at the local high school during my morning class. Ben personified the very definition of conservative law enforcement, and the long-haired class was not listening. "Hey man, where'd you get your haircut?" one metalhead asked, laughing.

Same place you didn't get yours, ya little weasel, I could almost hear Ben thinking. But Ben handled the rest of the class well for the hour.

A local probation chief approached Ben with a young teen boy after class. "He needs to talk to you," the officer said.

"Come on," Ben said, leading them to a private corner.

The boy was a cousin of the one who made fun of Ben in class. "Please, you gotta help Donnie," the boy pleaded. "He's into the devil, big-time. Last week, he talked to me in the hallway during lunch, and he was shaking and crying. He told me he went with his group, and he watched them kill a little kid. Suddenly, his 'leader' grabbed him and slammed him up against the lockers and told him to keep his stinking mouth shut or he'd be dead. So Donnie shut up. He's so messed up, you gotta help him, or I think he's gonna die."

Ben came over after lunch, introduced me to the probation chief, and explained the situation. The chief took us and the boy's cousin to the grandmother's house. She was raising Donnie. It was 1:30 p.m. We had a short time before Donnie was supposed to be home. We had to convince Grandma we needed to search Donnie's room.

"No, it's not true!" she protested. "Donnie's a good boy! He doesn't use drugs! He'd never do anything bad like that!"

The cousin pleaded, then got mad. "Grandma, wake up!" he shouted. "He's not your good little boy! He does use drugs, and he worships the devil, and if you don't let these people help, he's probably gonna die!" That shocked her enough to allow us to search.

We found metal posters and death metal tapes. We also found Ninja clothes and a woman's garment with bloodstains. They bagged that for later. But I was frustrated. I sensed there was more, but we were running out of time. "Let me look one more place," I said. I searched every inch of Donnie's dresser. There in the bottom drawer, taped to the back, carefully hidden so it would not be found until a later date, we found this note:

Read This Goodbye at My Funeral

Everything I own, burn! Burn it all to ashes and leave nothing. Every piece of paper, cloth, wood, steel, plastic, BURN IT ALL! To rid my body, don't bury me! Burn me before bury me. It is written ashes to ashes before dust to dust. If it's against the law, break it for me, please! Tell all my friends, I'll miss you! You meant so much to me. Stick together, and don't let what happened to me happen to you! Leaving you, my friends, was one of the hardest decisions I had to make. I hope you'll remember me when I'm gone. Think about me, and I'll be there in your heart forever.

To the family I didn't have, you all brought this on. I had to look for friends, 'cause it wasn't there in the family. Each one of you will pay the price, I won't let this pass!

And to the angel that meant so much to me, I love you. I always will, death will not keep me from you. Leaving our love behind was the hardest thing I ever had to consider. You've been through so much, and I wanted to love and care for you, like no one else . . . I'll be with you forever. I wish I could hold you, I'm so lonely. Being with you was the only time I felt safe. Not having you is too much for me. Heaven is where I want to be, but they tried to take you away from me, and left me in hell. Please forgive me for doing this to you, but my tragedy must end.

Grandma, keep my dog safe. If he's too much for you to handle, then kill him and send him to me. He and I shared a love no one will ever know about. He was a part of me.

"When's his birthday?" I asked them.

"Monday, why?"

It was Friday; the note was dated for that Monday. To many devil worshippers, their birthday is the most important holiday, and for a number of groups, committing suicide on your birthday was the ultimate sacrifice. I believe he was planning on taking his life on his birthday.

Grandma now knew this was deadly serious. By God's grace, because we found that note, probation was able to intervene and get Donnie some help. We were able to save his life by a mere three days.

Unfortunately, many kids' lives did not have a good ending.

I met Renee in 1988. She was a street-smart, savvy lady in her mid-thirties who had endured her own traumas and later became a private investigator. She was an advocate for ritual abuse victims.

"I need your help," Renee said when she called late in the summer of 1988. "My nephew and his girlfriend disappeared over the July 4th weekend. I know they were into devil worship. I'm afraid they've been kidnapped. They might have been sacrificed. If you can do anything to help, I'd really appreciate it."

I tried everything I could. I was in Midland, Texas over Halloween week, and I pleaded on live radio for information from anyone about Shane and Sally's whereabouts.

They found Shane and Sally's bodies a little over a week later on Veteran's Day near Twin Buttes Reservoir, seventeen miles from where they were last seen. They had been murdered with shotgun blasts.

(Note: Much of the following information was obtained from friends, family, and law enforcement. If anyone finds any discrepancies or information that proves it to be not true, please contact me.)

Shane and Sally were in their mid-teens. They got involved with a group called "The Lost Boys," based on a teen vampire movie of the same name. They probably thought it was just playing a game like *Dungeons and Dragons* at first—a seemingly "harmless" role-playing fantasy game that is packed with ancient occult imagery and demon-ology. (I was told later that Shane and Sally's *Dungeons and Dragons* pewter figurines, which identified their characters in the game, were found in their jeans' pockets.) It was probably a game to them when more occult aspects entered into it. But reportedly, "The Lost Boys," was a satanic ritual gang, and Sally was reported to have attended some of these gatherings.

According to *Unsolved Mysteries Wiki*,

In January 1988, Shane and Sally moved into an apartment together. In March, Sally called the police and claimed that some members of the cult were involved in criminal activity. They gave an investigator a gun that a cult member claimed was involved in a robbery/murder. He determined that it was stolen, although he was unable to connect it to a murder. Shane and Sally told him that they feared that they would be harmed by members of the cult. Six weeks later, they moved out of their apartment and left town separately. However, by early summer, they both returned to San Angelo. In mid-June 1988, Sally called Helen and told her that they were afraid that they were going to be killed.[6]

My sources told me that Shane had left town to start over in Oklahoma; he wanted to escape the drugs and the darkness that had entered their group. He wanted to get a job and come back for Sally. She may have been carrying his baby.

On July 4th weekend, he allegedly went back to San Angelo, pleading with Sally to leave with him.

The next day, they were gone.

I don't know what was harder for me—standing at the spot where their lifeblood had poured out into the ground at the lake, still visible —or going to the funeral and hearing no hope being given to the crying, devastated school friends who had come to say goodbye. "The Lost Boys" were standing on the fringes, Lost Boys jackets and all. They showed no remorse. No tears. Just calm, knowing detachment.

The killers are still free.

Kids dabbling? That's such a glib, careless response. I remember around that same time, a "Christian" book titled *When the Devil Dares Your Kids* by Bob and Gretchen Passantino had this to say about kids and the occult and white magick practitioners:

> Contemporary witches are generally positive, gentle, creative, and respectful of others and of nature. The contemporary witchcraft system, represented by the beliefs listed above, don't encourage violence, destruction, criminal behavior, or divisiveness within families. Many witches are positive assets

to their communities, responsible citizens, good employees, and devoted family members. *The average teenager who dabbles with the Goddess religion is at little risk for destructive occultism.*[7] (emphasis added)

I realize they were talking about Wicca. But I am astonished that any Christian publisher would print this lie. Anyone—I mean anyone —who has been in the occult, as I once was, will tell you in no uncertain terms that any form of occultism, from Ouija boards to Wicca, from Tarot cards to seances, is a deadly poison and is addictive and deceptive.

Perhaps we shouldn't be too surprised that this grossly misleading and dangerous statement came from the same couple who were behind a big part of the "satanic panic" narrative. (Even a major witchcraft publication reviewed this book with glowing accolades, saying, "Thank you, Passantinos!"[8])

Nonetheless, the point should not be missed. It was completely irresponsible that "Christian" writers would even suggest that kids who "dabble" are at very little risk for "destructive occultism." It is reprehensible and a lie. Little risk? Tell that to Donnie. Tell that to Sean Sellers or the families and loved ones of Tommy Sullivan.

Tell that to Shane and Sally's families.

Shane Paul Stewart and Sally Ann McNelly

Arise, cry out in the night: in the beginning of the watches pour out thine heart like water before the face of the Lord: lift up thy hands toward him for the life of thy young children, that faint for hunger in the top of every street. (Lamentations 2:19)

16

A Tale of Two Towns

Once upon a time, there was an obscure little town off the beaten path in the southwest desert I will call Helltown. People drove through just to get gas and then drove right back out again. The population was small, and there really wasn't much to do there but soak in the hot springs or pick up snacks and beer before heading out to one of the local lakes for a relaxing weekend.

My pastor friend Daniel* called me just weeks after he moved his family there to take over a small and struggling church. Daniel and his wife, who are white, had two adopted black children.

Daniel told me that within just a short time of their moving in and taking over the pastorate, the phone calls started. "You better leave town and take your n***** kids with you" and other even worse threats. There were some nasty folks in this little town—and dangerous ones. But that was just the tip of the iceberg in this otherwise unremarkable town off the beaten path from the desert highway.

Daniel got right to the point. "I need you to come up and teach Sunday school for me for a while," Daniel said to me about six months after having taken the church post. I paused, assimilating his request.

"You are aware that you are a two-and-a-half-hour drive from here, right?"

---

*Not his real name.

177

"Yes. It's important. I really need you to do this. You'll understand when you get here and see the class."

I made the drive that weekend and immediately understood why he wanted me there. There were about thirty kids in the class. This particular state is about 86 percent Native American and Hispanic. But here, in this tiny town in the middle of nowhere, was a class full of children ages six to fourteen years old, and all but a handful of them were blond-haired and blue-eyed. The implications were chilling.

Daniel filled me in on the lay of the land in Helltown: Large amounts of drugs were continually going through. Officials appeared to be on someone's payroll. Certain juvenile and child protection officers would do "favors" for you if you did "favors" for them—of the sexual variety.

A multimillionaire who had a huge ranch about a hundred miles away flew in every week like clockwork on his private plane to have a buffalo burger at a downtown greasy spoon, then flew back home again. Very odd in a state that also was the nearby residence of the wealthy and notorious pedophile/child trafficker Jeffrey Epstein. In addition, there was a pimp in a big Cadillac who frequently cruised the town with a carload of underage teenage boys he rented out. Everyone knew it, but no one did a thing about it.

What about the kids of the town, several of whom came to the Sunday school class? Some lived in trailers with their parent or parents, some lived with their parents by the river in tents, and some kids were living alone . . . by the river . . . even the younger ones. Child Protective Services was useless. One set of parents allegedly sold their teen boy to their dealer for a large amount of meth.

In the child trading/porn industry, blond-haired, blue-eyed kids are known as "high dollar" merchandise.

It seemed clear to me that someone was transporting children and young teens through this vile little town. It was perfect for this, and someone was no doubt covering all the tracks. Helltown was in an area we had long suspected was a hub for transporting people and children for the sex trade industry.

But what could we do about it? We kept track. We would try to get some authorities outside the area to investigate matters. And for the next year or so, we just loved those kids and tried to give them Jesus. It was painful not to be able to do much else.

Daniel and his family moved on after about six years. With Daniel's departure, I lost my only contact in this little hellish town. A couple of years later, the news came out that a man from the village adjacent to Helltown was arrested. He had been torturing and videotaping women in his trailer for years, women he had kidnapped or lured in. Mentioned only once and conveyed to me by an officer who was on the original crime scene team and not recorded as far as I know, the alleged torturer told the authorities, "I am a Satanist. I make videos for our groups." It was never spoken of again. But as if to give credence to his claims, besides an electrified coffin and various torture implements that littered the inside of the trailer, there was a sign as you entered the "torture room" that read, "Satan's Toy Box."

While the trial dragged on, a judge died, and a key witness died. There was a mistrial. Upon retrial, the Trailer Monster was finally sentenced. The case was closed, and everyone forgot about this weird little slice of criminal America.

Meanwhile, during the Trailer Monster's first trial, in the offices of a data-entry enterprise a state away, a woman had begun to confide in a friend of mine, very slowly at first, because she was so scared. She had escaped a deadly situation a few months earlier and was terrified that they would find her again. But she had to tell someone.

For weeks, my friend Mary* took voluminous notes as the lady, Donna,* had told her the terrifying details of her ordeal. Concerned because of the implications that this was an ongoing criminal group, Mary took extensive notes and sent them to me. It just so happened that I was spending some extended time in the very area that Donna was talking about. Every day, I took bits and pieces of the information and did the footwork to attempt to determine the veracity of her story. Everything that could be validated was, and nothing in the information was demonstrably false.

Donna had been married with children. When she got hooked on drugs, her husband left her and took their kids with him. She was sold by her dealer to a group in another desert state. The group she was sold to, according to her, did it all: drug running, gun running, human trafficking, prostitution, child pornography, and snuff films (a film in which the victim is sexually assaulted and then murdered at the end).

---

* Not their real names.

The ringleaders were a three-generation family of used car dealers. Cops were on the payroll. Their clients included important politicians and wealthy people who were flown into the airport in the middle of the night. Many of the adult victims, as well as the children, were kept thirty to forty miles out in the desert at a biker compound. Anyone who got too close to the compound was shot at or disappeared. The other compound was right in the middle of a small town, a trailer-park biker compound with trees that were so thick that you would need a helicopter to see inside of it.

Donna was forced to be a prostitute. She was also tasked with taking care of the children until they were transported, sold, or eliminated. She once was made to hide a gun that was used to murder a grandfather and his grandchild who were trying to escape. She escaped by being rescued by a Hell's Angel biker who felt sorry for her. I tracked down every bit of the voluminous information I could.

During this time, a news clip came on the television while Mary and Donna were taking a lunch break. It showed one of the prostitutes who had been captured and tortured before she escaped the grip of the same man previously mentioned who had a trailer in which he tortured women.[1] Donna became almost hysterical. "She was with our group!" she sobbed. The prostitute, a key witness, was scheduled to testify against the Trailer Monster. She died, as I said before, before being able to testify. The Trailer Monster died of a heart attack in jail shortly after his conviction, just before he was interrogated by state police on other issues. Contact with Donna was lost, but we were able to turn over a strong case file to the FBI, as well as to a personal friend in the DEA, in hopes that something would come of it all.

In 2021, a large group of victims of human trafficking were set free by a multi task force in the state Donna came from. Whether this was a result of our information, in part because of it, or even if it was the same group Donna was in, I do not know, but it was a great encouragement to keep fighting, keep teaching, keep making contacts, and keep trying to bring these people to justice.

Maybe, just maybe, something will break, and this vile network will be dismantled, the perpetrators brought to justice, and the children and teens in their clutches set free. It may not be right away, but as the saying goes, "The wheels of God grind slowly, but they grind exceeding fine." In the meantime, we wait, we work, and we pray.

The *Real* "Satanic Panic" Story—Part 1

Fear them not therefore: for there is nothing
covered, that shall not be revealed; and hid,
that shall not be known. (Matthew 10:26)

Shots Across the Bow

I admit that this chapter is very personal to me. I have been able to stay fairly dispassionate about a number of issues concerning the occult and Satanism: their protected legal status and their claims that they do not break the law. I am not now, nor have I ever been on a "witch hunt." If people want to worship Satan, Baal, or any other thing that's not of God, I wish they wouldn't, but that's their right to do so. Only if they use their god or religion to injure others is it an issue; and this has always been the foundation of the work I have done with both the church and especially law enforcement. I worked to help criminal justice workers understand the many aspects of occult crimes and crimes against children. We worked to help them pursue legitimate criminal cases and to avoid frivolous and distracting lawsuits by recognizing activities that may be the antithesis of what they believe but are nonetheless legal. I wanted to facilitate their efforts to help victims find healing and protection from real criminals.

I have learned more than I ever thought I would along the way. In the beginning, my hope was to educate churches and youth groups about the spiritual dangers of the occult. But then I came face to face with the crimes, crime scenes, suicides, and murders done in the name of the occult, Satanism, devil worship, or other fringe groups. That's when my education began in earnest.

I learned that it is not as easy as saying, "Satanists did that, or witches did that." There are as many occult groups as there are denominations in Christianity, maybe even more. Each has its own doctrine, philosophy, and practice. Identifying different ritual elements at a crime scene or recognizing occult clues found in a room or in a house search became a crucial part of pursuing a case.

The Tentacles of the Beast

There is a definite hierarchy—whether spoken or unspoken—in the occult world. There are what has nonchalantly been dubbed occult "dabblers"—kids and adults who dabble in horoscopes, tarot cards, palm reading, crystal magick, New Age teachings, and so on. This is kind of the lower end of the threat scale. Then, there are organized groups like the Church of Satan, the Temple of Set, and more recent groups like the Satanic Temple. One was a legitimate 501(c)(3) "church." Not a huge criminal threat, though a number of their followers were deeply enmeshed in the teachings of these organizations and found justification for some of their nefarious activities in manuals such as *The Satanic Bible* or Aquino's *Crystal Tablet of Set.*

There is white magick, black magick, grey magick, chaos magick, Gardnerian witchcraft, generic witchcraft, Italian Strega witchcraft (nasty stuff), and everything in between. Some groups and practitioners are fairly benign from a criminal perspective, and some are deadly.

All of these are really at the lower end of the scale as far as criminal activity is concerned. The Illuminati, an organization of elite occultists and global leaders that was formed in 1776 by Adam Weishaupt, has long been rumored to be a powerful secret organization. But even they are somewhat of a front group for the real-world power players in the occult world that stretches from White Light groups—a very hidden group—to the Luciferians. And that is where it gets really serious.

That is where we discovered more organized criminal activities such as human trafficking, cartels, and human sacrifice.

The musicians and actors who claim to have affiliation with the Illuminati probably did make a deal with the elitists in the occult world in the industry to attain their wealth and fame. And yes, there are blood contracts. According to one insider, there are Luciferian "Men in White" who come into Hollywood with millions of dollars to place it where they want to have the most influence.

The more we climbed up the ladder to see "who was who" in the dark mix, the more pushback we got. And the more we did this, the more we saw a larger picture emerge of an international cabal of bankers, politicians, judges, military leaders, and more, who were all part of a real-world organized entity. They were and are hell-bent on creating a world reborn in the image and likeness of Lucifer. They believe Lucifer to be the rightful heir to this world, and they consider the God of the Christians to be evil and that His influence must be eliminated in this world and His messengers silenced.

As with some modern satanic groups that don't claim to believe in a real Satan, for some, Lucifer is a principle: you don't even have to believe in Lucifer as a being to be part of them. Luciferianism is a principle that teaches that man needs to be enlightened by "Lucifer," the light-bearer, in order to throw off the chains of Christianity and Judaism—to become as gods. Secular Luciferian thought is all that is required to belong to this group—but those who are true believers, they say, wield the real power of global dominance. One of their last obstacles has been the Catholic Church, which they have been attempting to secularize through the influence of Luciferian bishops within the Vatican itself since the early 1960s.[1] Two issues have stood in the way: homosexuality and abortion. When these are completely written out of the church canon as being sin, then they will have become the secular church they have been striving to create.

Who exactly are the Luciferians? You will never really know. And they do not necessarily go by that name, though that is what they are. They are easily the most secretive group on the planet, and they plan on keeping it that way. In fact, Malachi Martin, a former priest and Vatican expert on Jerusalem affairs, and author of *Hostage to the Devil*, points out that their mottos are, "The guarantee of our tomorrow is today's perception that we do not exist," and "Un avulso non deficit alter" ("Where one is cut off, the other will succeed.")[2] The occult has always operated by attaining higher degrees. You never stop attaining higher degrees by doing ritual workings and ritual magick. It is probably a fallacy that Masonry only exists up to thirty-three degrees. We debriefed a former thirty-third-degree Mason who said he was recruited into much higher levels through being a courier between different groups, from the Rosicrucians to an Illuminist group in DC.

It is also likely true that top leaders of Luciferian-type groups generally keep their hands clean from blood rituals, having attained ranks where that is no longer necessary except perhaps as a reminder of where their power comes from.[3]

The ability to discern between these different groups was an ongoing learning experience. After a while, it became fairly easy to discern the difference between a wannabe Satanist, a LaVeyan Satanist (wannabe devil worshipper with credentials and a mainly clean criminal record), a mix-and-match occultist who used a bit of everything, a criminal occultist, a Wiccan, a generic pagan, a Santerían, a Palo Mayombe practitioner, a Santa Muerte practitioner, and so on.

But at some point, it became very obvious that we were not just dealing with low-level players, especially when we got involved in cases that were in the court system, the political arena, or well-moneyed socialite circles. They pushed back. They made things disappear. They had cases mysteriously shut down. People died, were suddenly fired, were discredited, reassigned, or dismissed.

When we bumped up against organized pedophile/child trading groups, things got very ugly.

How do you know there's a deadly spider in a hole, in a rock wall in your yard? You put your hand in and start poking around. "Oh, that's just a conspiracy theory. You can't prove there's a spider in there!" No—but I would be glad to show you the bite marks. And feel free to stick your hand in there and find out for yourself.

The "bite marks" didn't show up right away. In fact, we thought we were doing quite well in the late 1980s. Yes, there were attacks.

But we thought we were making serious inroads and causing major damage to the enemy. We felt we were winning. How naïve we were. We were about to get sideswiped and gutted. Skeptics were expected; we had our share of educators, cops, and psychologists who were not just skeptical but sometimes quite hostile. One psychologist became so enraged that he had to be bodily removed from one of our conferences.

Despite the continuing stream of solid information and good leads that we passed on to the authorities, there was a great deal of unbelief about the dangers of organized occult groups in our city. Since El Paso was a major hub for drugs, child porn, and child trading, we weren't too surprised at the lack of interest.

Two of El Paso's most notorious child molesters had been in operation for years, one having been a child pornographer in business for almost a decade. Our team investigated both of them thoroughly through surveillance and victim interviews, and as a result, a thick file was acquired on each of them. The FBI found out and requested a meeting with us. They acted very enthusiastic and were impressed with the work we had done. We turned over all our files to the FBI with their assurance that they would pursue these cases most vigorously.

We never heard back. After several months of silence, we had a federal marshall check on the status, and the reply stunned us: *Back off; they've got official protection.* One of these men, previously mentioned, was a high-level devil worshipper who hosted teenage parties and took pornographic films of the kids. We had debriefed people as old as thirty and as young as eighteen who had been to his house parties—some of them who had been drugged and "used" there. His house, according to several witnesses we interviewed, was one giant pornography setup, with video cameras everywhere, especially in the basement bedrooms. As previously mentioned, there were secret tunnels leading out from the basement so they could get underage kids out if the police were called. His porn collection was well-known even to the New Mexico police—but he couldn't be touched. I later had an opportunity to look inside the house while it was undergoing renovation, and it was exactly as it had been described to us by the victims who had been there.

A number of law enforcement officers denied there was ever any problem in El Paso. A few of them were so superstitious that they did everything they could to avoid going out on calls regarding satanic crime.

In the '80s, several women were raped, murdered, and buried in the northeast El Paso desert. We interviewed some of the mothers and relatives of the victims. They were convinced the killer was a devil worshipper. (We were never able to confirm that.) The cops dismissed them as wackos and hysterics. One sister of one of the victims was interviewed and taken on a long drive out to the crime scene while the person kept telling her about the power of the devil while writing "666" on his notebook so it could clearly be seen by the relative. She was scared to death.

We looked into it ourselves. That was back in our naïve days when we'd go investigate the sacrifice of animals at ritual sites or photograph occult graffiti. About two weeks after the crime scene had been processed, we spent nearly all day in the northeast desert where one of the bodies had been found. It still had the remnants of the crime scene tape hanging on the bushes.

What we found there was disturbing. We found a fire pit with dozens of adult and children's underwear around it. There was at least one sacrificed dog lying at the edge. There were cremated ashes and bone fragments within the pit. To the left of the area was a ranch with a fence that had ten upside-down plastic crosses made from Christmas tree branches tied along it.

There was a mesquite tree where a page from a book was nailed, which described how to eviscerate a woman (the same age as most of the victims) from sternum to pelvis. We also found a Clorox bottle with thirteen I.V. needles and tubes inside. (Thirteen is the number of a practicing coven. We learned from a law enforcement contact that one of the victims had been found completely drained of blood.) We bagged up what we could.

I called one of the detectives at the northeast substation to tell them what we'd found. "Not interested," he said. Ten minutes later, a detective called me. "Bring the items down right away."

I told him about a man who came to us for help because he was terrified. He had been out in the northeast desert, walking his dog late at night. He saw a bonfire over a sand dune, figured it was a party, and thought he'd go cop a beer. He parked his car and climbed the dune, then he heard loud chanting and saw a group of people in black robes. He ran back to his car. They spotted him and gave chase, shooting at him repeatedly at ninety-plus miles per hour until he lost them along the seventy-five-mile stretch to Alamogordo, New Mexico. He was so terrified that he kept his bullet-riddled car under a tarp in his garage.

"So, what makes you think they were devil worshippers?" the officer asked me.

"Sir, when you're out at midnight and see people in black robes chanting around a bonfire, it's a good guess it's not a Sunday school class," I replied. It was hard to get some people to look at these things for what they were.

We gave him everything we had. To this day, I am not sure whether they did anything with it.

Retaliation came in many forms. For me, it seemed to come from everywhere. There were death threats by phone, death threats by letter, and death threats by fax. There was a virus-induced computer wipeout, public ridicule, and secret slander.

One day, I had been away from home for several hours, and when I returned home, there were dozens of red cat paw marks running from my living room into my office and to other rooms. No one had access or a key to my house. I took pictures because I knew no one would believe this unless they saw it. It turned out to have been done with washable ink, which I was glad for. Still, it was unnerving to know they could so easily get into my house in such a short time, leave their "calling card," and then leave without a trace. I suspect it was just done to let me know how easily they could get to me whenever they wanted to.

In Midland, Texas, a man had telephoned three times at Crossroads Rehab Center, where I worked with the youth, trying to find out when I was speaking at the rehab-sponsored conference. At the conference, he showed up and stayed silent through three presentations by other professionals. The minute I began to lecture, he stood up and attacked my credentials and facts, quoting the inaccurate statement by FBI expert Kenneth Lanning that organized satanic crime was nonexistent.

In other words, he wasn't going to let me lecture. I finally had to call a break, at which time he was escorted out of the conference and given a full refund.

In Waco, Texas, Sue Joyner and I were lecturing to over 1,000 attendees at McClellan University. An irate man threatened to sue us for defamation before we even began to speak. Then, while I was telling of someone who was forced to participate in the murder of a young teen when he was a child, a stranger opened the side auditorium door and yelled, "Did they confess to being a murderer? Isn't that what they are?" I was furious. "Listen. Jesus said if you've thought about murdering someone, you've done it. How many people have you killed?" The door slammed. These people were everywhere now.

During the largest ritual abuse retrial in Texas in 1987, a "freelance reporter" approached me and two of our kids from our youth group outside the courtroom. She wanted to ask a few questions. Being very naïve, I answered her questions as best I could, including giving a little of my own history of involvement in the occult.

Two years later, I flew to New York to tape the *Geraldo Rivera* special on the Matamoros murders. As mentioned before, I spoke on camera in disguise in order to protect my parents from any possible retaliation.

Several months later, this "investigative reporter" blew my cover and exposed my real name, current location, and prior history in an article she wrote for *The Texas Observer.* She didn't just blow my cover; she misquoted nearly every single thing I told her. She went on to become one of the star "de-bunkers" and apologists against ritual abuse claims, as well as a de facto crusader insisting on the innocence of accused pedophiles and child abusers.

A couple years later, when I flew to Los Angeles to tape the *Montel Williams* talk show, I brought a young woman, Denise,* who had been used in teen porn and devil worship.

I didn't know we'd have other guests on the show—two devil worshippers. As we sat in the "green room," waiting to go on, Paul Valentine, head of the Worldwide Church of Satanic Liberation, sat with us. He sat next to Denise. "I'm sorry. Do I make you nervous sitting next to you?"

I chuckled to myself as she deftly replied, "No. Do I make you nervous? You should be." I smiled quietly at her boldness.

In the course of the conversation, Lauren Stratford's name came up. Lauren, the author of *Satan's Underground*, was a dear friend of mine. (More on that later.) "Oh, yes," Paul replied. "I met her when we did the *Sally Jesse Rafael* show together. She seems like a kind, compassionate person. She was very nice to me."

Paul was then called to the set, and within five minutes, the likable person he presented disappeared. He called Lauren a fraud, completely backtracking on what he had just told me. I was furious.

Paul sat on the set next to Rex Diablo Church, who looked like an exact replica of Church of Satan founder Anton Lavey, only younger. He was a second-generation Church of Satan member. Denise stayed hidden behind a screen offstage to hide her identity. She did an extraordinary job, telling her story without any fear at all. I was also thankful that ex-devil worshipper Charles Evans, who was a solid Christian, was also a guest on the set with us.

But these two "devil's boys" wouldn't let me talk! So, I blew up on national television. I had seen enough talk shows to understand how they try to make victims and Christians cower, and I was sick and tired of it. So, I exploded. My breaking point, along with the constant interruptions, was Rex Church informing the audience that Satanists were an elite group that only accepted the best into their membership. That was it for me. "Hey, I've got a membership form

---

* Not her real name.

to the Church of Satan!" I yelled. "Fifty bucks, and you can become a member. That's how elite they are. This is bunk!"

Williams' eyebrows went up, and when Paul and Rex tried to change the subject, Williams said, "Whoa, wait a minute, I wanna know about this fifty dollar membership!"

After a while, Williams asked me if satanic crime was real. Paul and Rex immediately cut in to say, "Oh, this is ridiculous! Even the FBI says there's no such thing. Are you saying you know more than they do?"

"Look, the FBI took twenty years to figure out that the Mafia existed!" I retorted. "You bet we know more than they do." Even as it came out of my mouth, I knew I was committed now; I had just succeeded in laying down the gauntlet to the FBI agency, which honestly knew next to nothing about ritual crime and, with rare exception, had only been an obstacle as we conducted investigations of this sort nationwide.

It seemed the show was over very quickly. After the show, Denise and I waited in the hallway for our limousine to the airport. Rex and Paul stood a few yards away, whispering and staring at us. When Paul left, Rex gave me the "evil eye." I raised one eyebrow returning his glare and grinned at him. Rex sprinted toward his limo and "satanic saluted" us as he jumped in.

I had not anticipated their being on the show, but I think we had been able to lay out a legitimate, factual case about the reality of ritual crime.

Months later, Paul called me at home. He told me he and his fiancée had been watching the tape of that show. He called to apologize for the rancor between us. *Thou art not far from the Kingdom,* I thought to myself. While being interviewed by radio talk show host Bob Larson, I was further surprised when Bob was handed a message from Paul that had been relayed during the show. He said that although he followed the satanic religion, he didn't believe it was right to hurt children. "It goes on," he said. "Greg needs to be heard."

It was strange to have an ally on the "other side," but I believe he meant what he said. I still pray for him.

Wiccan Backlash

I began to get heavy backlash from the Wiccan community after my extensive work training dozens of criminal justice workers, police departments, and school educators, especially in east and central Texas. My classes were an A-to-Z on the history of the occult, crime scene investigations, threat assessment, ritual child abuse, and teen Satanism. A Wiccan high priest and his high priestess wife were both educators in the public school system, and they did their best to undermine my work both before and after my workshops, spreading slanderous and untrue stories about who I was and what I taught. They attempted to get my classes canceled before I even arrived. I never feared these obstacles because I was more than willing to have the two of them show up and find out for themselves exactly what I taught. The irony is, though not surprising, they never bothered to attend.

They weren't alone in spreading disinformation. In fact, in one criminal justice class, I actually had to confront a pastor who was there spreading false information. He was claiming that Wiccans at Fort Hood army base were killing babies, a statement with no evidence to back it up. Also in that class was a police officer, a Wiccan high priestess, who told me she had expected my class to be filled with lies, but after she heard me, she wondered if perhaps she needed to warn her own groups about possible criminal elements hiding among their covens!

It wasn't until a few years after I started getting slandered by Wiccans that I was contacted by a source who had intercepted an e-mail from a Wiccan high priest police psychologist that was sent to covens around the country, wherein he vowed to "stop me," "have my CEU's revoked (continuing education credits given to class attendees), and "expose me" so I would not be able to teach in Texas again. I took that e-mail to my lawyer, who assured me it was actionable, but after praying about it, I had a clear impression I was not to pursue it. This was the kind of behind-the-scenes subterfuge we were having to deal with all the time.

And always, there were the bizarre e-mails like this one I received in December of 1998:

Dear Sirs,

I'm sorry to relay this message to you. After a fit of fervent prayer, Jesus told me your organization is under control of Satan. Unless you and your Godless followers repent and proclaim that Jesus wants you to love mankind and stop your spreading rumors. [*sic*] You will all go to Hell and burn in the eternal fire. Satan is your Lord because "by the fruit ye shall know the tree." Your fruits are lies and misconception and Jesus, Lord and Savior, will take a chainsaw to you!

(Written by a pagan, a disgruntled Christian, someone who was mentally ill, or a satanic troll? It was hard to tell.)

The Battle Widens

Ugly communications, threats, and retaliation certainly weren't limited to attacks against our little group or to me.

By 1990, the tide had most definitely turned against us. The False Memory Syndrome Foundation had arisen and was doing significant damage. The False Memory Syndrome Foundation was founded by Pamela and Peter Freyd, parents whose daughter, Jennifer, had gone to therapy, came to terms with her father's sexual abuse against her, and confronted them. They denied. Jennifer never went public until after her parents forced her to by founding The False Memory Syndrome Foundation and accused her of having "false memories" and being mentally unstable. She never recanted her claims. In fact, she was a respected academic at a major university.

The False Memory Syndrome Foundation became a powerful organization that denied claims of sexual abuse and ritual abuse and promoted the "false memory" "diagnosis." And as one expose states, The False Memory Syndrom Foundation "created a defense for countless sex offenders."[4] They came to be the child abusers' and pedophiles' best friends—eager to defend their innocence, often in blatant disregard of the evidence.

The most well-known board member of The False Memory Syndrome Foundation was the late Dr. Ralph Underwager. He was paid multiple thousands of dollars as a court "expert" on behalf of people accused of child abuse across the country. His main tactic was to call children fantasizers who were incapable of telling the truth. He was the oft-quoted, rising star of The False Memory Syndrome Foundation, that is . . .

Until . . .

He was interviewed in the Dutch pedophile journal *Paidika*. His words speak for themselves:

> . . . Pedophiles need to become more positive and make the claim that pedophilia is an acceptable expression of God's will for love and unity among human beings.[5]

> Pedophiles can boldly and courageously affirm what they choose. They can say that what they want is to find the best way to love . . . Pedophiles can make the assertion that the pursuit of intimacy and love is what they choose. With boldness, they can say, "I believe this is in fact part of God's will."[6]

On March 23, 1993, as a guest on *Good Morning America*, Dr. J. Gordon Melton, a United Methodist minister and false memory syndrome proponent, spoke about the "healthy" aspects of cults (not satanic, necessarily, just cults in general) when he said:

> Many cults can actually improve a child's life. Overwhelmingly, they are anti-drugs. Overwhelmingly, they are strong on discipline . . . so cults can have some very positive effects.[7]

He also attended and reveled in the partying at 1997's "Dracula Convention" in Los Angeles.[8] Another "false memory" and "satanic panic" narrative proponent, Benjamin Rossen, was also on the editorial board of *Paidika*, the same Dutch pro-pedophile journal in which Dr. Underwager had been quoted.[9]

It was apparent that the false memory proponents attracted these kinds of "experts."

It was a shock when a significant number of Christian publications, such as *Charisma Magazine* and *Christianity Today*, supported the claims and purposes of the False Memory Syndrome Foundation. And these "false memory" proponents became the most oft-quoted "experts" by the Christian media. And not one major Christian voice was brave enough to challenge them or even look at our evidence, which we tried repeatedly to get them to look at.

The *Real* "Satanic Panic" Story—Part 2

Bringing out the Big Guns

This next part was very difficult for me to write. The consequences of the following events were grave and damaging to all we had endeavored to do.

Our network of professionals—which included therapists, law enforcement, pastors, educators, medical personnel, criminal justice officers, and social workers who were working together to rescue children and teens from dangerous cults—had weathered our share of threats and personal attacks. But though these threats and attacks—ranging from assaults on personal and professional reputations to getting fired from job positions to actual death threats—seemed to be growing in number and consistency, we could not pinpoint them as being "organized" attempts, per se. Not yet. At first, they seemed almost random and scattered.

My first indication that things were about to change came in the year 1989. A message was conveyed to us through a cult member we were speaking with: "They will be more than happy to provide you with all kinds of occult scenes, animal sacrifices, or whatever else to keep you chasing your tails. But when you try to pull their children and youth out of their world, they will retaliate."

I didn't know what to make of it. Another message came from a pagan group: "You are fools if you don't realize that we watch every single thing you do in public, in workshops, or on the Internet." (They did, and they still do!)

I knew of several people who were considered frontline warriors in this fight. One of them was Mike Warnke, a man I mentioned in chapter 11. He was a former devil worshipper who renounced Satanism and the occult, had his testimony *The Satan Seller* published, and went on to become the top Christian comedian of all time. When the pandemic of occultism and occult crimes hit like a tsunami in the mid-1980s, because of his background in devil worship and the flood of people contacting his ministry for help to get free of occultism, Mike became a consultant to nationwide law enforcement who found themselves inundated with bizarre and ugly crimes done in the name of Satan. I'm sure Mike didn't expect this, and he was unprepared with information or resources to help them deal with these situations.

Suddenly and unexpectedly, Mike became the target of a serious journalistic attack on his story, his character, and his ministry by church journalists. I am not going to get in the weeds and answer all their allegations. (Mike has already responded to these things in his book *Friendly Fire* and posted his thorough response online, which you can read for yourself at http://www.mikewarnke.org/about/faq/ and look for "What about the controversy we heard about?" then click on "Tribunal Board Hearing.*¹*)

I want you to see the bigger picture and understand that this was bigger than an attack on one man. Mike was a figurehead. Mike was a public face of opposition to satanic crimes and the occult.

I did not personally know Mike Warnke then. I simply knew of his book *The Satan Seller* (which I had not yet read) and his comedy through his numerous albums from Word. But in 1986, when I began to step into this work, Mike was becoming known not just as a law enforcement consultant but as someone whose outreach became a crucial referral ministry for occult victims. By the time I became fully engaged in this field in 1987, we were becoming overwhelmed with requests for help from all over the world. Ritual abuse and occult crimes were being found in every state and nearly every country. Our

WATCH Network was a very small group with very limited resources. But we could call Warnke Ministries at any time, day or night, and they provided help: counselors, pastors, youth pastors, safe houses, physicians, criminal justice officers, you name it. It was a godsend. We absolutely relied on it, and Mike was never anything less than helpful and genuine in all our dealings with him. His ministry was a lighthouse in the storm for kids and victims in trouble. And Mike was leading thousands of kids to Jesus, many out of the occult.

And that, of course, was the real issue.

It did not take long for us to discover that there was a growing behind-the-scenes concerted effort to discredit, demoralize, smear, attack, question, destabilize, and ruin credible and vital ministries that helped survivors, victims, children, teens, and parents who were devastated by occultism. We knew to expect any number of measures to stop our work. And why not? In some ways, if you exchange the term *mafia* in place of "organized criminal occult group," it makes sense. The mafia would not allow dissent, would not tolerate traitors, killed those who talked, and bought off people who were in high places. And anyone who tried to take them down could expect a full measure of their wrath and retaliation. You should not think it a stretch to understand that the "dark side" employs the same tactics as the mafia and worse. For example, there were certain occult symbols that were sometimes left on the bodies of those who had been murdered for being a "satanic traitor"—someone who broke the oath or tried to get out.

In the late 1980s, Mike Warnke came to perform at the civic center in our town. He packed it out. I went to observe and see what he would address about the occult crime issues. I also wanted to see who might show up. Our own small meetings and conferences were attracting a number of occultists, from Satanists to Wiccans, from wannabes to real players.

Coming in and sitting in the third row, I did not expect to see the man we knew was the high priest and overseer of the occult world in the southwest region. He had long silver hair and walked with a cane. The minute I saw him, I knew Mike was being carefully watched by the "other side." Simple curiosity? I doubted it. The only reason I believed the high priest would have to be here was to find out what Mike was saying and, I speculated, network with others to devise a plan to take Mike out of the fight. Mike's ministry was a threat to the "occult cartels." As they had already informed us, once we started getting youth out, they were going to retaliate. I was concerned about what they would do after that meeting, what schemes they would or could devise to take Mike out. Or any of us, for that matter.

Later, finding a "destruction ritual" for sale on the Internet that had been done against Mike Warnke just served to confirm the fact that the satanic world dearly hated Mike and wanted to eliminate him.

From a "big picture" standpoint—and I am not going to draw a "conspiracy theory" picture here (although the definition of a conspiracy is when two or more people agree to conspire to do something, and there was plenty of evidence of that already)—it seems as if four entities rose up at once to oppose our work: They came from the psychological community, law enforcement, the occult community, and, most shockingly, the Christian community.

I am not saying that the people responsible for the events that led to the domino effect that ensued were necessarily devil worshippers, Wiccans, witches, occultists, or any other such thing. But I am also not saying they were not. And in a way, it doesn't matter. What matters is what was done, how it was done, how it affected the victims and our work, and what the end result of it all was. I will leave it to others to decide what it all points to.

Concerted "attacks" from the occult community—from Wiccans to Church of Satan-style groups—were to be expected. They were the ones who began screaming "witch hunt" early and often. Then Special Agent Kenneth Lanning from the Behavioral Science Department of the FBI began telling people he had never seen any evidence of organized criminal occultism, not one hair, not one drop of blood, that indicated any kind of organized crime. We knew this statement was in opposition to the facts we had, and I will simply grant Special Agent Lanning the benefit of the doubt and say he may have thought he was just doing his job, and he did it through the filter of bureaucracy, predetermined ideas, and established lenses. We hoped it was not just part of a planned disinformation campaign. Regardless of what it was, his claims became the salvo that was repeatedly lobbed at us, followed by the expected, "What? You're a better expert than the FBI?" We always replied that there were no experts in this field, and those who claimed to be, including the FBI, were more likely to be misinformed and inaccurate. Those who want to know the truth simply needed to follow the trails to find out where they led; we weren't asking for people to blindly accept what we were uncovering. We were simply asking for an honest investigation. Unfortunately, we were sometimes not granted that simple request. The "official" FBI stand caught on like wildfire.

Soon, other people in law enforcement were parroting the party line, saying that it was all "conspiracy theories" and nothing else.

In fact, during one of the last Ritual Crime Conferences in Texas, we were stunned when a law enforcement officer gave an entire training on investigating a ritual crime scene. He had with him a complete outdoor setup, including "sacrificed animals," courtesy of the animal control department, which were specially staged and dressed to mimic a ritually slaughtered animal scenario. The training involved each participant going to the staged ritual setup with all the occult trappings, evaluating, taking notes, and writing their conclusions about what they saw. Everyone came back after the outdoor training and reported their findings. When their reports were finished, the trainer informed the class that they weren't likely to ever encounter anything like this because ritual crimes and satanic abuse crimes were largely just conspiracy theories and village folklore. Several of us just sat in complete, utter disbelief. It just smelled so much like the typical satanic mind games

> "Not only do skeptics such as Lanning choose to ignore eyewitness/victim accounts of ritual criminal activity, they apparently also choose to overlook the significant number of cases of ritual abuse in which perpetrators have confessed to their crimes."[2]

we had already encountered. I wouldn't dare suggest that the teacher was ill-intentioned—but he was definitely a useful tool to the "other side," undoing so much of the hard and legitimate work of years of law enforcement training we had done on occult crimes. It also flew in the face of the actual real crime scenes we had seen with our own eyes—murders, suicides, animal sacrifices, and more, not to mention the testimonies of those who had suffered because of the occult and satanic crimes. It was infuriating.

And, as it happened, within ten years, we found that nearly all our work had been forgotten or undone. The number of our law enforcement associates and other professional helpers was beginning to dwindle—not just because of disbelief but from pressure from departments to quit investigating these kinds of crimes. (This included one major case that was personally shut down by a state senator because the case was leading to uncovering an ugly ritual abuse case within his own religious denomination—Mormonism.[3]) People were also quitting from fear, burnout, overwhelming and inexplicable spiritual attacks, and worse.

One of our top people—and one of the most credible, too—was hired to work as a consultant on a Hollywood series that involved an episode with Santeria. He had been on site for about a week when he got a panicked call from his wife. She had received a packet of photographs in the mail, which included their children walking to school and pictures of her in the bathroom of their own house.

He immediately quit his consulting job, his work training police and investigating occult crimes, packed up all his training materials, and retired from training on and investigating occult crimes shortly thereafter.

How far do occult hands reach? That far.

I have already outlined the damage the False Memory Syndrome people did. Before long, every court case that we advocated for on behalf of children who had been abused was overturned. In large part, this was thanks to false memory "experts" and therapists (including the aforementioned Ralph Underwager) who were paid exorbitant "expert witness" fees to take the stand to convince the jury that kids are liars, that they make up stories, that they get their "sick stories" from their parent's porn collection, and worse. In my opinion, they were just as bad as the monsters who abused these children.

"Conspiracy theory" was the first "mantra" repeated over again, followed by what soon became the primary mantra to try to shut people up for good—"It is all false memories." One of the falsehoods that the "false memory" people vehemently put forth as truth was that the therapists that some of the children had gone to were conspiring together and used techniques that they learned from each other for the purpose of implanting false memories in the children. That is such a bald-faced lie. The therapists I had met (and some that I knew quite well) had no idea what they were encountering with the traumatized children who were disclosing, and they had to learn as they went along. And none of them I knew had read *Michelle Remembers*, a biography about a woman who had survived childhood satanic ritual sexual abuse. The vast majority of these therapists did not even know each other! The timeline of these cases shows that they broke spontaneously and, in some cases, simultaneously to one another. You have to remember that this was happening all around the country and even overseas. None of the therapists I knew had any reference point whatsoever for the horror stories the children were disclosing. Hundreds, if not thousands, of them came forward with outcries of nearly identical abuses.

Satan is no longer feared, but his very existence denied on the onehand, or his superhuman ability ridiculed on the other. How different was the behavior of Michael the archangel, who, when he disputed with the great adversary, durst not rail, but said, "The Lord rebuke thee!"[1]

Harry Ironside (1876-1951)

19

The *Real* "Satanic Panic" Story—Part 3

Assault From Within

The wave of attack initiated by one segment of the Christian community was swift, overwhelming, and totally unexpected. We were blindsided. Ambushed, really. Before this happened, we had, by and large, receptive audiences in many churches and in the few Christian media outlets that covered us. We were trying to raise awareness of occult issues so believers could protect their children and understand why it is crucial to engage believers in prayer. We counted on them to hear us and to have our backs in prayer as we outlined the serious nature of our efforts and the need to have them standing with us as we sought to expose the devil's schemes.

Yes, there were a few hucksters and frauds exploiting genuine occult issues just to sell books and promote themselves. We did have to undo the credibility damage that was done through instances of false information and testimonies, such as John Todd, which unfortunately gained audiences in some churches. None of that discounted the real testimonies and real occult crimes we were discovering both inside and outside the church.

Sometime after Mike Warnke came to El Paso to speak at the civic center, I learned that *Cornerstone*, an alternative Christian magazine that was a branch of a Christian hippie commune in Chicago called Jesus People USA, had released an extensive exposé about Mike Warnke in July 1992. (A follow-up book, *Selling Satan* by Mike Hertenstein and Jon Trott, opened their book with a quote from notorious devil worshipper Aleister Crowley![2] Not a Scripture, but a piece of filth from a well-known Christ-hater.)

> As a Christian and a minister, I was responsible before God for searching out the truth about these things.

As a Christian and a minister, I was responsible before God for searching out the truth about these things. I was responsible for carefully examining this exposé about Mike, regardless of my own personal feelings. And I did. From page one, I felt nauseated at the way it was written. All my warning lights turned on. Does that seem strange to you? It really shouldn't. The way a subject is presented tells you an awful lot about the ones who present it. And from beginning to end, the article against Mike came across as accusatory and vicious.

The accusations against Mike were written with such a furious barrage of "facts" that no one would dare, much less be capable of, challenging them all. (Even if someone did, no one was willing to even print an opposing thought.) It is true that Mike had sins and failures. He exaggerated some elements of his story in his comedy shows. He made a few things up. Comedians do that. And his personal life was spiritually out of order at that time. Mike did not attempt to defend himself. He admitted his faults and sins and placed himself under the accountability of a group of Christian pastors and leaders who made sure that his ministry and his personal life were in order. Mike was very open about certain exaggerations, admitting, for example, to overstating the size of the satanic group he led. However, Mike has never recanted the basic facts of his testimony and stands firm in it. (My friend was fully restored and continues to this day to minister and lead others to Jesus.)

Most of the accusations in the *Cornerstone* hit piece were along the lines of, "Mike was a liar, he had a big ministry and was a fraud and a bad example to the church," and so on.

They essentially ambushed Mike. He had no time to prepare for the onslaught.

With numerous moral scandals and downfalls of Christian leaders in the 1980s, why did *Cornerstone* spend all that time, effort, and money to go after Mike? And who bankrolled it? Basic questions never answered by *Cornerstone*, never allowed to be asked. It seemed to me that perhaps it was because he was the only one who had such a powerful influence on young people, packing stadiums, warning them of the dangers of the occult, and leading them to Jesus Christ.

To me, the big-picture goal was fairly clear, especially considering the barrage of other major efforts from secular and occult sources determined to silence the voices of those who contended that ritual abuse, satanic crime, and occultism were real and needed to be confronted: Silence the messengers, and you stop the message. Mike was but one in a list of the most well-known voices, ministers, and spokesmen who were pursued and viciously attacked in the media. More would follow. It is of interest to note that the ones we knew to be demonstrably fraudulent were never pursued.

Whatever the motives behind the attack on Mike may have been, they were essentially irrelevant to me. I knew the Accuser of our brethren (Revelation 12:10) well enough to understand that he would use any vulnerable or willing vessel he could to do his bidding. In some ways, I consider those who participated in the onslaught, secular or Christian, as simply pawns used to create the "satanic panic" narrative and make sure the occult and satanic world grew and flourished unopposed.

In my thinking, the attack on Mike and the others was rather like the druidic practice of decapitating the enemy and placing the head on a pike. The warning was clear: Come after us, and this will be you. And it worked, for by the time they were through, most churches wouldn't get anywhere near exposing or even learning about the occult world and satanic practices.

Satan's Underground

The attack on Mike Warnke was not unexpected. Three years earlier, I had seen how the *Cornerstone* authors had gone after Lauren Stratford. Lauren was the author of the best-selling autobiography

Satan's Underground, originally published by Harvest House in 1988. *Cornerstone* magazine released a smarmy exposé, "Satan's Sideshow," (released in volume 18, issue 90, 1989)[3] authored by Bob and Gretchen Passantino—the very same people who said Wicca was harmless to kids[4]—along with co-author Jon Trott. The article claimed Lauren was a fraud and that her entire story was a hoax. Indeed, it essentially painted her as mentally ill. "Step right up!" it began. "It's Satan's Underground! A hundred thousand copies in print! Featured on radio and TV, from 'Geraldo' to the '700 Club'! Stories of satanic rituals, snuff films, and human sacrifice! Author Lauren Stratford survived to tell us all about it! Now judge for yourself . . ."

Their message right from the start was that Lauren was a publicity-seeking fraud, simply doing this to sell books. Nothing was further from the truth. This was my first introduction to the Passantinos. I was stunned by the fashion in which it was written: arrogant and cynical, clearly filled with half-truths, and un-Christlike in its wording, artwork, and approach. It was, to me, nothing more than character assassination. The whole tone of the article came across as utterly heartless. One preacher said that if you must preach on Hell, at least do it with tears in your eyes. The architects of Lauren's undeserved public humiliation were in no danger of such tears. (In fact, my two subsequent personal interactions with the Passantinos confirmed just how cynical and arrogant they were about all they had written and done.)

It felt so familiar. Over the years, I had also been similarly targeted, as had many of my associates, by occultists and pedophile-friendly "reporters." I remember, as I read this article about Lauren, thinking that Anton LaVey and Michael Aquino would be so proud. It was executed in true satanic style—going right for the jugular. It was a tactic I expected from Satanists, but I was not prepared to see it coming from proclaiming Christians.

I suppose such an ambush should have been expected from at least one of the *Cornerstone* writers, who wrote in an article about having spent hours with Anton LaVey[5] and yet did not spend one moment face-to-face with Lauren.

I first became aware of Lauren Stratford in March of 1988 while watching her stunning testimony of ritual abuse in the face of Temple of Set founders and practicing occultists Michael and Lillith Aquino on the *Oprah Winfrey Show.*[6] Lauren went on Oprah Winfrey's show with Johanna Michaelsen, author of *The Beautiful Side of Evil*, and together they confronted the Aquinos. Lauren didn't hesitate to testify right to their faces that she had been redeemed by the grace and love of Jesus Christ. The look on the Aquinos' faces spoke volumes, and I began to pray fervently for both Lauren and Johanna, as the Aquinos were no small players in the occult world, and they were not happy. I was concerned about what might be set in motion against Lauren and Johanna.

I then read Lauren Stratford's book, *Satan's Underground*, and found it to be a brutally painful and believable account of Lauren's early life of sexual abuse, child pornography, and, later, forced involvement in devil worship. The very essence of her story rang true to me, coinciding with dozens of other testimonies of survivors I had heard and documented. Reading it only solidified my confidence in the foundational genuineness of her testimony.

I contacted Lauren shortly after the release of the Passantinos' article in 1989. After that initial contact, we spoke by phone. We became friends, and through her, I eventually met Randolph and Johanna Michaelsen. We talked, I listened. The more I learned, the more appalled I became at the systematic way in which the attack against her had come about. Some questions raised in the *Cornerstone* article were unanswerable:

- "Prove you were pregnant!" (She couldn't; she had had a hysterectomy.)

- "Nobody ever saw Lauren's alleged pregnancies!" (There are innumerable cases of women who themselves did not know they were pregnant until they found themselves unexpectedly giving birth.)

- "Prove you had babies that were sacrificed at these rituals!" (Really? How do you go about doing that?)

- "Her mother categorically denied ever having abused little Lauren as a child!"

Maybe. But if Lauren's allegations were true, what exactly would the Passantinos have expected the mother to say? Did they really expect Mommy to burst into tears and thank them for the opportunity to confess everything that she had "allegedly" done to little Lauren? I don't think so. Let's be realistic; most of us would be hard-pressed to prove many elements of our own lives and testimonies. I am sure Paul the apostle could not "prove" that Jesus appeared to him. But it happened, nonetheless. It is absurd to think that the degree of proof that was demanded of Lauren by the Passantinos could have ever been met, especially when dealing with high-level satanic groups. They are experts in disposing of evidence.

• "There are too many inconsistencies in your stories, so clearly you were lying." Lauren had something to say about this in her book *Stripped Naked*:

> There have been times in these past several years that I wish I had never spoken publicly about the atrocities that none of us want to believe are happening in our country. The tendency to find an easy escape into denial does not eradicate the fact that sexual abuse, incest, ritual abuse, and ritual murders do occur. If no one dares to speak out, then history will continue to repeat itself!

> There *must* be a starting point for each survivor. If survivors have to be silent until all the puzzle pieces of their lives fit seamlessly together with no inconsistencies, no time gaps, and no errors, there will be no voices to stand up and warn us of the dangers for the next generation of children.[7]

Lauren answered the questions they asked to my satisfaction. It was clear to me that the essential details of her story were true. It was also clear that much was altered or changed to protect others or because of gaps in her memory. Trauma has a way of doing that. To add to this, when the article came out, "someone" anonymously sent this *Cornerstone* article to churches Lauren was going to speak at in an attempt to have her talks canceled, as well as all the shows she had appeared on and media outlets that had covered her. Secret agreements were made even before the article was released to make sure Lauren wouldn't find out about their "investigation" in advance. Who would do that?

The Passantino/Trott article utterly devastated Lauren. Over the following months, I listened to the Passantinos on the radio concerning these issues—and I was completely dumbstruck at the cavalier way they conducted their "campaign" to discredit Lauren in the name of "defending the truth." *What kind of people could do this so casually, unconcerned about who they might injure?* I asked myself. I was beginning to formulate an answer.

Miraculously, a relative of Lauren's stepped forward in 1992 in support of Lauren and in corroboration of her testimony.[8] And despite what everyone has been led to believe, even though Harvest House pulled Lauren's books, it is my understanding that they never pulled their endorsement of Lauren. In fact, Harvest House made it clear in a letter to her[9] just how much they regretted having to make the decision to pull her books but that the spiritual and emotional pressure brought on by these attacks were too much for them to contend with—not to mention, by the way, the financial pressure brought about by the threats of protests, boycotts, etc.

Despite these attacks, Lauren continued to write books and conduct seminars for pastors, therapists, survivors, law enforcement, and anyone else who wanted to know the truth. And there were many. She was given this endorsement from someone with far more credibility than the ones who attacked Lauren's credibility, Dr. Judith Reisman, PhD., Investigator for American University, Washington DC on a federal grant program on Child Abuse/Pornography.* Concerning Lauren, she wrote:

> Based on my knowledge of the staggering increase of child sexual abuse and of the escalating brutality of that abuse, *Lauren Stratford's story is only too credible.*
>
> When you talk about a child who is able to emerge with a clear voice out of the abusive circumstances in which she has

---

* Read about Dr. Reisman here: https://www.thereismaninstitute.org.

been demeaned, degraded, and lost, that is a miracle of God.
*It is absolutely crucial that Lauren, as one of these precious
few, speak out. But it is even more crucial that we listen to her
story.*[10] (emphasis in the original)

(Note: After the *Cornerstone* exposé, Lauren was contacted by one of the most well-known singers/songwriters of our time after having read Lauren's book. She, too, was a satanic ritual abuse survivor. Though I am not at liberty to share her name, most would recognize the name instantly. Lauren both ministered to her and kept her identity private.)

Satan's Underground was later republished by Pelican Books in 1991 and saw worldwide distribution. She wrote two other excellent books also published by Pelican: *I Know You're Hurting* (1992) and *Stripped Naked* (1993). She continued, in part, because the Christian backlash against survivors brought on by the Passantinos, Jon Trott, and *Cornerstone* left in its wake a demolished mass of survivors who had once hoped to find Jesus' healing in the church. They now feared being disbelieved, ridiculed, and rejected. Lauren knew we had to continue to extend Jesus' love to them, or they truly had no hope. I stood by Lauren without reservation. She kept going relentlessly in the face of one of the ugliest smear campaigns I've ever witnessed, and I was proud of her.

I confronted the publishers of the hit piece on Lauren by phone, demanding to know their sources, and they refused to give them up, citing "confidentiality." Without this, of course, one can neither prove nor disprove their sources and what they have said. Very convenient. The authors of the article prided themselves on having contacted some of those who had been implicated in Lauren's book. Of course, they denied everything. Incidentally, the real names of the alleged abusers were not disclosed by Lauren but rather by the authors of the *Cornerstone* article. Lauren had legally changed her name to protect herself from those responsible for her abuse.

Lauren, like many people who write memoirs of abuse, changed key details to protect the privacy of individuals so that they would not be readily identified. Too much time had gone by, and actual hard evidence in her case would be impossible to come by. Nevertheless, Lauren wanted to tell her story—not for herself, but for the victims. She knew she could never stop the "bad guys," but longed for her story to provide healing for the hurting. Other elements she simply could not remember.

When I saw Mike Warnke in 2012, I began to talk about Lauren, who had died ten years before. Mike's eyes welled up with tears. "It's too hard to talk about," he said. He loved Lauren. We all did, in spite of the efforts to make her look like a dangerous mental case. She helped more people in the course of her life than the authors of the hit piece ever did.

When confronted with the relative's letters, legal documents, restraining orders, and personal testimony that corroborated Lauren's story, the authors of the hit piece refused to publish it. There were no retractions or corrections from *Cornerstone*, the Passantinos, or Jon Trott. If this "Christian" publication was run by genuine truth seekers, why would they not let the readership know the evidence that clearly contradicted the picture they had painted of Lauren? Those who demanded that she provide proof of her innocence, in the end, refused to let that proof be made public to their readership audience, clearly choosing to turn a blind eye to evidence that conflicted with their narrative.

But this was only the beginning. Over the next few years, *Cornerstone* and friends, later aided and abetted by Hank Hanegraaff's Christian Research Institute, went after all ministries and victims who were claiming that ritual abuse was a reality. Articles and books such as *The Satanic Panic, Selling Satan, Satanism: A Taste for the Dark Side, When the Devil Dares Your Kids,* and so on proliferated like loco weed. And somehow—overnight, it seemed—nearly the entire Christian media began to parrot their words. Before long, they were all quoting each other—the Wiccans, Ralph Underwager, the Passantinos, J. Gordon Melton, the False Memory Syndrome Foundation, Michael Aquino, et al., until the average person would be led to think there was no other truth than the one these people had espoused.

And there we were, with scores of injured kids, horrific case files, murdered innocents, devastated families, and teen suicides. Under the cover of one big sweeping smoke screen, we had nearly the entire support of the body of Christ ripped out from under us, leaving nowhere for the victims to go, nowhere to find help and healing. In an ironic twist, victims were forced to seek more compassionate support in the secular world—but without the deeper, true healing that only Jesus Christ can provide.

In looking back, I realized that the timing of these "Christian" attacks on those who sought to help victims, as well as on the victims and survivors themselves, coincided almost exactly with the rise of the false memory empire. All the information they disseminated, the experts they quoted, and the discrediting methods employed were nearly identical.

To this day, if anyone in the church brings up the subject of Satanism, satanic crime, ritual abuse, or the "satanic panic" era, they generally (if they have any memory of these things ever having been an issue at all) bring up two names: Mike Warnke and Lauren Stratford. (Other names are occasionally mentioned but never seem to be attacked as brutally as Mike and Lauren because their books and stories were clearly not as much of a threat and were easily dismissed.)

Mike and Lauren came to the forefront, partially because their stories were so clear and dramatic, but mostly because they were thrust into the media spotlight during a time when Satanism and devil worship were a hot topic for the media—it was the "crisis du jour"—sensational stories designed to gain top ratings.

I found it ironic that Dr. Walter Martin, who in the early 1970s took the Passantinos under his wing and allowed them to assist him in his growing ministry, had released a newsletter in 1989 titled "Satanism on the Rise," written several weeks prior to his death. In that newsletter, he fully affirmed the reality of satanic crime and pledged his ministry, Christian Research Institute, to combat it. His article urged the church to take it seriously. He pointed out the influence of entities like the Church of Satan and the Temple of Set and outlined real-life occult murders such as the Matamoros murder of college student Mark Kilroy (see page 35). Dr. Martin opened the article by saying:

> Today, we are witnessing an unprecedented rise in Satanism all over the world. The evidence for this is overwhelming. At Christian Research Institute, we have been consultants to over a dozen and a half police departments. They generally inquire about whether there's any significance to what they have come across in their cities. They may ask about the meaning of something written on a wall, satanic symbols or numbers, animal sacrifices, grave robberies, ritualistic child

abuse (some satanic groups require molestation of children for initiation), the game *Dungeons and Dragons,* "blood pacts" with the devil, and vandalism with satanic overtones. With so many police departments inquiring about the same things, it is clear that they are all having similar encounters and experiences with Satanists. . . .

As terrible as this kind of blatant Satanism is, there is a far more subtle way that Satan is working in our world today. I am referring to the fact that he has penetrated the Christian church. For me, Satan is not only served by satanic High Priests, Black Masses, and blood sacrifices (animal or human). These things are more or less an outward symptom. The bottom line in Satan's strategies is to undermine the very foundation of the Christian faith—not just without but also within the church.[11]

Dr. Martin concluded this prescient article by committing CRI to pursuing these matters, saying:

At CRI, we are committed to standing against the activities of Satan, whether within or outside of the church. We are intent on exposing his [the devil's] work wherever it crops up. And certainly we will draw flack for this—from both the physical and spiritual realms. But like Harry Truman said, if you can't stand the heat, get out of the kitchen. We at CRI are not getting out of the kitchen![12]

Soon after Dr. Martin's death on June 26th, 1989, Martin's "assistants" Bob and Gretchen Passantino, became well-known after their exposé of Lauren Stratford. They had already gained a measure of credibility from writing their 1981 book, *Answers to the Cultist at Your Door* published by Harvest House Publishers. They became a major voice in creating the "satanic panic" narrative that would later become "gospel truth" to a world and church that were unaware of the facts and who, quite frankly, didn't care enough to find out. The Passantinos also made a name for themselves by writing the aforementioned *When the Devil Dares Your Kids*, downplaying the dangers of the involvement of kids in the occult, garnering the praise of the Wiccan community for their softball treatment of the occult in general and Wicca in particular.

Within a short period of time, the Passantinos were doing programs on CRI with Dr. Martin's purported heir-apparent Hank Hanegraaff, talking about, among other things, redeeming Halloween for Jesus.[13] Within a few years, they were speaking at JPUSA's (Jesus People, USA) Cornerstone Festival (1984-2012), a Christian music festival which in its heyday drew close to 20,000 attendees but which had begun to resemble a pagan fest like The Burning Man at an "Imaginarium" "Day of the Dead" exhibit where they had a coffin, candy skulls which are eaten during the "Dia de los Muertos" celebrations, played horror films, and so on.[14] They became the spokespeople for the satanic panic narrative for the very transformed post-Walter Martin Christian Research Institute.

It's easy to say Dr. Walter Martin would have been rolling in his grave, but I rather think he would have roared out of it, rebuking these people not only for their heretical perspectives on the occult but their utter betrayal concerning a very real and deadly problem that Walter had committed to tackling shortly before his death. I felt as though Dr. Martin's words were being trashed; and his underlings gained fame and power by doing so. I had been so encouraged by Dr. Martin's willingness to stand on the battlefield on this issue. And now this.*

It seemed inexplicable that people right under Dr. Martin's nose turned out to be the very ones who disavowed his message on Satanism.

Because I had befriended Lauren, I was able to get real insight into her attackers. I saw first-hand how her life was destroyed, humiliated, and dismissed through the power of writers and a magazine, *Cornerstone,* which, at the time, no one dared criticize or question for fear of legal retribution. Lauren had no opportunity to defend herself. She died before she realized fully what was happening to her.

---

*In the Winter 1992 (Vol. 14, No. 3) issue of the *Christian Research Journal*, CRI published an article by the Passantinos titled "The Hard Facts About Satanic Ritual Abuse," which was an effort to debunk satanic ritual abuse.

Thankfully, to this day, I continue to get letters from survivors whose lives were touched and healed by Jesus because of Lauren's books and because she reached out to care for them when no one else did. "[T]heir works do follow them" (Revelation 14:13).

The Final Trap

Lauren fell into one last trap in the latter part of her life when she was befriended by some Jewish folks in her apartment complex. Lauren, who was adopted and had no idea who her real parents were, had begun to wonder if she might be Jewish. That was not out of the realm of possibility. Many people in the last thirty or so years have discovered they have a Jewish heritage. By invitation from one of the ladies in her apartment complex, she began to attend the local synagogue to learn more.

Unfortunately, Lauren met a "Holocaust survivor" named Benjamin Wilkomirski, who had come to speak at the synagogue. He convinced her that he remembered her from one of the Holocaust camps when she was a three or four-year-old child. She began to wonder if this was where she had developed the anti-thrombin 3 deficiency disease that would eventually take her life. Her world went spinning. It was enough that she remembered so much of her abuse—but this, too? It seemed outlandish and yet possible. She pursued the idea, and therein lay the trap. This man who claimed to be a Holocaust camp survivor was completely discredited. But by then, it was too late for Lauren to disassociate herself from him. Defeated, tired, and sick of the relentless attacks, she gave up and went home, essentially, to die. It was just a matter of time.

That, however, did not stop the attacks. She called me one morning in absolute hysterics when she learned that a couple who perfectly fit the description of the Passantinos, albeit wearing cheap wigs and floppy hats, had gone to the post office where Lauren received her mail. Posing as "concerned family members" who were worried about "poor little Lauren," they tried to get the postmaster to give them her home address! The postmaster refused and called Lauren because he was alarmed and concerned for her. Then she called me. Apparently, the Passantinos were doing "research" for a follow-up hit piece on Lauren.

After being on the periphery of these attacks for nearly two years, I had had enough. I tracked down the number of Bob Passantino and had an extremely volatile two-hour conversation with him. I confronted him about everything—why he was stalking Lauren, who they were, why they defended occultists—everything. I can only say that he treated it like one big joke: he laughed at my concerns, cynically responded to my questions, and answered sarcastically to everything I confronted him with. I told him in no uncertain terms that it may have been easy for them to go after a fragile woman in her sixties but that Lauren wasn't alone in this, and if they kept pursuing her, I would get involved with anything at my disposal, including legal action. He laughed. And really, that summed it all up for me as to who they were and what was in their hearts.

I was not surprised when I got a call from Gretchen Passantino just a few months later asking if Lauren wanted to respond to the "new charges" against her about her claiming to be a "Holocaust survivor" since I claimed to be such a good friend of Lauren's. So, I was right: they had never stopped stalking Lauren. They wanted to get a second story out of it. I was, in a word, infuriated and pulled out all the stops to let them know I considered what they were doing spiritual murder. And they laughed. Again. Heartless laughter—again, yet all the while claiming to just want the truth because they loved the truth. It was one of the darkest and ugliest exchanges I've ever had with anyone. Trying to talk with them was like being trapped in a demonic house of mirrors.

Their article was published, and that was it for Lauren. She just . . . gave up. It broke our hearts.

But she never gave up on ministering to others; in fact, she never stopped corresponding with survivors, praying for them, loving them. If the fruit of the Spirit is what defines us as believers, Lauren had a tree full. The others only bore poisoned fruit.

After the damage had been done by the *Cornerstone* authors and several more articles had been published, the satanic triad of "experts" was complete: The FBI "expert" Ken Lanning said ritual abuse is not real; the false memory people said it was made up; and the folks at *Cornerstone* and the other Christian publications said it was all village folklore and should be ignored in the name of Jesus.

Still, the attacks persisted. Lauren was contacted by a reporter who said he wanted to interview her and get her side of the story. The meeting was a setup. He had no intention whatsoever of presenting Lauren's side of the story but rather, he began the interview by attacking her before she pulled the plug on the interview. The interviewer was Martin Bashear, the very same unscrupulous reporter who was denounced by the Royal Family and BBC for his unconscionable setup of Princess Diana. Bashear had given Diana false information that convinced her that the Royal Family was out to get her, and therefore she agreed to let him interview her. Some, including her son Prince William, believed that the interview led to the snowball events that culminated with her tragic, untimely death.[15]

This was the quality of folks who were spokespeople for the "satanic panic" narrative. Brutal, uncaring, and destructive, with not one ounce of concern for the people they were writing about or who they would hurt.

Lauren died on April 8th, 2002, her little body not able to survive any longer.

Given the barrage of attacks on Lauren's testimony with no chance of her being able to respond before her death, I felt it was important to add a very crucial part of the story in light of those who called her a fraud out to get famous by writing and selling books.

Perspectives

Johanna Michaelsen met Ken Wooden when they were both guests on the *700 Club* on the night of Halloween in 1985. Ken was one of the most nationally respected experts on child abuse and child exploitation, and the founder of Child Lures, a program that educated thousands of parents and children across the country on how to recognize and prevent child abuse. He was also a former special investigative reporter for ABC News' *20/20* and the author of *Weeping in the Playtime of Others* (1976) and *The Children of Jonestown* (1981). He was nominated for the 2010 Pulitzer Prize Lifetime Achievement Special Award and gave expert testimony to the United States Congress (from 1973—until the time of his death in 2023.)[16]

Johanna found his expertise and information impressive and invaluable, especially in light of the number of sexual and ritual abuse allegation cases being raised across the US, including the McMartin case in Manhattan Beach, California. Johanna had done several TV and radio programs discussing child abuse and Satanism and had spoken with Hal Lindsey about doing a program with Ken.

On March 25th, 1986, Johanna received a call from a woman named Laurel Wilson. (It would be two years before she would be known legally as Lauren Stratford.) Laurel had been speaking with some of the McMartin parents about the reality of child abuse, and one of the parents felt that Laurel should contact Johanna and her husband, Randolph. They got together on March 27th and spent over seven hours together, at which time some of the most horrifying, gut-wrenching stories of ritual child abuse poured out.

She stayed with Randolph and Johanna for the next several weeks as more of her horrifying story was revealed in bits and pieces. It became evident that some of Laurel's abusers were still in touch with her, and she needed protection.

Johanna contacted Ken Wooden for advice. Ken agreed to fly to L.A. to interview Laurel to determine the veracity of her story. He arrived June 30th, 1986, and then the next day, July 1st, 1986, he spent five hours in Randolph and Johanna's living room debriefing Laurel. Laurel was excited about the opportunity to present her story to someone with Ken's expertise. He questioned her on every detail that she could remember of her testimony and memory concerning her abuse and details concerning ritual abuse and mind control. After that in-depth and exhausting session, Laurel excused herself and went to lie down.

"So what do you think about her story, Ken? What's your conclusion?" Johanna asked.

Ken looked straight at Randolph and Johanna and said, "I wish I had met her years ago. She knows more about the inner workings of Satanism and mind control than anyone else I have ever met. You don't get that level of understanding by reading a few books like *Michelle Remembers*. She knows what she is talking about. She's the real deal."

Clearly, Ken's professional evaluation, based on decades of experience, carried immense weight. The next night, Wednesday, July 2nd, 1986, Hal Lindsey hosted a three-hour program with Ken Wooden, the Michaelsens, and Laurel on child exploitation and ritual abuse. Laurel was interviewed with her back to the camera, and the abusers were on notice that even though she was choosing to remain anonymous, Laurel was no longer alone.

Two years later (1988), Laurel's book was published by Harvest House under her legally changed name, Lauren Stratford. It was published knowing that her memories were incomplete and that there were aspects of her story that she had modified to protect everyone's safety and privacy.

It carried several powerful endorsements, including one from Ken Wooden, who said:

> Lauren Stratford's moving account of prolonged and treacherous exploitation by the occult is *a work of national importance.* Her experiences and insights provided the missing links in an evil power movement that is spreading across the American landscape.

> This personal story is more than a book. It is *a triumphant epic of courage and hope* conquering hatred and death.[17] (emphasis in original)

Now, after Lauren's passing and after all the vicious attacks by the "truth lovers" who told respected ministers they either must stop supporting Lauren or they would take them down the way they did her, I decided to return to the one expert whose credibility on these matters was unimpeachable, Ken Wooden. I managed to connect with him just months before he passed away in 2023. Barely able to talk, he understood my wanting to verify that initial meeting and said he would email me. His last message to me relayed that the meeting with Lauren did take place and that, "YES, my gut told me then, and now: I believe Lauren."

I will take his carefully and expertly arrived-at conclusion over a hundred self-appointed critics who never even met her and knew virtually nothing about the subject of ritual abuse and child exploitation.

Were there flaws, gaps, and inconsistencies in Lauren's story and in other survivors' stories? Of course, there were. Trauma creates that. And so does forced drugging, sexual torture, and mind manipulation that disorients and confuses victims—especially children. It is important to know that these things all work together to ensure that enough inconsistency will be present in testimony that even a mediocre attorney could easily drive a military SUV right over the children on the stand, and the case would be dismissed. Victims are often told during the abuse that no one will ever believe them. How tragically often this proves to be true.

So, you can make up your own mind on these things. But you need to know who and what—and maybe a little of why—these attacks came. And it all succeeded in a spectacular way in making sure that the voices of nearly all survivors—especially those who went public—were silenced and making sure that all means of research would be completely glutted with the "satanic panic" narrative so that a "casual" researcher would quickly conclude that there was no issue at all about satanic and occultic crime.

Still, survivors come forward. Still, children are abused in ways so demonic and horrible, often in the name of occult demons and gods, that just reading about them will give you nightmares for a lifetime.

I look back—and I realize, as late as 1990, I had over 250 contacts, friends, and associates who were committed to stopping satanic crimes. And now? I can count those still in the fight on both hands. The few of us left have endured unbelievably hard things and attacks.

In retrospect, I have had to ask myself: Who stood to benefit the most from all these attacks by The False Memory Syndrome Foundation and so-called Christian investigative journalists? The answer was and is clear to me: devil worshippers, pedophiles, and child pornographers. Who got hurt the most? Victims! And the ones trying to heal them! I would not dare suggest that all these Christian folk were knowingly aiding and abetting the enemy, though my opinion is reserved concerning some of them. But in the end, it doesn't really matter, does it? Every tree is known by its fruit. And the fruit of what they did has been absolute devastation for the victims. I see absolutely nothing of Jesus in any of what was done. Like it or not, they have expertly illustrated the enemy's plan: "Deny everything. Blame the victim." Didn't I tell you? It worked. It works still.

With all the efforts that have been made to discredit ritual abuse, people might find it surprising that Sarah Young, the author of the best-selling book *Jesus Calling* (having sold over 45 million copies, published by Thomas Nelson) writes about the reality of satanic ritual abuse in the introduction to her popular book. In describing "satanic ritual abuse,"[18] she states:

This form of Satan worship involves subjecting victims (who are often young children) to incredibly evil, degrading tortures.[19] (parenthesis in original)

In that same introduction, Young refers to a satanic ritual abuse survivor she counseled in her former Australian counseling practice. Young writes:

[A] counseling client who was an incest survivor began remembering experiences of satanic ritual abuse. . . . My courageous client and I walked together into the darkness of her memories.[20]

I bring this up, not to promote *Jesus Calling*,[21] but here we have a book that has been read by tens of millions of people where satanic ritual abuse is recognized as real and is published by the largest Christian publisher; and yet even as currently as 2025, there are still efforts being made in Christian venues to discredit and demolish the reality of ritual abuse. A case in point, in November of 2024, while this new edition of my book was being prepared for press, *Christianity Today* began an eight-part podcast titled *The Devil and the Deep Blue Sea,* debunking ritual abuse. The final episode was released in May 2025 and was titled "Forgetting What Happened: The Satanic Panic may have faded, but its legacy lives on—reshaped into modern conspiracies, political crusades, and weaponized fear."[22]

Interesting timing for this series to come out. The last time I know of that *Christianity Today* came out with something on satanic ritual abuse was thirty-two years ago in their June 21, 1993 issue, an article titled "Memories of Satanic Ritual Abuse: The truth behind the panic."[23]

And so . . . it never ends.

Nevertheless, this battle belongs to the Lord. And He already won the battle on the Cross.

Again, I wrote this book because I was there. And those who say nothing happened are misled, misleading, or outright lying about it.

May God break through these lies so that the victims who come forward in the future will have a safe place to heal and people to believe them.

Ritual sexual abuse . . . is this calculated physical and emotional cruelty many people find difficult to accept. The "fantastic" allegations made by children and adult survivors of childhood ritual abuse cause people to turn their heads, and cause the media and the courts to discredit the reports as fantasy. The bizarre aspects of the victim's stories are dwelled upon in the press and in the courtroom. The fact that there is usually conclusive evidence of sexual abuse becomes obscured.[1]

From the Department of Justice's Virtual Library

20

Occult Crimes and Sexual Abuse: The Pedophile Connection

He hath showed thee, O man, what is good; and what doth the Lord require of thee, but to do justly, and to love mercy, and to walk humbly with thy God? (Micah 6:8)

I was informed back in the 1990s that human trafficking, child pornography, and child trading were likely an eight billion-dollar-a-year industry or more. That was over three decades ago. I have been told that it's closer to a 250-billion-dollar industry today. Let that sink in for a moment.

Human slavery has been going on since the beginning of time. Now it is called "human trafficking;" and thank God, things are finally being done to try to stop it. But there's only so much that can be done. It is an industry with monstrously huge money resources, and, as they say, money talks and people walk. The larger the network, the more powerful will be the people involved, and the less likely the perpetrators will be brought to justice—if, in fact, they are even found.

The sad fact is, as of this writing, due to the horrendous failure of our government to control our border crisis and the cartels that are fueling the massive immigration influx, those seeking to rescue victims from human trafficking are being thwarted because we are no longer able or capable of keeping track of the victims—especially children—and they are now freely being shuttled from one trafficking house to another. It is horrifying to know that, as of this writing, our government has lost track of over 85,000 children who have entered this country![2]

Many times over, we found the lines blurred between those who sell human flesh and those who traffick in human souls. Numerous pedophiles have been found to be deeply involved with every level of the occult, including devil worship. And numerous occultists have been found trafficking in children, child pornography, and so on.

Human trafficking is a flesh-peddling "corporation" that steals the souls—and often the bodies and lives—of innocent children, and even adults.

With the advent of the Internet, this "corporation" from Hell has made access to child pornography both easy and more discreet for hundreds of thousands who are addicted to watching adults have sex with children and underage teens.

There are at least two huge international Internet "Boy Lover" websites that defend their activities as being a good thing. They have dozens and dozens of links to other "boy lover" sites, from "picture sites" to "story sites" about sex with kids to personal websites of other like-minded "boy lovers." They also state that they are against child abuse. But to them, "abuse" means parents hitting their kids. They say they are against child pornography. That is why they only have pictures of little boys and teens in swimsuits or underwear and only occasionally nude. You can be sure, their secret cache of explicit child pornography is always well hidden. P.R. is everything. And getting caught is to be avoided at all costs. By their definition, sexual abuse is when a teen or a child doesn't *want* you to have sex with them. Yet, when you listen to these predators, you'll find they actually believe that kids and children ask for it—and flirt with them for it! One predator lobbying for a lowering of the age of consent stated that even infants can give consent.

It is a small wonder that one "boy love" site listed The False Memory Syndrome Foundation as one of their "helpful resources."

There are many groups actively lobbying for the social acceptance of pedophilia. One is NAMBLA—the North American Man-Boy

Love Association; and the other is the Rene Guyon Society, whose motto is, "Sex before eight, or else it's too late."[3]

The media has been most helpful to them. On any given talk show, when they do a program about sexual abuse against children, they usually interview someone currently in jail or who has been arrested for such a crime in the past. When asked why they did it, what is their answer every time?: "I was abused myself as a child." And everybody buys that lie. Yes, some *were* abused, but studies of sexual predators in prison found that the majority of those who said they were sexually abused as children—actually were not![4] Yet, at every seminar and law enforcement or probation training I have done, I have to un-brainwash folks who have accepted this lie as being true.

Another wake-up call for people is when I ask them if they know what "pedophile" means. They do not. It means "child lover." So, in effect, these predators have managed to get the whole population to use the very name they prefer to be known by: those who "love children." They are *not* child lovers; they are predators!

While it is not true that those who have been sexually abused always become sexual abusers (in fact, this is rare as I explain in my book *The Color of Pain*), you should be aware that nearly every teen devil worshipper I have met was abused. Devil worship became the tool they used to handle their rage, to protect themselves, and to seek vengeance for the horrible crimes they endured.

Predators have more recently updated their agenda and fashioned it after both the civil rights movement and the LGBTQ+ political movement. They are positioning themselves as victims—persecuted people who, through no fault of their own, are attracted to children and need to be given rights and respect like everyone else. I predicted this would happen twenty years ago, and now it is here. In fact, they refer to themselves as "MAPS—minor-attracted persons"—in order to make it sound more palatable and socially acceptable.

And most frighteningly, I have recently found that teenagers are frequently becoming the ones who are promoting these ideas. "Who are you to tell me I can't have sex with an adult if I want to?," one teen poster declared. I have seen a growing number of "positive" memes supporting the idea of "transgenerational relationships" coming from youth culture. It's a predator's dream come true.

What does this have to do with my work to help children and teens? Well, this may be the biggest "demon" of all the ones I have ever confronted. And often, I have found predators, child pornographers, child traders, and devil worshippers working hand in hand for their mutual goals.

It makes sense: if a predator wants access to child porn, a criminal satanic ring can get the film and pictures, either through their own children being sexually exploited for the camera or through the many networks of brothels, ranches, and child trade "stables" they connect with around the world. After all, criminal devil worshippers do not lack cash. Between drugs, gun running, and child trading, they have plenty of money to work with.

On the other hand, if a devil worshipper needs a child for a sacrifice or needs to make more movies to make more money, then there are plenty of child traders who can fill the order.

It is no secret in our world of investigations that criminal devil worshippers have a great investment in supporting and maintaining the child-peddling network. It is big money for them. I learned from my contacts that a "snuff film,"* which shows a blond-haired, blue-eyed boy or girl being raped and murdered on camera, can go for as much as thirty to forty thousand dollars per video. We also heard that a person can pay ten thousand dollars in cash per viewing in a private setting. The client is taken to a secret location wearing a blindfold. He sees the movie, and they take the cash and take him back. Nothing to trace, no one to give a location to the authorities. No evidence at all.

---

*Some antogonists have tried to say there is no such thing as snuff films (or photos) or that they are very rare. But this is a lie. As just one example, a colleague of mine visited the L.A.P.D. in the late 1980s, while investigating a sexual abuse case. While there, one of the detectives showed her a wall of lockers and said they were filled with snuff films and photos. The officer said, "You don't need to see these ones. These kids were all murdered." And that's just one city, forty years ago.

I get a lot of phone calls around Halloween about whether the rumor of a blond-haired, blue-eyed child really is the preference for these groups. And the answer is absolutely yes. Why? There are several reasons for this, and I will give you two:

First, the satanic philosophy and the Nazi/Aryan/KKK white supremacist doctrines are nearly identical (which is why these groups work so well together). It is all about the survival of the fittest, the "elite," the elimination of the weak, and the belief that blond-haired, blue-eyed children are the chosen, the perfect, the highest bloodline. (See chapter eight, "Grooming the Young and Fatherless.")

So, why sacrifice the children? Aleister Crowley said, "A male child of perfect innocence and high intelligence is the most suitable sacrifice."[5] Devil worshippers believe if you want favor from Satan or demons, you have to offer a sacrifice. The more favor you need, or the more power you want, the more valuable the sacrifice must be; so, sacrificing one of the "chosen" is the most valued sacrifice of all. Unfortunately, they also believe that "energy" is released from the victim which goes to the sacrifist at the victim's death, and the more that child is tortured and in pain before death, the more power the sacrifist receives.

The second reason "blond/blue" children are preferred is because they are what's called "high dollar" kids. For some reason, predators prefer them and will pay an extraordinary amount of money for this child pornography or to buy the child outright.

This works very handily for the criminal devil worshippers. They have the kids, sometimes born and raised by them, other times stolen and kidnapped. They know addicted predators will do anything to feed their evil lusts for children.

While we spend millions of dollars on studies trying to figure out how to "cure" sexual predators, the fact remains that the average predator can molest hundreds of children and teens during the course of his lifetime. They are usually repeat offenders who are jailed only for short periods of time and then released and free to offend again. In a legal system where we at one time had a "three strikes, you're out" law for drug dealers, predators often get probation and therapy and are often returned to the very home in which they have sexually assaulted their own children in the absurd belief that the family must remain intact at all costs.

Just as I believe a devil worshipper can be redeemed, so too I believe that a predator can be redeemed. But never should we place forgiveness for a sexual offender above the safety of a child. I have spoken to far too many Christian counselors and pastors who are much more concerned about forgiving a person who molests kids than they are about protecting the child from being re-abused. Most Christians have a very dangerous and wrong understanding of grace and forgiveness on this issue, forgetting that Jesus said whoever causes one of these little ones to stumble would be better off with a millstone tied around his or her neck and cast into the sea (Matthew 18:6). This doesn't mean a predator can't be forgiven. But it does make it very clear that Jesus Himself does place sins against children in a very grave light indeed. Because of this misplaced priority among many Christians, we have been blocked over and over again from protecting children in the churches. Surely, this is not at all what God would want.

Unfortunately, those who are unwilling to face and deal with the serious damage that child abusers do are often the same ones who deny even the possibility that satanic criminal groups abduct, rape, and kill children. Actually, it's understandable in some ways: Who wants to even hear about these kinds of awful things? Yet, to deny it because that's an easy road to take, is wrong. The fact is, horrendous crimes do take place against children in the evil world of child pornography and child trafficking.

A friend of mine passed on to me intel that had been obtained from a high-level military official in 1990 about a train that was detained in Stuttgart, Germany on a tip. It was found to be filled with children and adolescents in cages, bound for transport to Japan and other places for sale on the human trafficking auction market. (The trafficking/pedophile/occult network spans nearly every nation, including the UAE, Bahrain, Brunei, the Balkans, and Japan, some of which were known hotspots for the sale of humans in the 1990s.)

We often found a sinister blend of the abuse and trafficking of children with the practice of witchcraft, Satanism, and black magick.

For example, in El Paso, a seventy-year-old man was found murdered in his downtown home. He had been stabbed repeatedly. Most people just thought it was sad that someone killed an old man, but those who knew this man and his reputation were not surprised. He was a well-known *brujo* (witch) who trafficked, sold, and rented underage teen boys from Juarez through the local gay bars and off the streets of downtown. Most of us just figured one of his victims came back to get revenge for having his life ruined.

Classic Conditioning

One thing people need to understand is that for true devil worshippers, the sexual assault of children is part of the conditioning process. Sexually assaulting children tears a hole in their souls, creating an opening for a lifetime of pain, distress, and at times, demonically inspired influences. Sexually assaulting a child destroys a child's ability to believe in goodness or God. Sexually assaulting a child produces hate in that child along with fear and compliance. While predators sexually assault children because they enjoy it, criminal cult devil worshippers do it because it is part of the process of creating a satanic child.

And it works. There is even a particular ritual that is performed on little boys in which they are sodomized, and demons are summoned to inhabit the child. This process is called "inculcation," and this ritual is called the "Magick Mirror." The abuse allows demons to inhabit the child so they can be used for divination and several other occult purposes within the group.

No one who knows the true nature of black magick and the occult is surprised by this. The twisting of sexuality and polysexual activity is deemed necessary to attain occult heights and "power." As Richard Cavendish said in his book *The Black Arts*, "The magician cannot become the One unless he becomes bisexual."[6] Even the worshipped goat Baphomet is hermaphroditic with both male and female parts.

A Note About Harry

While we are on the subject of the Goat of Mendez, I would be remiss if I did not point out something about J.K. Rowling, the creator/author of *Harry Potter*, who is responsible for introducing real magick to an entire generation of children. While parents defended it as fantasy and fiction, Rowling included several real-magick elements, including "The Hand of Glory," which was an actual ritual where the severed hand of a thief was made into a candelabra and used in ceremonies. Rowling very much knew her material.

And as previously mentioned, Rowling got a tattoo with the two words "solve" and "coagula" inscribed on the right and left hands of the Baphomet.[7] So much for innocent literature for kids.

I know some of you are saying to yourself that none of this could possibly be real. Believe me, it is. And of late, the occult world has released little glimpses of their real-world activities in the media. The movie *Midsommar,* released in 2019, was a ghastly, demonic, but extremely accurate depiction of the ritual practices and beliefs of ancient druidic, Germanic, and European pagan death rituals and rules.

Hollywood has been a cesspool of predators for decades. Movie director Roman Polanski was arrested and charged with the rape of a thirteen-year-old girl and has spent decades in exile to avoid prison. Polanski's victim, Samantha Geimer, showing a clear picture of the confusion victims deal with, sued Polanski in 1988 for sexual assault but recently said that she never had a "problem" with being drugged and raped by the director when she was just thirteen years old.[8]

In 1995, Disney produced the movie *Powder,* a strange little film about a teen boy who was struck by lightning and gained supernatural healing powers. Something about the film felt so wrong it made me squirm. There was a reason for that, which I soon discovered. Right around then, a brave young man named Nathan Winters and his family and friends picketed the movie. Nathan had been the victim of the film director, Victor Salva, when Nathan was just a boy. Salva had met Nathan and offered him a part in a small movie he was making called *Clownhouse.* He groomed and molested Nathan during that time.[9] Salva went to jail for a couple of years and, shortly after his release, was once again making movies, beginning with *Powder.* The movie makers made excuses when the director's pedophile criminal history was exposed. (Funny, since Disney himself was an FBI informant.)[10] They tried to blame Nathan for doing the protest, saying he just wanted to get publicity for himself. Disney spokesman John Dreyer said, "What's the point, other than you want to make headlines?[11] The movie was released, and Salva went on to do all the *Jeepers Creepers* horror movies. *Hollywood protects its own.*

Predators often get away with abusing children, and worse, for years. One researcher postulated that a single predator could molest hundreds of kids before ever getting caught or coming to the attention of law enforcement. That's staggering. One predator, Dean Schwartzmiller, kept detailed notes of his abuse of children. He molested thousands of children over a thirty-year period across the United States as well as in Mexico and Brazil. Police discovered binders full of child pornography and numerous logs with lists of more than 36,000 children's names—mostly boys—with codes that appear to indicate exactly how he abused them.[12] Thousands of other predators have risen up to take his place.

Protecting Children in Churches

A word of caution to churches: I am glad that many churches have finally understood the necessity of vetting children's volunteers, youth workers, and pastors. It's a step. But you also need to be aware that, again, just because someone passes a background check doesn't necessarily mean they are "clean" or safe. In fact, most of the in-church predators I know of had no previous records or charges.* As I said before, many predators molest children for decades without being caught or even coming up on the radar of law enforcement. They are very good at hiding in plain sight. So, my recommendation is to, as much as possible, move away from the "they have skills and talents with kids and youth, and they passed the background check" mentality and move more toward Paul the apostle's recommendation, "know them which labour among you" (1 Thessalonians 5:12). This is hard in our megachurch age, but vital. Better to hire a trainable

---

*An excellent discussion on how churches can protect children from being sexually abused is Stacey Shifflet's book, *Wolves Among Lambs.* Also read Sergeant Patrick Crough's book, *Seducers Among Our Children,* which offers excellent advice on how to protect children.

person whose integrity, biblical foundation, and doctrine are solid, one that many people vouch for, rather than a person with skills and talent who is actually a wolf in children's or youth ministry's clothing.

A Local Case and Lessons Learned

My former youth ministry partner, Tim, had joined with another minister, and together, they opened a soup kitchen downtown. They also conducted youth meetings every week. I was traveling during much of that time and could only attend the youth meetings about twice a month. However, my friend Mary helped in the ministry and attended almost all these meetings. She was a passionate protector of children and had a radar for predators that was sharp and unfailing.

When I returned from one trip, Tim told me that while he had been counseling a young man in the back office after a meeting, Mary observed a man come in whom she had not previously seen at the meetings. He had been invited to the meeting by Tim's son. This man had previously approached the son at a Christian biker event and told him he was a youth minister. He expressed an interest in seeing what we did at our youth center. This was the man's first visit since being invited by Tim's son.

Mary watched as this man began performing magic tricks for a couple of the kids. It wasn't but a few minutes before he was surrounded by nearly every child and youth in the building. The kids were fascinated by his skill and tricks. Mary barged into Tim's office and said, "You need to get out there right now. There's a child molester with the kids!" So, Tim went out, took the man aside, and engaged him in conversation to try to ascertain if what Mary said was true. He didn't confront him but waited to talk to me after I returned from a trip to see if I was up to meeting the man to determine who he was.

"Do you want to meet this guy?" Tim asked me.

"Absolutely!" I replied.

In late November, Tim and I met with the magician (whose name we learned was Lloyd), at his duplex. Lloyd asked us a lot of questions and then began to tell us all the things he had been involved in. He said he had worked for the Texas juvenile lockup, helped found the

Big Brother program in our city, and worked with the Boy Scouts. We just let him talk.

I had learned that the best way to find out what a predator is up to and who his victims are was to just ask him about the kids he has "helped," and he will name every victim he's ever molested in a short time. Sure enough, this man began to talk about this kid, and that boy, and where they lived, and who got along with whom, and so on. Halfway through, I feigned a bad allergy and asked if I could use his restroom. It gave me an opportunity to see what was in there and to turn the tape over on my microcassette recorder. I couldn't find any hard evidence to confirm our suspicions in his restroom.

After about an hour, Lloyd got the idea that we weren't really his kind of people. We politely took our leave with a strong conviction that Mary was correct in her discernment.

Shortly thereafter, Tim's daughter came down to the center, waving the front page of our local paper, which featured a prominent picture of Lloyd. He had been arrested on child molestation charges. As I recall, he was eventually charged with over fifteen counts of molestation of ten children over an eighteen-year period of time.

I made a cold call to the sex crimes unit and asked to speak to the lead detective on the case, Detective Doris Provencio. I assured her I was not a "cop groupie" but that I had done legitimate work with sexual abuse victims and had worked on criminal cases. I told her I had some information on the case she was working on. She agreed to meet with me.

After formally introducing myself to her at the meeting, I handed the recordings over to her and said, "Here are two tapes we recorded at our meeting with your suspect. I think you'll find that he mentioned most of his victims on these tapes. And here's a book I wrote for male survivors of sexual abuse. If you have an older victim, it may help him." I kept my time with the detective short and to the point. Meetings like these either ended up with the detective throwing the information in the trash or taking it seriously. Detective Provencio took it seriously.

Detective Provencio called me two hours later. "Thank you for the information," she said. "Really helpful. And yes, he named all his victims. I gave your book to our oldest victim, who is eighteen. He may be our lead witness. He took it and read it in an hour and wants to meet you." The book *Orphans in the Storm* (now titled *The Color of Pain)* is specifically designed to prepare parents and others to identify predators and how they work. The second part is heart-to-heart, real discussions about the damage that abuse does—and how to find healing from sexual abuse.

That night, I met with the young man, Ben,* and told him about Jesus Christ and that I understood personally what he had lived through. He called me later that night to tell me that he had given his heart to Jesus. I was so grateful; that is what makes this work worth everything. (Thirty years later, Ben found me again on Facebook, and he's still walking with Jesus.)

Lloyd, the perpetrator, had a long history of abusing boys. He had slipped through every crack. By the time law enforcement got to him, he had a whole "stable" of boys from eight to seventeen years old. He had groomed the older boy since the boy was ten years old and now had been using him to find other kids. Can you imagine the guilt that boy must have felt? The fear that he might go to jail too? Thankfully, the attorneys assured him he was as much a victim as the younger kids and would not be charged.

Lloyd had used magic tricks, occult lures, affection in the place of absent fathers, mind-control tricks, and you name it to win the trust of his victims. Disturbingly, he often had a boy or two picked up for a few hours by a man in a military uniform whom they called "The Colonel."

Just a few weeks before the start of the trial, Ben called me in a complete panic. One of Lloyd's older "boys," who had also been abused, came by his house, banging on the door around 11 p.m. Ben opened the door and asked what he wanted. "Hey, I just got back from visiting Lloyd in prison. Lloyd said you better change your testimony and tell them nothing happened. He wanted you to know that he has a very, very long reach from jail." Ben slammed the door in his face and ran to the phone to call me.

---

* Not his real name.

"Stay by the phone," I said. "I'll call you back in a few minutes." I immediately called Detective Provencio. She was nonplussed.

"That's great," she said confidently. "Tell Ben not to worry. Tomorrow, I'm going to slap another ten years on this guy for terroristic threats."

Lloyd took a plea deal before his case ever went to trial. This, thankfully, spared the victims from the hell of having to relive their abuses at trial.

He was sentenced to, I believe, thirty years. But he was given time served and was put back on the streets. He essentially skated completely with little or no punishment for his horrendous crimes against kids.[13]

Nearly fifteen years later, I had a college-age lunch Bible study at my house. It was a great group of about twelve to fifteen young people. One Wednesday, I shared a bit about this case in context with the Bible study instructing us to defend the defenseless.

After lunch, one of the young men stayed to talk. "I was one of Lloyd's victims, too," he said. He saw my shock and somberly unraveled his own nightmare of being taken in as a hurting boy and wrecked by this evil predator. His mother had just seen Lloyd working at the local hospital. This predator served *almost no sentence* for making these kids suffer *a life sentence* for what was done to them. I just thanked God for this young man's bravery in telling me and for the ultimate victory he got in Christ as he went on to become a teacher, a loving husband, and a wonderful dad. The devil didn't win this one. He and Ben are living proof that God is able to heal even the deepest wounds.

The Nebraska Case

Paul Bonacci was a young man who tried to expose one of the largest child-trading rings in the United States, whose clientele included senators, the police, and high-ranking government officials. One alleged stable boss was a Nebraskan banker who sang at the 1984 and 1988 Republican National Conventions. Paul was discredited, railroaded, and imprisoned for his efforts to go to the authorities and expose this trafficking ring. (The entire case can be read in the book

The Franklin Cover-Up by former state senator John DeCamp. I recommend this book one-hundred percent to anyone who wants to understand the evil depth and extensiveness of trafficking networks that go up into every level of society.)

Paul Bonacci detailed the transporting of underage teens to the convention to trade them to Washington's elite for sex, as well as the satanic involvement of some of the stable bosses. Paul even detailed the forced trip he took with a small boy, where the boy was sodomized in a remote area outside Sacramento, California, and had to watch the boy's head blown off while it happened—for the purpose of filming a snuff film.

When I heard that Paul had confessed to being part of one of the most well-known child abduction cases, my attention was riveted to it. It was the case of Johnny Gosch, barely-a-teen Iowa boy, who was snatched away in 1982 while on his paper route. Paul said he was forced to chloroform Johnny when the perpetrators threw Johnny into the car, and Paul was also present when they "broke him in" when they stopped at a hotel that night.

I am sure that Paul suffered a thousand emotional/psychological deaths from that, even though he was barely a kid himself when it happened.

Paul provided verifying evidence to Johnny's mother and father, with details only they could know about Johnny, including specific physical characteristics.

Investigators knew the name of the man who was the "mule," the one who traveled around the country snatching kids and taking them to their designated drop-off. But since he constantly traveled by van, no one caught him, and few law enforcement people except for *America's Most Wanted* had ever even taken an interest in trying to find him. Our intel indicated that he had possibly died of AIDS in Mexico.

I traveled to Nebraska in 1992 to speak personally to the investigator for Paul's court case and was able to review his material. I have to admit, I was not prepared to find that Paul had named some of the exact locations for the rape and holding of children that I had been given just a year earlier by the officers on the Houston, Texas case. Paul also wrote down a nearly identical, slightly varied set of "mind-control codes" that the perpetrators used on the victims in the Houston case, which were a combination of Greek letters and numbers.

Most people who have worked on this case believe that Johnny Gosch is still alive. The big question is, why doesn't he come home? Apparently, he made contact with his mother. But come home? When you're a thirteen-year-old boy who has been kidnapped, sexually assaulted, and held captive into your twenties, no doubt having seen and done everything *unimaginable*, it would be devastatingly hard to come home. The shame, the guilt, the fear, and the dissociation from trauma may be the only things keeping Johnny from coming home. Just like every male sexual abuse victim I've ever met, bar none, he no doubt thinks he is the guilty one and that his parents would never be able to love him if they knew all he had done and had been done to him.

In 1989, I was on a layover from Salt Lake City back home via Dallas. It was just a week before Halloween. I was watching a television drama based on true stories of satanic ritual abuse called *Do You Know the Muffin Man?* and it absolutely wrecked me. It was chillingly accurate in portraying the details of how children are abused, how the perpetrators (aided by slick lawyers) cover their tracks, as well as how the victims felt—especially the little ones.

During the movie, a flash came across the television and announced another abduction.

I had learned too much those past few years. I was trained, as were all my counterparts, to look for abductions close to satanic holidays. And Halloween was so close at hand.

This was when the battle became deep and personal for me.

I tacked up pictures of the many children I had been involved with helping, and I also had pictures of those who were still missing—the ones I was sure were taken by this criminal network. I prayed. I wept.

And then one morning, I lost it. The helplessness of it all hit me. It seemed like I could do absolutely nothing about all of it. I yelled at God, "Why do you show me these things when you know I can't stop it?" I vented my anger for quite some time and then bitterly told Him, "Solomon was right. There's no justice on the Earth." And as clear as I can ever remember God speaking to me, I heard Him say, "There may not be justice for these children in this life. But there can be love—if you will love them—if you will love them for Me." I broke down crying. I committed my life to this battle once again. I may not be able to do much. But as long as God gives me breath, I will do everything in my power to help every child, every victim, every innocent youth ruined by predators and devil worshippers that He will bring to my attention.

This is what everything is about for me: Innocent kids whose lives are snatched away from their parents, their lives, and their friends; and all the while, "experts" were saying these kinds of things didn't happen or that it was just a small handful of kids. But that this should happen to even one child is unacceptable. You can say that it doesn't happen often enough to warrant concern. But then, it isn't your child, is it? I'm sure John Walsh, whose son Adam was kidnapped and decapitated, would tell you—that it is every child; they are our children, and we cannot turn our heads away and pretend it isn't significant enough to matter.

The longer I have investigated, the clearer ties I see between criminal occultists and pedophiles, child pornographers, and child traders. They are murderers and destroyers of children. Jesus made it plain,

> But whoso shall offend one of these little ones which believe in me, it were better for him that a millstone were hanged about his neck, and that he were drowned in the depth of the sea. (Matthew 18:6)

If on the off chance you are one of these people, turn to Jesus while you still can. There is mercy even for you. But if you do not turn to Him and repent, rest assured that there is a God who will fulfill this very word toward you.

I will continue to pursue those ties between occult criminals, child rapists, and murderers and help authorities track down every single one of them that I can and bring them to justice, cost what it may.

To the best of our knowledge, Johnny and many others may still be alive. My lifetime prayer is to see them come back home.

By God's grace, perhaps I can at least prevent one child from suffering this fate. I have to try.

Johnny—we will never forget you.

21

The Cries of the Children

Children are such perfect victims. Small enough to be terrified into silence, weak enough not to be able to ward off sexual assault, innocent and trusting enough to believe anything adults tell them.

Yet, in spite of that, many children began to speak of the horrors they had endured. And many adults believed them. But then came the backlash. We have written of those who tried to convince people that the children's cries of sexual and satanic ritual abuse were fantasy—wild imaginations at play. And I guarantee they have never held one of these shattered little angels in their arms or dared to look at the fear and torment in their eyes.

I'm not an expert on children's memories and how they think. But I'm convinced that many of the skeptics aren't either. Just listen to the arguments of some of the more prominent people who attacked the testimonies of the children:

- It's all false memories.

- Therapists brainwashed them.

- They got all this sex information from their parents' porn collection.

- Their parents made them lie.

- They have overactive imaginations.

Does it sound like these skeptics were even slightly willing to consider the unacceptable and unbearable possibility that these children could actually be telling the truth?

I do consider myself somewhat of an expert on pedophiles—child molesters—partly because I spent decades investigating, tracking, and even helping to see some of them jailed and partly because I have worked with victims for five decades to try and see them healed and get justice. Through it all, as I stated earlier, I learned the abusers' modus operandi: deny everything and blame the victim.

I cannot stress strongly enough the damage to victims and their families that the "false memory" notion has created, especially for children. Right after the "satanic backlash," I received a call from a family whose son had outcried having been molested at the Presidio Army daycare center in San Francisco, which resulted in the investigation in which Lt. Col. Michael Aquino was accused of abusing kids. The parents didn't discover their son's molestation until sometime after the abuse when they were stationed overseas where their son felt safe enough to tell them what had happened to him.

It had been years since the molestation at the Presidio daycare. The boy, who was now barely a teen, was in and out of therapy as a result of the severity of the abuse.

His parents had the support of their church. That is, at least, until the year all the "satanic panic" articles and disinformation came out. This caused their son to have a breakdown, and he had to be hospitalized. The pastor called the parents, and after a short talk, he said, "Aren't you glad that you found out it was all false memories about devil worship?"

"What?! What are you talking about?" the incredulous parents cried out.

"You didn't read the article on false memories in *Christianity Today*? The article said it's all false memories!"[1]

In one swift blow, the parents' whole spiritual covering and support had been cruelly ripped away from them because of gullible Christians who printed something without knowing all the facts. I almost think some Christians are only too happy to have an excuse to deny the terrible truth that this sort of evil is not only in our world but is completely focused on harming children.

That is why this book is so important to me. Because ultimately, it's all about the children, and they are the ones who suffer the most from our fear, our ignorance, our gullibility, and our absolute denial of the facts.

It does little good to engage in the debate with these deniers since not any amount of evidence would change their minds or change their course. So, I will simply let the following stories speak for the children, for the older survivors, and for me.

You've no doubt heard of the McMartin Preschool ritual abuse case in Manhattan Beach, California. It was the most expensive case in California's criminal history. And the juries in the various connected trials acquitted the defendants on all counts.[2]

What you no doubt heard from the media, aided by an HBO special about the McMartin case, was that it was a case of hysteria, a witch hunt, where innocent people were falsely accused.

But, you say, if it wasn't false accusations, what actually happened? Here is my own personal opinion, as well as some inside information:

- In my opinion, the well-meaning but overzealous prosecutors botched the case.

- Much of the evidence and testimony of the children was never admitted.

- Eighty percent of the children interviewed had physical evidence of sexual abuse. That was never made public.

- The defense was slick, convincing, and thorough—not to mention brutal—accusing, scaring, and, in the opinion of some, essentially re-abusing those children on the stand. It just reinforced what the children were told by their satanic perpetrators: *No one will believe you.*

- The children's stories were too unbelievable for people to accept.

Let me elaborate on this last point. "Unbelievable" does not necessarily mean untrue. It means it may be so bizarre that people simply can't process it. As one prosecutor said about another case, having to accept that adults want to have sex with little children strains the limits of a jury's threshold of pain. When you throw in rituals, blood drinking, and the killing of babies for Satan, well, you've just lost the case. Most juries will rule not guilty rather than dare to face the horrific possibility that these things actually happened.

This is exactly what criminal devil worshippers count on. They make the abuse so bizarre, so unbelievable, that the children sound psychotic or like liars, making up wicked fantasy stories. But do they? According to Major Barbara Perry, Beaumont Army Medical Center Nurse, out of 300 children interviewed concerning alleged sexual abuse, only two percent (six) of the children were found to be lying. Those six were caught in the middle of custody battles. It is a proven fallacy (untrue) that most children make up stories of sexual abuse.[3]

Criminal devil worshippers indulged in theatrics. They dressed up in cartoon costumes. Who would believe that "Mickey Mouse abused me"? No one. Or, how about this: A coven member dresses as a cop. He tells the child, "Tell anyone, and you'll see someone dressed like me. We'll know you told, and you're going to jail." The child tells: then here comes a cop to investigate; the child denies it all.

Or this: In a satanic ritual, the members will often have black robes. "If you tell," the child is told, "you'll see a man in a robe like this, and we'll know you told, and we'll kill your mommy and daddy." If the child tells and goes to court to testify, she sees the judge walk in—in a black robe.

"I made it all up," she will say. "No one hurt me."

Made to Forget?

Add to this the mix of sedatives and hallucinogens given to the child, along with the child's silence, and the devil worshipper's safety from discovery is virtually assured.

Can victims really be caused to forget such horrific traumas? According to a study by Linda Myer Williams, 200 children were treated for sexual abuse. One in three did not recall the sexual abuse that had been documented in their hospital records!

How much they recalled depended on a number of circumstances, but in general, the younger the child and the more violent the experience, the greater the likelihood and severity of amnesia.

Confused Memories

You can drug children and make them believe they saw a murder when they *really* didn't because it was merely acted out and staged. Or you can make them forget that they actually did see a murder. I am astonished that so many professionals ridicule this notion. Child pornographers and pedophiles have been using these methods for years to silence their victims. In 1987, law enforcement and other professionals compiled a potential list of drugs that would have or could have been used: scopolamine, ketamine hydrochloride, and in the 1950s-1960s, the very effective Nembutal—advertised back then by doctors as useful in sedating your child and making them compliant![4]

The use of drugs was clearly a component in ritual abuse settings. In fact, in the early days of our investigations, as I already mentioned, intel indicated that one of the drugs used to cause victims to forget the experience was scopolamine. It reduced the victim to being fully aware but completely compliant and unable to resist, unable to talk, and unable to fight off the perpetrator as well as being left with a diminished short-term memory.

Confirmation came of this in the late 1990s and early 2000s as law enforcement issued warnings that a highly concentrated powder made of the substance that scopolamine was derived from (something called "devil's breath") and was being used to dose victims without their awareness. As an example, the powder would be placed on the edge of a business card and the unsuspecting victim would be approached and asked for help in getting directions for the address on the card. The powder would be instantly absorbed through the skin as they took the card, and then they would be taken and forced to empty out their bank accounts and open their houses or apartments so the thieves could rob them. They would then be on a park bench or somewhere else hours later, having no idea how they got there or what had taken place.[5]

Does that make you understand a little better how ritual child abuse atrocities could have taken place (and still do), and the children's memories can be scrambled, confused, or even completely repressed?

Abusers often top all this off with additional threats. For example, a little girl is sedated. The abuser lays her on a table and tells her he's going to do "magic surgery." He moves the edge of his hand across her stomach. "See, I'm putting a magic bomb in your stomach. Now, if you ever think of telling someone, or if you do tell, you'll feel the bomb ticking, and you're going to blow up and die."

The child desperately wants to tell. But what happens when you're afraid? You get "butterflies" in your stomach. The little girl feels the butterflies and is sure it's the bomb. Would you tell if you were a little child?

Are these actual techniques of trickery hard for you to hear in these very real incidents? Imagine how hard it must have been for the children to live through them.

Yes, the stories that came out in the McMartin trial were bizarre, including stories about underground tunnels underneath Ray Buckey's office at the preschool, trips to Disneyland in an airplane, sacrificed bunnies, and people dressed up in masks and costumes.

You also need to know that after the acquittals, when the trial concluded, proof of the existence of those tunnels *was* found. And they also found animal bones, a paper plate from Disneyland, a child's scrawled drawing of a satanic pentagram, and many other things that corroborated the children's testimonies—all from the filled-in tunnels found underneath Bucky's office.[6]

My phone rang one night nearly ten years after the end of the McMartin ritual abuse case in Los Angeles. It was a young man in his early twenties who had gotten my number from someone who worked with victims. "I was a McMartin kid," he said, quietly crying. "Will the flashbacks ever stop?" He apparently had run out of places and others to help him. It broke my heart.

First Case

My firsthand involvement with a ritual child abuse case was in El Paso, Texas. Several children had come forward in 1985 with horrific stories of being sexually and satanically abused and forced to be involved in child pornography at a local daycare center. It went to trial, and both female perpetrators were convicted—one with a 20-year sentence, the other with life plus 311 years.

In 1988, they held a retrial on a technicality. At the first trial, the children's videotaped testimonies were used so as not to re-traumatize the children by making them face their perpetrators in open court. A defense attorney contested the convictions, citing the law that an accused person has the right to "face" his or her accusers.

And face them, they did, but it emotionally devastated these brave little kids.

The parents called us before the retrial, and we met with some of them to hear their stories of all that happened.

Mark, not even eight years old, came home one day from the daycare center. His parents were devout Christians and always said grace at supper. But this night would be different when Mark recited the Lord's prayer over supper. It wasn't the Lord's prayer he'd learned in Sunday school. Mark recited it backwards—perfectly. His teachers taught him, he said. Mark's parents were in shock and incredulous and might have slipped all the way into denial, if not for Mark's subdued behavior in more recent days, which told them something was amiss even before this incident.

Discard the phony false memory myth that parents want to believe and hear this stuff from their kids. These parents just listened in shock. Even though this was the last thing they wanted or expected to ever hear. They were a decent Christian couple who knew nothing of devil worship. And now their little boy was reciting the Lord's prayer backwards! (Reciting the Lord's prayer backwards is a standard black mass blasphemy.)

They decided to talk with their neighbor friends whose children also attended the same daycare that Mark went to. It turned out that several parents had their own nightmare stories to tell, each thinking they were alone in it—until now.

Daniella was a single mom with an eight-year-old boy named Anthony. One afternoon after daycare, Daniella had Anthony take his bath and get ready for a nap. He lay down on his bed on his stomach in his underwear. It was a family ritual: Mom would rub his back, and they'd talk until he went to sleep.

"Mommy?"

"Yes, honey?"

"They taught us a new game in school today. Can I show you?"

"Sure, you can."

Anthony turned over onto his back, pulled down his underwear, and began violently masturbating, in a trance, calling out the names of his daycare teachers.

The parents got together and went to the authorities. The children's stories came gushing out. Stories of sexual abuse, photographers, having to do nasty things for a camera with adults, nude games, killing animals for the devil, trips to teacher's house to take pictures, and seeing a werewolf (remember, perpetrators sometimes use costumes).

As I said before, the two perpetrators were convicted and sentenced. "You're safe now, honey," the parents, who naïvely trusted the justice system, told their little ones. "They won't hurt you anymore. You're safe. The bad people are in jail."

No, they weren't safe at all.

We met some of the parents before the second trial got underway. Some parents had moved, and some refused to let their children go through another trial. And I can't blame them. The defense attorneys did as much damage to the children as the rapists that hurt them. "Not again," the parents said. "We are not putting our kids through that again."

Mark was going to be called to testify. We met him with his parents. I will never forget his vacant, haunted, pain-filled eyes as long as I live.

I attended the trial. It was a mockery of justice, a perfunctory, obligatory, half-tried case.

The main perpetrator made ugly, frightening, mocking, hateful, and threatening faces at the children as they testified. And the prosecutors did not once object.

The prosecutors "prosecuted" not at all, allowing the defense attorney to condescendingly tear down and dismiss the children's testimonies.

Within days, acquittals were rendered on all counts for the main teacher. (The other teacher's retrial and acquittal would follow shortly thereafter.) She did the usual, "I thank God that He acquitted me because He knew I was innocent," which I've heard every time from pedophiles and child molesters who managed to escape justice. And the children, of course, now felt that they were not safe, ever, and that good did not win over evil.

Later on, we learned why the prosecution was so weak. They were told, "Just get this case off the docket. It's cost too much money already." So, they sacrificed the children on the altar of judicial expediency and economic concerns.

After the trial, a photo was found of a Halloween party for the daycare workers. The janitor was dressed head to toe as a werewolf. But these children just made up these stories about a werewolf, right? Who could believe such a wild idea?

A year after the trial, an FBI associate told us that they believed it all. But they lacked sufficient evidence to make a case.

Seven years later, I received a call from the mother of one of the children. Her son Ryan was now twelve. She caught him dressing up in her clothes. He was sexually confused. She called me because they had gone to Album Park the week before to have professional school pictures taken of Ryan's baseball team.

At the park, she found that Ryan had climbed up a tree and was screaming and crying. "Mommy, that's him, that's him!" Ryan screamed and pointed to the photographer who had just arrived to take the photos of Ryan's team. "He's the man who took the bad pictures!"

While perpetrators go free, aided in no small part by our own denial and the lies of the "false memory" people who claim all this is just a fairy tale, remember that victims serve a life sentence without parole. I am so grateful that Jesus can give freedom to every victim from the cruel sentence that perpetrators have inflicted on them.

Even Parents and Grandparents

Jimmy was eight. His mom called us from New Mexico and arranged to come to El Paso to meet with us.

Jimmy's mom had a history of drug abuse but had gotten clean and was raising Jimmy alone. She thought they had a pretty safe and stable life.

That is, until one day, Jimmy came home from daycare, and he wasn't wearing any underwear. He screamed when his mom tried to bathe him. He had crisscross scratches all over his back.

Then, she found his bloody underwear in his knapsack.

Jimmy would not tell her what had happened or how he got the scratches. Terrified, she called her mother and had her come over to the house with a camera. The last thing Jimmy's mom expected was the angry and vehement denial by her own mother that Jimmy could have been abused. "He probably got those scratches roughhousing!" her mother insisted adamantly. She didn't bring a camera.

It wasn't until Jimmy's next bath that Jimmy's mother understood. "Mommy, mommy, you got to save the little kids!"

"What little kids, Jimmy?" his mother asked.

"The ones Gramma and Grampa kill! You gotta save them!"

Jimmy's mom was in shock. "Where, Jimmy? What little kids?"

"The ones they keep in the mancaves!" Jimmy cried. The "man-caves" were old mines and caves outside of Albuquerque. Jimmy's mom was very upset; she found out about us, called us, and conveyed the situation to us.

I believed Jimmy's story. Just north of El Paso in Oro Grande, New Mexico, the old mining town had caves and mines as well. From two different victims—one, a former devil worshipper and one former child trading "mule" (as mentioned before, this is someone who procures children)—we were told that caves, and in particular caves in that area, were used to hold children and trafficking victims in transit.

We went out to investigate those Oro Grande mines. After a half-hour descent into one abandoned mine, we found a metal door attached to the side of the cave wall. On the outside of the door, the words "Keep out," along with a death's head, were painted. Opening the door, we found a crawl space about four feet high and five feet deep, big enough for two adults or three or four children—and painted on the inside of the door were the words, "You're dead." There was an unlocked padlock on the outside and no light on the inside once the door was closed. The only handle was on the outside.

Further down, there was a rope tied to a mining car rail that ran above a drop so deep that it took a rock five seconds to hit bottom.

We tried to pull up on whatever was tied to the rope at the bottom, but it was so heavy that we could not bring it up. (At that point, I'm not sure I wanted to know what it was.) We decided to leave and come back the next day with rappelling equipment and rappel down. On our way out, two rednecks were sitting on a truck hood with shotguns resting on their shoulders, watching us come out. We waved, said, "Have a good day!" and left before we risked ending up being at the other end of a rope.

When we returned the next day, the rope had been cut, and whatever had been tied to it was gone.

Caves and tunnels and abandoned mines riddled New Mexico, Arizona, West Texas, and Nevada. In the ensuing years, dozens of people have independently told us about the many tunnels and caves that were used to transport children and hold them in cages in transit like animals. The smoking guns were out there. But of course, with hundreds, if not thousands, of such hiding places that stretched across four states, the chances of actually finding them (with a crew as small as ours and especially because there was little to no interest from the authorities) were slim to none. So, my thoughts returned to the "man-caves" and the grandparents that Jimmy was so upset about.

Jimmy's grandparents—naturally—angrily dismissed Jimmy's accusations and tried to get custody of Jimmy, claiming that the mother (their daughter) was an unfit and unstable parent. The grandparents fit the profile. Grandma worked for a powerful politician—and Grandpa was a pharmacist. Mom did the only thing any decent parent would— she denied her parents any access to Jimmy, moved out of state, and started over again.

The mom had no ax to grind, no custody battle to fight. Everything in her wanted to believe that her parents couldn't possibly be involved. She had no recollection of having been abused herself and had no reason to believe her parents were involved in something so awful. But Jimmy's nightmare prevailed over her own denial, and Jimmy's safety and healing were secured, although it was at a terrible cost to his mom.

Multiple Cases

Danny and Trisha were seven and eight years old. Their abuse by their father and grandparents was clear and detailed in many of their drawings. The mother had called us for help. There was no prosecution. It was a total surprise two years later to be involved in a case of two children from the Dallas area, three hours from where Danny and Trisha grew up, who drew and described in detail the very same house in Fort Worth Danny and Trisha had described and drawn. One of these two children, ten years old, came forward after he was found on the school bus carving a pentagram into his hand with a razor and not even feeling it. His father, he said, worshipped the devil.

It was not unusual to find children from across the country in separate ritual abuse cases with separate therapists, drawing nearly identical depictions of some of the horrors they endured.

Invasion in the House of God

A transient couple and their three-year-old daughter had been hired as live-in caretakers at the El Paso Eastside Assembly of God Church. They were given a little room at the back of the church in exchange for their caretaking and had been there for less than a month.

Our team was called in to talk to the parents and pastor.

A week earlier, the parents had awakened to find their daughter gone from her cot.

They quickly searched the building and found their child in the girls' restroom, hands around her knees, shaking, disheveled, and the bottom of her feet covered with road tar and dirt.

After much questioning, she told her parents and the pastor what had happened. She'd heard a knock at the door by the restrooms. A mail flap opened, and two teen girls told her to open the door. So, she did. The teenagers took her to two nearby houses. At the first one, she was undressed and described what was some kind of ritual where the people ate what she called "bad cereal" (she was likely abused there). Then she was taken to another home by a man wearing white, where she was dressed in white, given "good cereal," hugged a lot, put back into her nightgown, and then taken back to the church.

At night, we surveilled the area around the church and went to the houses the little girl had pointed out; we were surrounded by flashing car lights signaling others, warning whistles—and a large male sentry watching our every move from across the street. The moment we pulled up to the two houses, the curtains were quickly drawn shut.

"Has anything unusual gone on at this church?" I asked the relatively new pastor, who had only been there for about six months.

"No," he said. "But we did find boxes of skeleton costumes in the attic when we took over the pastorate."

"Skeleton costumes?" I asked, a little stunned. "Pardon me, but I know the Assembly of God Church does not celebrate Halloween at all. Why would there be boxes of skeleton costumes up there?" The pastor grew very concerned, looking at it in the light of this event with the little girl.

The couple were the only live-in residents that the church had ever had. My best guess was that a satanic group had free reign midnight access to this church until the caretakers moved in. And now, they were going to reclaim their territory.

My theory was partly confirmed when the pastor arrived early Sunday morning to find a bird slaughtered on the altar inside the church.

There was also a message left on the church answering machine. A man said, "I don't care what you do or what it takes, we're going to have your church even if we have to kill you."

The pastor called my co-youth director, Tim, at three in the morning several days later to ask us to come down to the church ASAP. Tim, his brother-in-law, and I rushed over. The pastor had received a panicked call from the caretaker.

The caretakers had awakened to hear banging cabinets and breaking glass in the kitchen. They rushed in to find that every church cabinet had been opened, and all the dishes and glasses had fallen everywhere, crashing and breaking and covering the floor. The couple was terrified. We prayed for protection for the church and family. We helped them clean up the mess. We made sure there was no one in the church and no signs of entry.

The week before the kitchen incident, the pastor and the caretakers had used binoculars to watch a house they suspected was involved in some of these demonic activities. A white limo had pulled over down the street from the church. At the time, there were about fifteen people standing outside of the house. A chauffeur got out of the limo carrying a tall paper bag. He rang the doorbell at the house where a big party was taking place. The door opened. The chauffeur gave a weird hand signal to the person opening the door, the bag was delivered, and the limo left. The pastor had taken down the license plate number of the white limousine.

We traced the plates on the limousine. The limousine was owned by a crematorium. The crematorium was owned by the pastors of a Baptist church, about which we had previously received credible reports that the church was being used for rituals in the middle of the night. (The church was one of the five Masonic-built churches in our city.)

We had found what was possibly our first lead in confirming that devil worshippers were using crematoriums to dispose of their victim's bodies. We could only speculate on what was being delivered in the bag by the limousine driver from the crematorium. We added that information to our growing file of evidence that something wicked had indeed come our way.

Within a short period of time, the pastor left the church. Not long after that, the church was apparently sold and razed to the ground. There is not even a trace to show that the church was ever there.

Shattered Lives

During a fall tour, I was speaking to middle-school kids in Killeen, Texas about devil worship and the occult and the terrible consequences that often resulted from these practices. I spoke to them in a way that only one who had been there and one who helped children and kids get out of those dark worlds could speak—carefully, straightforwardly, and with a lot of understanding. They were a rowdy bunch, but they were good kids with lots of good questions. The school, near an army base, had begun to see a growing number of kids involved in occult and satanic activities and had asked me to address the issue. Kids were beginning to draw satanic and occult drawings on their notebooks, their clothes, and their skin. Many schools asked for our intervention during that time to address this growing youth phenomenon.

After I asked for questions, an eleven-year-old boy raised his hand. I had just finished telling them about some of the things I had endured as a result of occultism. "Yes, son?" I asked him.

"Sir, do you still have flashbacks?"

"Yes, I do," I answered.

"I do, too," the boy solemnly replied. "My parents are in the military, and when we were living in Germany, I had a friend whose parents were selling drugs and were into the devil. He told me that if he told anyone, they'd kill him. He died right after that. I keep having flashbacks about it and all." The class went completely silent.

"I understand, son. I'm so sorry you had to go through that." The class ended.

The same boy came right up to me after class. He was shaking and really scared. "God loves you, son," I said, putting my hands on his shoulders and watching his tears flow. "I won't forget you. I will be praying for you."

"Thank you," he said. Unfortunately, the school was on a tight schedule, and I had to leave him to get to the next class.

After the final class that day, as I was about to get into my car, a teacher rushed over and handed me a note. The note said, "The boy's name is David. He is desperate. He is asking for you. Please come to the counseling office immediately." I rushed over. David and I spent over an hour talking together. I was pretty sure that he had experienced far more than the death of his friend while in Germany. This eleven-year-old told me about coming home from Europe feeling like he had some kind of evil power in him. He was being visited by demons in the night and believed he was able to curse people and they would die. He wanted Jesus to take it all away. So, we prayed together for him to give his life to Jesus. I will never forget him or that encounter. I knew there had to be hundreds of kids like him, slipping through the cracks because no one was talking to them about these things and giving them permission to tell their horrible secrets. I vowed to do everything I could to get more access to the schools to meet these kids right where they were. Thankfully, I was able to speak to many schools over the years.

Arresting the Rescuers and Betraying the Innocent

In 1994, I received a call from the mother of a six-year-old boy named Jeremy. His parents were, on the surface, amicably divorced. Mom had primary custody, but she had no problem with Dad's frequent visits to California from his home state of Texas to take Jeremy on two to five-day "vacations."

That is until Jeremy's personality totally changed. Almost overnight, he became angry, withdrawn, sullen, and terrified. His speech patterns became almost infantile. His mom, unsure of what to do, took him to a speech therapist who recognized a bigger problem, and a children's therapist was called in. Before long, so was Child Protective Services. Jeremy began pouring out volumes of specific details about being sexually hurt by his father, his father's new wife, and strange men and women in the motels where they stayed. His language was that of a child's—pee pee, poo poo, and bottom to name a few. The details, however, were chilling and so intricate that it was worse than a triple X movie. They took pictures, he said. They went to "bad motels." As the authorities drove around the town where Jeremy claimed he was abused, he pointed out those motels while screaming in terror. They were exactly where he said they would be and what they would look like. The mother confirmed that Jeremy's father had stayed with him in these exact motels.

Jeremy continued to deteriorate. He went into trances, hid in closets, and screamed, "I'm bad, I'm bad!"

Jeremy's mom and grandparents sought any help they could get. Some people in the local state authorities said, "If we were you, we would never allow his father to have access to him again."

But since it was a two-state custody matter, the father called the FBI, and the mother was ordered to return Jeremy to his father for visitations or face arrest.

So, they fled. Grandpa and Grandma sank their entire life savings into hiding and protecting Jeremy and his mom.

When they were found, the mother was jailed and given an outrageously large bond—a bond not even required of some accused murderers and rapists. And all she had done was hide and protect her shattered child.

The grandparents lost the rest of their money; they had to get their daughter out of jail and ready for trial.

Halfway through the trial, someone paid to have the boy's lawyer fly to Las Vegas for a three-day conference on the false memory syndrome. When he returned, he asked the judge to take him off the case. "I don't believe your boy's stories anymore," he callously told the mother.

Jeremy's father ended up being granted full custody of his son— and Jeremy went silent. The mother was allowed one hour a week of visitation, with police supervision. All Jeremy's mom and grandparents could do was pray for a miracle. The fact that a local deputy, who was accused of child pornography and molestation, killed himself on Jeremy's father's property just days before the trial, never did make the news. If it had been thoroughly investigated, I am convinced that Jeremy's abuse would have been verified.

I still feel nauseated just remembering what I read in the volumes of graphic outcrying from Jeremy that his therapist let me read—descriptions no child could make up or even be coached to say.

Nor will I ever forget his words to his grandmother: "Nana, God told me I'm not bad! He told me I'm a superhero!"

Indeed, he is. Wherever Jeremy is today, I pray he was delivered out of the hands of evil people and found a good life in Jesus.

Broken Children and a Broken System

My final witness is the one that touched me the deepest.

One evening, a woman called me. "I got your number from a Christian bookstore. They said you could help."

"What can I do?" I enquired. The woman, Julie,* proceeded to pour out her story in fragmented and disjointed details. I could tell she was traumatized and numb. Her children told her that her husband had taken them to Mexico, where they were sexually abused by adults.

---

*Not her real name.

Her son, Johnny, was ten years old from a previous relationship. Her six-year-old daughter, Rachel, was from her current husband.

She didn't want to believe her kids, especially her son, who told her that her husband had sodomized him. But the children begged her to go look at his car. (He had gone to work in Mexico that day in their second car.) They told her that they had hit a block wall on the way out of Mexico. She checked the car, and the right fender and headlight were smashed up. Her husband had not mentioned anything to his wife about having an accident.

She searched the house while her husband was at work. She found a pair of Johnny's underwear stained with semen. She bagged it, took some of her husband's papers and some strange personal items—one a packaged drug, which turned out to be an aphrodisiac and a note which said, "Cebele Puta"—which translated means, "Whore of the Goddess." She packed up the kids and fled. "What do I do now?" she asked desperately.

"Take the kids to Sierra Medical Center. Have your son examined for sexual abuse."

"Okay," she agreed. "I'll call you back."

When she called three hours later, she spoke in a monotone voice, clearly in shock. "The doctor just came out. He had tears in his eyes. He said, 'Your son has both old and recent severe anal scarring. I'm so sorry. Your son's been sexually assaulted, and not just recently.' We're leaving the state. I'll call you." I didn't have a chance to stop her. She just suddenly hung up.

She called me again a few days later from a hotel in Albuquerque. I could hear the children crying and screaming in the background. "No, Mommy, don't open the door! It's them, they're coming after us!" It turned out to be their grandmother at the door, but the kids were absolutely terrified, thinking that their dad had tracked them down.

When the Albuquerque police interviewed Johnny, they dismissed him and told him his story "didn't wash," that his story was "all washed up." Then they confiscated the evidence that the mom had taken from her husband's possessions as well as the damning evidence from the underwear.

The husband was able to track them down, and he told her he didn't remember doing anything bad to the children. He cried and begged her to come home, and he agreed that if she came back, he'd take a sodium pentothal test to prove his innocence.

The mother fell for it. They flew home, and Julie was arrested for kidnapping the moment they stepped off the plane at the El Paso International Airport. Johnny and Rachel were placed in protective custody until the authorities could sort out the truth.

When the children were interviewed, they were believed one hundred percent by the El Paso authorities and were returned to their mother, whom had been released from jail. The authorities sent out an arrest warrant for the father who managed to take Rachel from school and was now on the run and facing kidnapping charges.

Julie asked me to come over to talk to Johnny. I went over the next afternoon. Johnny and I went out back to talk. He was nervous, antsy, and scared. He'd already recanted his story to the authorities the day before. "I made it all up," he told me when I asked about what he had told the police his dad had done to them.

"Why did you do that, Johnny?" I asked as we sat under the gazebo.

"Because my dad beats me. I wanted to get rid of him."

"Oh, okay," I said. That might have sounded plausible to someone who had no other details, but in light of the evidence from the hospital report, I wasn't buying his explanation.

"Can we go throw a football or something?" he asked. "I can talk better when I'm doing something."

"Sure," I agreed, and we went out front and threw the football around for an hour.

I went for a long pass, tripped over a cement lawn edging, and was sent flying ending up sprawled out on the lawn, sunglasses twisted on my face with my leg cut and bleeding. Johnny was laughing his head off; so was I. I think at that moment, he knew I was safe. We flew kites until dusk. We didn't talk about what had happened. We just talked about random things like who his favorite superhero was and what he liked to do for fun. "Can you come back again?" he asked.

"Sure, Johnny," I replied.

"When?" he asked.

"Soon," I told him. "I promise."

Two days later, they found the father, and he was jailed. Rachel was returned to her mother who took the kids with her to the battered women's shelter. At Johnny's next therapy session, Johnny poured out their story again to his therapist in rage, pain, and anguish.

I met them in the park later in the week. Rachel and her mom went off in one direction while Johnny and I walked the other way to talk.

"Johnny, why did you tell me you made it up, then told the therapist it was true?"

"I was scared," he said.

"Why?"

"My dad was still out of jail." Of course, it made perfect sense.

"Did he threaten to hurt you?"

"Yeah, all the time. He said if I told on him that he was gonna kill my sister and mom and sell me to some old guy in Mexico."

"Do you think he would?" I asked.

"Yeah!" he said, getting worked up and agitated. "I saw 'em! When we lived in Laredo, a lady that was there at the house where they did bad things to us tried to leave with her little girl, and they took a gun and *bang!* They shot her right here," he said, pointing between his eyes, "and threw her on the fire. I knew he'd do it." Johnny even told me the name of the little girl—Trudy—and said they burned Trudy in the fire before they shot and burned the mother.

My stomach began to churn, and I had to fight back my tears so he wouldn't see them. "Johnny, you're one heck of a tough, brave kid," I told him. "I knew a kid like you," I said, about to launch into a story about myself.

"You're talking about yourself, right?" he asked, clearly proud of his insight.

"Well, I guess you got me. Yeah. I know how you feel. And I'm here for you. I'm your friend."

We walked back to where his mom and Rachel were. I was wearing a necklace with a little sword and a jewel. To me, it represented Ephesians 6:17, "the sword of the Spirit, which is the word of God." But not to Rachel. "You have a knife!" she exclaimed, with fear in her eyes when she saw it. Then she hung her head. "My daddy and I had bad knives!" she spat out. I tried to process this unprompted outcry as I explained to her that I wasn't one of the "bad people." I knelt beside her and assured her that I was one of the good people and that I was going to do whatever I could to protect her.

Later, as I was about to leave, both kids ran over and hugged me. This one moment of trust was profound after all they had been through with other adults.

The attorneys and the prosecuting attorney called me. Lynette, the D.A. prosecutor, was determined to see this child molester punished to the maximum extent of the law. I agreed to meet with Lynette and her attorneys at the mother's request.

The meeting was a disaster. I innocently walked in, videotapes and books in hand, thinking I could just feed them some good information on ritual abuse cases. Instead, I found myself questioned, grilled, and interrogated by the attorneys. Not about the case; about me. Why was I interested? What made me an expert? Why hadn't Johnny told me certain things? Lynette, who apparently really wasn't expecting this, just sat by helplessly. They grilled me for almost an hour; and since I had just agreed to meet with them, hoping to be of help, I was completely caught off guard. I admittedly didn't handle it well.

I told them of Johnny's disclosure to me of seeing a woman killed.

"My God, I don't even believe that!" another of their attorneys said.

"And you're his lawyer?" I asked, astonished. "You better believe him!" Everyone was silent for a moment.

"We appreciate you coming down, but we won't be using you to testify."

At that moment, I understood. "Do you think I came down here so I could be an expert witness? Is that what you think this is about for me?" I snapped my briefcase shut and got up. "I'm not here to testify, and I'm not here for you. I'm here for those kids. That's all." I stormed out.

I felt a hand on my arm in the hallway. It was Lynette. "Please don't take it personally," she said. "That's how they work. It's their job."

"Okay," I said quietly.

"Please don't bail on Johnny," she said. "He needs your support. He listed you with his therapist as his best friend." That was the last thing I expected to hear. It touched me deeply.

"I won't, Lynette. I'll stay with it, no matter what. I won't let him down."

During the time they were preparing for trial, I had been trying to help the mom and her kids any way I could. One week, I took a golf break in Tucson, Arizona with an old college friend, staying at a resort hotel I had been going to for years.

One evening, we were about to leave for dinner when there was a knock at the door. I opened it to find an evil-looking, burly hispanic man staring at me with steel deadly eyes. "Can I help you?" I asked. He took a drag off his cigarette.

"Mis-TAKE," he said coldly. I got the message.

"Yeah, whatever," I said and slammed the door.

"Lock all the windows and the porch door," I told my friend as I filled him in on what happened and told him I believed it was a threat because of the case I was working on. He was skeptical until we stepped outside and saw the man hiding behind a Mimosa tree smoking, watching us. I took a quick look at the parking lot, found a shiny new truck with Juarez plates, and walked over with a pen and paper to take the plate numbers down. The man literally ran to his truck, got in, and peeled out. We jumped in my car, and we peeled out after him and chased him at speeds up to seventy miles an hour before he took a quick turn up a dark street, and we lost him. Honestly, I was only recklessly pursuing him out of blind anger at feeling so helpless about these children. I had neither the authority nor the legal weaponry to do anything about it and was later grateful God protected me—and others—from my own reckless actions.

It was pretty clear that Johnny and Rachel's abusers were not at all happy about my involvement in their business. I had gotten too close. Now, they were giving me a message—which I promptly ignored. I would have risked almost anything to try and save Johnny and Rachel.

Inexplicably, the mother returned to the abusive husband (who was out on bond) just days before the pretrial hearings—with the kids! On the stand at pretrial, Johnny denied it all. Again. As I knew he would if he was returned to his stepfather. His stepfather made it clear what he would do if he told anyone.

"You know you didn't lie, Johnny!" Lynette pleaded with him, in tears, after he took the oath and then denied everything. "You've got to tell the truth!" He didn't. Of course, he changed his story! His stepfather was back in the house. Johnny knew that his life, and that of his mom and sister, might be at stake if he told the truth.

Case dismissed. It was a devastating loss.

I researched this case far back. The family had, it seems, left a paper trail from San Antonio to McAllen, from Laredo to El Paso. Brutal beatings, drug abuse, outcries of spousal and child abuse.

I reached the Child Protective Services worker who had handled the outcries two years before, and she was infuriated that the abuse had not stopped. She vowed to do everything she could to pursue this case.

After the case was dismissed, I carefully reviewed everything the children had revealed, and it sickened me. From one Texas town to another, the children had given volumes of details about the abuse at the hands of their father and others. The mom and grandma had previously provided their own journals and accounts to me. Johnny's accounts were the most detailed. Little Rachel was too young to articulate much.

Johnny said it started in San Antonio when his stepdad took him and Rachel to a house where there were other children—and adults who hurt them. A few months later, the stepdad moved the family to McAllen. From there, the children continued to be abused in a house across the border in Reynosa, Mexico. Julie had her husband arrested once again after he beat her severely, which is where Child Protective Services (CPS) first intervened.

But Julie kept going back to him.

They next moved to Laredo, then El Paso, which is when the children began to be taken at night to Juarez, Mexico, right across the border.

"Didn't your mom know what he was doing to you and Rachel, Johnny?" I asked in one of my original conversations with Johnny about being taken to Mexico.

"No. He always put some white powder in her nose when she went to bed. She'd sleep all the next day. She felt sick and slept all the time."

Johnny and Rachel described colored robes and dances, animals being killed and having their faces painted, and lots of strange chanting.

Johnny described a house in Juarez, Mexico, in great detail. He drew the best map he could for a ten-year-old who was taken in the dark to another country.

Johnny and Rachel described the "old witch"—"La Bruja"—with white hair and strange jewelry, who owned the house. Johnny said there were pictures of both Jesus and the devil. Anyone familiar with Mexican witchcraft will not be surprised by this weird duality.

I had already heard about that very same Juarez house of child traffickers from three other victims long before I ever met Johnny and Rachel. Those victims also described the white-haired ringleader—the old witch—La Bruja—just as Johnny had and in the exact same details. They each said that many well-known city officials were participants. And, although we haven't yet found the house, it's surely there, and children are no doubt still chattel for sick, evil child rapists. Unfortunately, Juarez is so taken over by the criminal world that investigation is nearly impossible.

Johnny said when they went to that house, he and Rachel were put into a room with toys and other kids. He said it was a really dirty room, and all the kids were crying and scared. Big men came for them, one by one. He watched a man take Rachel, and when he brought her downstairs an hour later, he saw the man kiss her on the mouth like his stepdad kisses his mom.

A man picked Johnny up and took him to a blue room that had a mattress with shiny blue sheets. He had to take his clothes off and lay on his stomach, and the man sodomized him. Then Johnny's stepfather took them back home before their mother woke up. This had been going on for a year in Juarez, and similar things happened in the other locations, Johnny said.

I'll spare you the worst details. Believe me, I'm being kind to you. It only all came out because little Rachel began crying one night when Mom was there and said, "Please, Johnny, please tell Mommy the truth, tell about Daddy taking us. I don't want to go to Mexico anymore!" Johnny had been whipped and sodomized by his stepfather for just small things. *What will happen if I tell everything?*, he thought. But

Johnny wanted to protect his sister. So, he told. And that's when the real nightmare began.

I paused while reviewing the notes and tried to take in the hell these children had been through.

I learned later that the kids had told their mom that they overheard that she was going to be killed at 3 a.m. that morning because she was getting too suspicious. Her husband had called her earlier that day, telling her to pick him up in Juarez at exactly 2 a.m. because his car had broken down. That's when she realized her kids were really telling the truth. That is when she called me.

I wish I could tell you it had a good ending—it didn't. The father's cruelty continued. Mom finally ran again with Johnny and Rachel and moved to Grandma's in another state to start over. Grandma called me a year later. The father had moved just a state away but had driven down and kidnapped Rachel. He was keeping her because he found a judge who ruled in his favor and ruled that he did not have to return Rachel. Isn't that amazing? In the previous story, Jeremy's mom had been jailed for refusing to return her boy to his abuser. Yet Rachel's father was given full protection by the law to keep her, and he was still frequently flying to Mexico. Justice is relative and definitely not on the side of children. I am amazed that no one asked why this man went through two jailings and two bankruptcies, yet within months, he was back on his feet and was able to buy new houses and cars. Someone was bankrolling this deal. In occult and human trafficking worlds, they take care of their own. Or they dispose of them if need be.

I heard later on that progress was being made, and Mom had gotten primary custody—thank God. Johnny, thankfully, had stayed safe, but without God's miracle, he's never going to talk about it again, and without God's healing hand, he has been altered for life. I will always pray for him and for Rachel. God alone knows all that they had endured.

As for Lynette, the DA prosecutor on Johnny and Rachel's case, she resigned and transferred to Lubbock, Texas soon after the case was thrown out. I will always be in awe of her courage and genuine love for those kids and for doing everything she could to go the distance for them.

I created problems for the local Child Protective Agency, refusing to accept the "There's nothing else we can do" mantra. But one cop I consulted told me, "Someone's got to be being bought off on this one. This should still be an open case."

In the end, through the help of the CPS worker in McAllen, at least El Paso CPS got thoroughly reprimanded at the Austin board, though unfortunately, it was too late to help Johnny and Rachel.

The last word on the case came from a grandmother, one of the assistant D.A.s who had been intimately involved with Johnny and Rachel's case. "I just called to tell you I've taken a position outside of El Paso."

"Why?" I asked. We were losing all the good people, it seemed.

"I have grandkids. We're not helping kids here. We're not protecting them. We're returning them to their abusers. It's a joke. I can't live with that. Maybe I can make a difference somewhere else." And I'll bet she has been doing just that.

In more recent years, a few good and caring people have come on board in El Paso. For the first time, we're seeing things turn around for the children. I've met some good people in local agencies. They want to learn. They want to do something. They want to make a difference.

It's hopeful, and I pray that together we all can turn things around for the children to come. We weren't ultimately able to rescue Johnny and Rachel, but this is all the more reason to persevere and do all we can to try to help the children still caught up in these monstrous networks.

Through all these things, I knew these were the risks we had to take and that we may not always succeed in getting the kids out. I still remember Solomon's words when he said there was *no justice in the Earth* (Ecclesiastes 3:16). And I also remember—and must not ever forget—the words God spoke to me in my darkest hours of anguish over the destruction of innocents:

> There may not be justice for these children in this life. But there can be love—if you will love them—if you will love them for Me.

May God grant us the courage to fight for the children and love them through their dark battles no matter what the outcome.

22

Where David Died

Thirteen-year-old David Cardenas was from a small town in the Rio Grande Valley town of Donna, Texas at the southernmost tip of the state.

David Cardenas, what dreams must you have had? New adolescent dreams of a girlfriend, joining the football team, or your upcoming summer vacation? Dreams of every normal child. Did you know, David, that your friends were pawns in the hands of the Prince of Evil? What was your last dying thought?

It was Good Friday, 1998. I was on South Padre Island in Texas taking some time off, trying to enjoy a few days on the beach, needing to salve the wounds of my father's passing and the wounds of this long, painful battle fighting occult crime.

It was 5:00 p.m., and I was attempting a nap. I was soon startled out of my sleep by a sudden urgency to turn on the news. A boy had been murdered. A reporter said, "Police originally speculated that it could be part of a satanic ritual, but now believe it to be gang related." And I saw a photo of young David's picture on the television screen. Since it was Good Friday, there was a good chance it was satanic.

The ten o'clock news did not mention anything about devil worship. On my way through San Antonio on the flight home, I called the newsroom in McAllen, near Donna, Texas. "First, they said it was; now they say it isn't. What's the story?"

"Well," the reporter told me, "At first, they thought, *maybe,* because we've had so many occult animal sacrifices around here lately." (That certainly didn't make it into the papers.) "But then, the authorities told us it was gang related."

MISSING

David Cardenas - 12 years old.
Green eyes - light complexion -
medium brown hair
Last Seen: Friday - 4 - 17 - 98 - t
    Cesac's Drive - Inn in Donna, TX
was wearing: Jenco blue jeans - light gray
    Sweater - black NIKE Sandals
Please Contact: Donna P.D. 464 - 4481

The morning after I arrived home, Officer Javier Garcia called me. He worked for Weslaco, Texas Police Department, right next to Donna. "Did you hear about the boy?" he asked me. (I had met Officer Garcia at the last Killeen Police Academy training in March. I had been an instructor on cult crimes that week. Officer Garcia and his partners had been there to learn.)

"Yeah, I did," I replied. "What do you know?"

"It looks to be occultic," he replied. "They cut the kid's arms and feet off, and the guy drank his blood while he was still alive. I've got officers from Donna on their way here so I can fill them in on what this might be about. Can you maybe talk to them?"

"Be glad to," I replied. Javier had taken in every bit of information that we taught during our academy training, never knowing at the time he'd be thrown into an active case so quickly. I trusted him. I knew he'd make sure the Donna officers would understand the possible implications in this case.

I talked to the officers to help them understand the potential larger implications of all this. They needed to understand this may not be just "gang related"—there were serious hard-core occult elements involved.

Three months later, Officer Garcia had me down to train their departments. At lunchtime, one of the officers took us from the training center in Weslaco over to Donna to see the crime scene. The minute we entered Donna, my flesh began to crawl. "We're in Donna, aren't we?" I asked warily.

"Just crossed the city limits," the officer replied. Donna had a very small population, but it felt as dark and evil as any big city I'd ever entered.

We stopped outside of a huge two-story house in the exact center of town. The officers wanted me to see the enormous stained glass pentagram symbol on the second-story window.

A lot of big drug money passed through Donna, a perfect connection for the trafficking of children, I thought. Devil worshippers would not be a big surprise.

We stood at the spot behind the abandoned building where David's body was left in a shallow grave. "He wasn't the good kid everybody thought," one of the officers said. "He smoked dope."

"Yeah, kids do that, unfortunately," I said. "But he was just a kid." The officer fell silent.

"I guess, yeah," he replied. My mind flew back to another thirteen-year-old teenager whose older body I now inhabited, and I knew David was probably much like me. Lonely. Lost. Wanting to be accepted and loved. Willing to go with whoever would accept him.

I stood at the place where David's relatives had lovingly placed a plastic cross and flowers on this killing ground. I restrained the deep,

deep agony and grief I felt so as not to expose my heart to those men who were doing a good job in an evil place. At that moment, I realized it wasn't about "proof" anymore. Here's proof. But how many people really cared enough to accept that proof? "Proof" of a satanic murder won't be accepted; it would only bring secondary explanations by the "experts." Proof will not bring David back.

Was it a "satanic ritual murder"? No, maybe not in the "technical" sense. But it did take place on a date when ritual sacrifices happen. And the way the body was desecrated, positioned, and mutilated certainly fit the profile. The murderer said he heard Satan telling him to do it, to kill him and to drink his blood. We may never know everything about what happened and what, if any, deeper involvement these kids, as well as the adults who tried to dispose of evidence, had to do with the occult. But it really didn't matter. Satan is a destroyer.

When I got back home, I wept for David. Just like every victim, they are brother, sister, son, and daughter to my heart.

No, it isn't about proof anymore. Believe me, I have seen enough proof to provide nightmares for a lifetime. After David's murder, something changed. I changed. It was about David. Every David. The skeptics and the "false memory experts" are irrelevant in the light of the real kids and real children whom we have seen sacrificed to evil.

I have stood on the killing fields of this war and wept at the innocent blood spilled for nothing. I will no longer acknowledge nor respond to skeptics.

I will only respond to the voice of Abel whose blood cries out for justice from this unholy ground.

23

Down in the Zero

Though I walk in the midst of trouble, thou wilt revive me:
thou shalt stretch forth thine hand against the wrath of mine
enemies, and thy right hand shall save me. (Psalm 138:7)

Over the years, the skills necessary for vetting people's stories became more crucial than ever, especially as the backlash against our work increased, and we had to make sure we were as discerning, accurate, and foolproof as possible. As I mentioned before, there were a number of people who came to us claiming to be high-level Illuminati, high priests, or relatives of famous occultists. We were always patient and willing to hear someone's story, but we were also able and prepared to unravel the truth in case it was a made-up story told to get attention. In spite of what the skeptics had accused us of, we didn't just wholesale buy someone's story in our zeal to bolster our case. Far from it. We always erred on the side of extreme caution. And yes, a number of stories turned out to be false.

The real cases were like battling at the very gates of Hell.

Our team met with a seventeen-year-old young man in 1990. He had called from a motel in Las Cruces, New Mexico. He was dying of AIDS. He wanted someone to pray for him, and he needed to confess some things and seek God's forgiveness.

He had been a street hustler ever since he ran away from home at a very young age. He became part of the "children of the night," the invisible population of hookers, hustlers, and drug addicts that had turned Hollywood into a nightmare world of sex and abuse, addiction, and tragedy.

He told us he had been hired recently for a particular party high in the Beverly Hills foothills where most of the wealthiest of Hollywood lived. He was a "party favor." Don't be shocked; ever since the dawn of Hollywood, it has been the scene of debauched parties and orgies attended by Hollywood's brightest stars. One well-known socialite was famous for bringing "party favors." Boys and girls, children, and teens of all ages from ten to sixteen were passed around like hors d'oeuvres at these parties to curry favor and wealth.

The young man we spoke to, Chad,* had been hired for several of these kinds of parties before, and he was well-paid. But on this one particular night, everything turned unexpectedly dark. Chad and the others were in a frenzy of a drug and alcohol-fueled orgy when suddenly the atmosphere changed. An outdoor staging was set up, and a number of people donned robes. In the midst of candles and chanting, a thirteen-year-old hustler, drugged and seemingly unaware of what was happening, was placed on a stone altar and sacrificed.

Chad was shattered by what he had witnessed, and he was able to escape in the night. He found his way to a dirty Las Cruces motel, praying to God and pleading for grace and forgiveness. The young life butchered by the rich and famous had been a friend of his.

In recent times, more and more significant information has come out about high-level pedophile abuse thanks to brave people like Cory Feldman—star of *Goonies*, *The Lost Boys*, and several other Hollywood films.[1] Information also began coming out about a number of Hollywood elites involved in all levels of the occult, from Santeria priests and priestesses to indulging in black magick. And when you see actual photographs of the *so-called* brightest and best media stars like Lady Gaga attending the ghastly (though legal) "human cake" parties put on by occult artist Maria Abramovich—who does her artwork in blood—and see people cutting slices out of a cake that looks like a life-like human, which is soaked in blood-like liquid confections, you realize the level of Hollywood depravity is deep and dark, and for many, has no boundaries.[2] Again, the truth for

*Not his real name.

those involved in real satanic/devil worship activities is that you conduct rituals to curry favor with demons, but the demon's price is high. And they don't do anything for nothing. The more you ask, the "purer" the sacrifice has to be. A child. Innocent. It has been going on since the days of Baal, where priests threw live babies into burning fires to appease their gods (Jeremiah 19:5). The only thing that has changed are the names—Baal, Satan, Moloch, whatever. It's a horrible and nightmare-inducing reality.

You'd Take a Bullet for Me?

It was late one fall evening when I received a phone call from a young man who was looking for help. He was reluctant to say much at first. He said he was staying at the Century City Hotel in Los Angeles with his mother and stepfather for a white-tux event. He was alone in his separate room when he found a Bible in the desk drawer. "I'd never seen one before," he told me. "I read a little and then saw a number in the front that said if you needed help, you could call this number. So, I called and told them a little bit about myself, and they referred me to a counseling person. That person couldn't help me, so they gave me another number, and it was an attorney who gave me *your* number," he explained. "I don't think you can help me, but I figured I'd call anyway."

I asked him a number of questions, wanting to make sure he was for real, mentally vetting his answers. The more he talked, the more my heart started to pound. This was for real. This boy was in trouble.

He said his name was Mike, and he was fourteen. He told me he was in a family that practiced the occult—even human sacrifice. He didn't think I would believe him. He definitely didn't think I could help him get out of his horrific situation. I believe I was his last hope. I listened to him talk for nearly an hour, trying to get as many details as I could, trying to form a mental game plan for how to help or extract a fourteen-year-old from a killer cult. "I gotta go," he said abruptly. "Maybe I'll call you again sometime." And the line went dead.

He wasn't playing around. This wasn't for attention. He was describing all sorts of things including rituals and settings that he just barely understood, except for the fact that it was all he had ever known. He gave me the name of his group. It wasn't something silly like "Satan's Little Worshippers" or "LaVey's Kids." It was a name that totally identified with the druidic nature of this group. He told me his father and grandfather had raised him in rituals. His father had died (been murdered, he told me) by the group, and now Mike was next in line. He was scared. He'd seen terrible things done to children, and he didn't want to be the next in line.

Every single thing he told me tracked with everything I knew about these groups and what they did.

He began to call me once or twice a week, usually for just a few minutes. Just to see if I had any way to help. Just to throw out an S.O.S.

After several weeks, he began the conversation with, "My real name is Lucas." I had gained his trust, and it both encouraged me and terrified me. What if I couldn't help him get out? I shared a great deal of my own history with him so he would know that I understood. I talked to him about Jesus. He was not opposed to listening, but he had no reference point to relate to Christianity. They worshipped a dark god. Jesus was different.

Lucas began to grow more panicked as he realized dates were approaching when he would undergo further initiations. He said they began to tattoo him as a child, starting with his ankle, and it would get added to with each initiation that took place, sometimes a year or two apart. He explained that the tattoo went all the way up to his upper back. It was about to be completed, at which point they would expect him to begin to step into the roles that his father previously had. It was like a demonic bar mitzvah.

He called one night in a complete panic. "You gotta help me, man, you gotta help me! I gotta recite my lineage tonight, and if I get it wrong, they're going to beat the hell out of me. Please, man, help me memorize this thing!" It was a surreal moment; I helped him remember his lineage as best I could. The recitation was elaborate and nothing a kid could make up.

He sounded so disoriented. "Did they give you anything?" I asked.

"No, I don't know. They took me and a couple of the other kids to town and gave us cookies and punch for lunch." I'd heard that before.

"Where are you Lucas, do you know?" I asked.

"Northern California, somewhere north of San Francisco, I don't know. It's got, like, a big iron gate with owls on it."

He was at the Bohemian Grove.

Every once in a while, in our work, we came across information that was so unreal and so unbelievable that we wanted to just dismiss it out of hand. Some of that information was concerning the Bohemian

Grove. It is a men's retreat camp in Northern California. It is owned and operated by the elites and hosts retreats that are attended by some of the most well-known politicians and world leaders—presidents, princes, kings, bankers, and other world rulers. They allegedly get together and have drunken weekends, and they discuss the big world chessboard and how things will play out in the world. At the end of these weekends, the participants attend a "play" conducted by a group of twelve men in black robes before a towering natural stone owl figure—the owl being their totem. They take a wicker effigy of a human and cremate it at the end of the play. They call this "The cremation of care." It is thoroughly druid. Two movies have been made about such rituals—one of which is called *The Wicker Man*. It is a fictional, though very clear depiction of real modern druid activity in the twentieth century. In the movie, the sacrifice was a human being burned alive in a huge wicker structure.

While a great deal of secrecy has been maintained by those running and attending the Bohemian Grove, I knew enough about it to be greatly alarmed when my young friend, Lucas, in a desperate moment, was telling me he was going to be initiated inside the gates of the Grove. Lucas had called me from a payphone at a convenience store but hung up before they took him and some other kids at the store back to the Grove. He had told their handler that he was going to call his mother.

It was weeks before I heard from him again, not knowing if he was alive or dead or simply too far in to be able to call.

His next phone call was very direct. "If I can tell you when and where they are going to have a ritual and sacrifice a baby, can you get the police or someone to stop it?"

"I can try," I said.

"No! Not good enough!" he argued. "Unless you can find some people and promise me one-hundred percent they will stop it, then I'm not going to tell you anything else. Sorry, I can't. Can you do something or not? It's just a couple of weeks away," he said with desperation.

"I'll do my best, I swear I will," I told him. We agreed on a call-back date and time.

It was crunch time, and all of my years of work in criminal justice, law enforcement, and other authorities were all going to be put on the line. Everything was crystallized in this moment. This was the moment of truth.

I began to make phone calls to California to any one I could think of. I had all the credentials and recommendations from people in authority from around the country to let them know that I was for real, this was for real, and we needed help to not only save a child, but hopefully Lucas too.

Not one police department or police officer would help. "Sorry, we don't have any cause to pursue it." "Occultism, devil worship, what? Never heard of this stuff around here, and we can't just go chasing rumors." And then the worst, the thing that enraged me and showed the extent of the damage the "satanic panic" movement had done: "That's all bunk," one sergeant told me. "It doesn't happen. It's not real. It's just village folklore."

I dreaded Lucas' phone call. "You didn't get anybody, did you?" Lucas said when I answered his call. I sighed.

"I'm so angry. I'm so sorry," I said with a heavy heart.

"Not your fault. I'm not trying to be disrespectful, but it looks like this time, our god won."

"It's not right that I couldn't get help," I said, almost in tears.

"Nothing you can do," he said sadly. "Kinda running out of time on things."

He said he was getting closer to the "final steps" for himself.

"You gotta tell someone, Lucas! Tell your mom; she doesn't know; tell her; she's got to help you!" His parents divorced when he was little, and they divided his time between parents enough so that Lucas could live in the two worlds without his mother suspecting much at all.

"You know what it's like, man!" he said in desperation. "You've been there! They said they'd kill my mom and my whole family if I ever said anything! You know why I can't tell!"

Yes, Lucas, especially since everyone would think it was just village folklore and laugh at you and dismiss you as an attention-getting teen. You're right, I thought to myself.

"Lucas, I swear, if I could stop them, I would. If I could get between you and them, I would. And I would do whatever I needed to do to get you out." Lucas went silent. Then I heard him sniffling, trying to hold back tears.

"You'd take a bullet for me?" he said.

"In a heartbeat," I said, through tears silently coming down my own face.

"Man, no one has ever stood up for me. No one's protected me before. Thanks, man. I wish you could."

There was little left to say as we came to an unexpected crossroad where two children who had been raised in darkness stood—one who was redeemed, one doomed without a miracle, as we were transfixed in a kind of timeless moment and realized the bond we had forged, as well as the hopelessness we both felt.

"I'll keep calling you every few weeks," he said. "Don't tell anyone about me, okay? It's kinda too late for me, but I'll try to keep calling. If something happens to me, and you don't hear from me after like a month or two, you can tell anyone you want. If I don't call, it's probably because I'm dead, or I'm too far in, and I can't ever get out, and I can't ever call again. But I'll try. Thanks, man, for trying."

"I'm here, Lucas," I said, sensing the sand in the hourglass about to run out.

That was over twenty-five years ago. I never heard from Lucas again. I choke up anytime I think about him or try to talk about him. He wasn't just a kid, some devil worshipping adolescent. He was a young life that was on the razor's edge and about to be fully plunged into a life of hell on Earth he did not want and could not escape from. He may yet be alive, though my heart tells me he probably didn't make it. I pray he reached out to Jesus if he knew the end was coming—and I believe he did. God did not connect us for nothing. I have to trust.

I know this is not a happy story; few of the stories in this book have been happy ones. But war doesn't have happy stories. And for believers, my prayer is that something of this true story will wake you up to pray for the many kids who, through demonic cults or human trafficking, are without hope, without Jesus. Please pray that God will send workers into this field, to rescue, to redeem, to repair, and to save them from slavery and death. *You* may not be able to go, but please help send those who can.

Lucas, wherever you are, if you are still out there, I would still take a bullet for you. And if you're not still walking this Earth, I pray you were redeemed by the One who took the ultimate bullet for you, who gave His life so you could be set free and spend eternity with Him. I remain, always, your brother and friend.

Rejoice not against me, O mine enemy: when
I fall, I shall arise; when I sit in darkness, the
Lord shall be a light unto me. (Micah 7:8)

24

Light in the Darkness

I t was early fall of 2012. My friend, Pastor Scott Hayes, had texted me about an upcoming event in the town of Spring, Texas where he pastored. "They are having the grand opening of the Luciferian Temple in downtown Spring the night before Halloween. Want to do a prayer walk?" I looked at the information he sent and texted him back.

"I want to do a whole lot more," I texted back. Within a few minutes, we had arranged a three-day event at Scott's church, which included training for the church on occult issues as well as my own testimony of deliverance from the occult world.

However, the central focus of our three-day ministry would be praying while walking around the neighborhood where the Luciferian Temple was having its grand opening. A handful of folks in the church had begun praying weeks before the grand opening. They just . . . prayed. No harassment. No accusations. Just asking God to intervene in the darkness.

I arrived in Spring, Texas the night before the Luciferian opening. I did a training on dealing with occult issues, and I gave my testimony about being delivered from the occult world. We met up with the prayer team and headed to downtown Spring. The team was fully prepped— pray, share Jesus, don't confront or attack people.

By that time, the grand opening of the Luciferian Temple had gained national media attention, and as expected, the media showed up in swarms. There were also a few committed Christians who were out to share the Gospel. Unfortunately, these events also attract disruptive, off-base, angry, and unloving religious people. One group stood across the street from the new temple, shouting angrily and carrying a five or six-foot statue of Mary on a platform. *Go home*, I thought. *You're not helping. You're giving the enemy fuel for the fire and a reason for people to laugh and mock those who say they are followers of Christ. You are doing nothing but underlining people's already distorted notions about Christians and Jesus Christ*, I thought to myself.

It was the night before Halloween, and the Luciferian Temple was having its "open house" where everyone was welcome. It broke my heart as I watched family after family taking their little kids into the Luciferian Temple, inadvertently exposing them to that darkness, thinking this was just a fun Halloween treat.

We had a team of about ten people with us. I had asked the team to try to keep the media away from me, as I had had 99 percent bad experiences with them over the years. But God apparently had other plans, as one of our team members told someone from a local news team that

Greg and Pastor Scott Hayes—2012

they should talk to me. I was able to explain that I came out of the dark occult world like the Luciferian Temple people were involved in and that we weren't angry; we were here because God loved them and wanted to bring them to Jesus Christ. Brief and on-point.

Despite the angry and not-unexpected demand from the occult Wiccan store owners across the street from the Luciferian Temple that we get off "their sidewalk," after about three hours, we went home without incident.

One of the church members texted me later, sending me the link to the news piece that the news stations did. They covered me accurately, which I was thankful for. But then they showed an interview with one of the Luciferian Temple leaders, explaining her beliefs. Then there was a brief flash—unmistakable—when something appeared in her eyes—something *other*—that looked out from inside her, and it was absolutely jarring. You'd have to see it to understand what a clear demonic manifestation it was. *Wow,* I thought to myself. *We really were on the battle line!* [1]

Some of the church team kept walking and praying for days and weeks after the event. No one expected that shortly thereafter the Luciferian Temple would close its doors, and the high priest would commit his life to Jesus!

It's been said that as believers, we've read the back of The Book, and we win. Watching God turn around the works of darkness, and sending them fleeing as He did in Spring, Texas, gave me courage and reassurance that the Lord is with us in this crucial battle with the power of the enemy.

Through the tender mercy of our God; whereby the dayspring from on high hath visited us, To give light to them that sit in darkness and in the shadow of death, to guide our feet into the way of peace. (Luke 1:78-79)

In 2023, The National Center for Missing &
Exploited Children received over 36 million
reports of child sexual exploitation with over 100
million files related to child sexual abuse.[1]

25

Now What?

Y
ou have read many difficult and painful stories in this book, but also redemptive ones, and Jesus Christ always remains Lord and God over all the forces of evil we encounter. I pray this book will help you understand that, truly, our battle is not with flesh and blood but with the demonic powers and principalities that are even now working furiously to paganize, demonize, and destroy generations.

In the end, we do what we can in the face of great evils, wars, human trafficking, occult crimes, crimes against children, and so much more. But ultimately, the answer is always Jesus. He is the only hope for a dying humanity that is headed not toward a glorious future but certain destruction in a world without God, a world that has made man his own god and whose breath is in his nostrils and will soon be gone.

The world needs Jesus Christ. He is the Hope, the Redeemer, the everlasting love, and healer, the only One who can truly save, set free, and make whole.

I know I have painted a very grim picture—one that is necessary in order to shatter the illusions and lies of the "false memory" crusaders and the cynical Christian skeptics. This wasn't intended to be a happy-halle-lujah book. This was intended to be a wake-up call.

I have spoken of both evil and redemption. As one writer said, "If you're out to tell the truth, leave elegance to the tailor." My lack of elegance in couching these things in softer terms is because they require sharp, unvarnished telling. Things as they are, as the great missionary Amy Carmichael said, not things as we wish they would be.

I know it's been hard to read. It's been hard to witness, believe me, and I've spared you of many details. But the point is, if it hurts this much to hear it, imagine how much it hurts the children, parents, and adult survivors who have endured these agonies.

And some didn't survive.

So—what do we do?

First and always—pray. Pray for all the children, our most precious future. Pray for the kids who need a real and strong relationship with the true Jesus Christ to save them from satanic snares, enticements, and death. Let us pray that God would deliver them and raise them up to be front-line warriors against the Evil One.

As God opens doors and opportunities, let us help them, guide and equip them.

How do we do that?

First, it's time to look around us and realize that the world and the devil are devouring the youth; decide to stop babysitting our kids in youth groups by giving them games, X-Boxes, entertainment, and a little Jesus snack at the end, thinking it's going to equip them to fight the evil outside of the church doors. It will not. Youth pastors need to take kids from the Romper Room to the Upper Room and teach them to pray, teach them to fight the good fight (1 Timothy 6:120), and teach them the Word of God.

Above all, let's love them, in whatever rebellious guise they come.

Pray for the victims. They have been disenfranchised from the church thanks to those claiming to be the "defenders of truth." Let the church be a refuge in the storm for those who have endured these monstrous things.

Pray for those who remain committed to the battle for lost souls who carry on the hope of saving just one child. Pray for the workers' protection, strength, and godly wisdom.

Second, as the Lord leads, let us help educate others about these issues, that others may understand the dangers and also the answers. Let us gird ourselves for battle and be willing to help victims find safety and assurance.

I am sounding an alarm, but I am not calling for hysteria. I'm calling for prayer and action.

If you peruse the bookshelves of the local Christian book store or online Christian book outlets, what do you find? Books on Christian self-help. Books on success stories. Comforting books on healing from dysfunctions and addictions. Lots of books on marriage, family, and relationships. But isn't it long past time we, as Christian believers, break out of our comfortable, "safe" world of church growth, successful tithing, and youth entertainment and lay down our lives so we can stand for truth?

Criminal devil worshippers fear little. They do not fear the law; they are stealth enemies that cover their tracks exceptionally well. They do not fear the courts. They do not fear the victims; after all, no one believes the victims anymore.

They aren't afraid of the church. Shouldn't that bother us?

The fact is, they will only take us seriously when we take our faith and the ensuing spiritual battle seriously: go after the kids, provide help to the victims, shut the door on the perpetrators, and pray that their network of pimps, predators, child traffickers, child pornographers, and devil worshippers will fail and be torn down.

Yes, it will cost. It may cost everything. It certainly cost Jesus everything. Why should we be exempt? And what value does God—what value do we—place on the life of a single child or youth? What if it were our own child? The God that calls us to defend the orphans and the innocent makes it very clear: They *are* our children.

I leave this book in your hands and the hands of God, knowing I have done the best I can to tell the truth. Perhaps some will question my agenda. I have none. "Then why tell it after all these years?" Because I was there. It was history untold. And now I have completed that telling.

This book has taken many years to complete. In its completion, I have closed the door on what was—and prayerfully have helped to prepare people for what may yet come. May God use this book to thrust a powerful sword to pierce the heart of the Destroyer of souls.

There *Is* a Way Out

If you are someone who is trapped in the dark world of the occult, Satanism, sexual abuse, or just know you are separated from God, there is good news! The Bible says:

> For God so loved the world, that he gave his only begotten Son, that whosoever believeth in him should not perish, but have everlasting life. (John 3:16)

There is no sin you have committed that God will not forgive you for, no hurt He cannot heal, no demonic bondage He cannot break. Jesus died on the Cross to save and deliver you out of the hand of the devil, evil, and sin, and bring you into His Kingdom of life, light, and eternal joy and peace.

The Scriptures tell us that "all have sinned, and come short of the glory of God" (Romans 3:23) and that "there is none righteous, no, not one" (Romans 3:10). Isaiah 53:6 says, "All we like sheep have gone astray; we have turned every one to his own way; and the LORD hath laid on him the iniquity of us all."

You can't save yourself. It's impossible, but with Christ, all things are possible. Jesus laid down His life so you could be forgiven and have eternal life. He can save you; that's for certain.

Becoming a Christian is the easiest thing in the world. It's so easy, most people just stumble right over it. And it won't cost you anything but your life. You don't have to earn it; you can't. It is a free gift.

> For the wages of sin is death; but the gift of God is eternal life through Jesus Christ our Lord. (Romans 6:23)

What do you have to do to receive it? To be set free and to be saved, it starts with acknowledging and repenting of your sin (repentance means to do a 180-degree turnaround), and believing on the Gospel (which is Jesus Christ's death on the Cross for all sin, His burial, and His resurrection (1 Corinthians 15:3-4).

When I became a believer, I was guided in a simple prayer:

> Jesus, I know I am a sinner. I know I can't save myself. Jesus, forgive me for my sins. Come into my heart and make me into a new person. I surrender my life to You. Make me into the person You want me to be. Amen.

If you have prayed a prayer like this, according to the Scriptures, you have been taken from the kingdom of darkness into the Kingdom of God.

> [I]f thou shalt confess with thy mouth the Lord Jesus, and shalt believe in thine heart that God hath raised him from the dead, thou shalt be saved. (Romans 10:9)

The battle ahead may not be easy because you have broken away from the kingdom of darkness—Satan's kingdom—and he doesn't like to lose. But don't worry—Jesus crushed the head of Satan while on the Cross, and He has given you authority to defeat him in every area of your life: "and having spoiled principalities and powers, he made a show of them openly triumphing over them in it" (Colossians 2:15).

Get a good Bible, and read it. It will feed your soul, equip you with the armor of God (Ephesians 6:11), and comfort you throughout all your remaining days on Earth. If you can, find a good Bible-believing church or fellowship where people will pray for you and support you. And learn to pray; Jesus Christ is the best friend you will ever have. Talk to the Lord; He loves to spend time with you. He will never leave you.

> Fear thou not; for I am with thee: be not dismayed; for I am thy God: I will strengthen thee; yea, I will help thee; yea, I will uphold thee with the right hand of my righteousness. (Isaiah 41:10)

Appendix: A Note About Deliverance— Rules of Engagement

The subject of "deliverance" is a hot-button topic for believers. What I write will no doubt fly in the face of the conventional thoughts regarding demons and deliverance. I do not have all the answers, but I want to pass on what I do know to those who may have ears to hear.

First, I want to make something very clear: I am *not* a "deliverance minister." Youthfire is *not* a "deliverance ministry," at least not in the way most people have come to think of that term. I have and do deal with occult matters. I have been involved in helping people with demonic oppression and sometimes possession. But I've also traveled to Indonesia, written books, painted a youth center, done evangelism, and even played Larry the Cucumber. (Do *not* call me for that job again!) I babysit a lot. But that doesn't mean I am a babysitter by calling. Sometimes I wonder if there is a connection there. You know how it is: Babysit a few times, you get on a list and people assume you are available to do this all the time. And if you do a few deliverances . . . the same thing can happen.

The reason I won't be tagged as a deliverance ministry is the reason I am very wary of deliverance ministries by and large. Praying for demonized or oppressed people is surely but only *one part* of a much bigger calling all believers in Christ should have. And once you are known for this, people will be sent to you or come to you in droves, and sometimes keep you from the full measure of ministry God wants you to do.

From that scenario, I have seen two things emerge: One, ministers get overwhelmed, caught up in the deliverance work and completely burn out. As one minister told me, "I never want to see another demonized person as long as I live." Two, many (though not all) of those who hang out a shingle advertising "deliverance ministry" have been some of the scariest people I've ever seen. If you mean by deliverance the overall healing and setting free of a person, I believe in that. If it is strictly a "demon business," I see no Scripture for that. I have seen the "fruit" of many of such ministries, and it is chaos, convoluted Scripture, and messed up lives. I think you understand why I don't want to be associated with that kind of ministry.

Is there a place for demonized people to get free? Absolutely, yes. It is in the church. Unfortunately, the high majority of believers are too terrified of the demonic to do their job; and thus, God has raised up those who are willing. It becomes specialized when it is something we should *all* be willing to handle if the need arises. " In my name shall they cast out devils" (Mark 16:17).

There are two situations in which I will engage the demonic: One, when a demon manifests. Two, when I have been made aware of a situation and have carefully prayed and gotten God's go-ahead to become involved.

I believe the first situation is the most frequent and the most biblical. Wherever Jesus went, demons manifested. They could not stand His presence. I truly believe if we are walking in the power of God as a church and individuals, this will happen, and we must deal with it when it does.

The second situation is crucial for me. I must know in advance, if someone is brought to my attention, if and when I should engage. I need to be prayed up; I need to be prepared and be sure. Many have been trapped because of getting a reputation for doing deliverance, and before long they are completely overwhelmed. You need to understand that not all demonized people want to be free. And if they do not, they will make the rounds of pastors and ministries, and their demons cause havoc.

Let me share, from my own experience over the years, a few essentials concerning deliverance.

We must set the rules and terms of "engagement." Sometimes people manifest in church. (Expect this to happen more as we approach a time of greater occult involvement in our culture.) We must determine by the Spirit whether to confront, deflect, or move the person into another part of the church to deal with it. A few years ago, I was confronted with such a situation. It was a large youth outreach at a church. I had just finished giving my testimony and was in the process of leading kids to know Jesus and dedicate their lives to His service when an ungodly scream came from the congregation and someone fell out of the pew in a demonic fit. Conventional wisdom—as well as "instinct"—would say to deal with it right there—but instead I felt the Lord urging me to have the elders take the person out and into the prayer room to pray for her. It was crucial, because a moment of eternal consequences was attempted to be sabotaged, and we could not allow it.

Sometimes demons are sent to be manifested to create fear, chaos, and confusion. Do not let them set the battle. Each situation is different and requires a well-discerned action.

I. Choose your team carefully.

Deliverance prayer is not a free-for-all. It's not a time for everyone to "give it a try." It is a time for order, discipline, and unity. Everyone on the team must come *cleansed*. Believe me, you don't want to carry any sin uncleansed into a deliverance. I have seen and heard too many deliverances where uncleansed private sins get very publicly detailed and exposed by demons who use it to fail the deliverance. But what is cleansed is untouchable. Make sure every team member is spiritually strong, humble, and ready for anything.

II. Maintain order.

One person alone should be the "point man." Everyone else should pray, support, and follow that person's lead. The worst situations I've seen are where there is no order at all and the person being prayed for is put through a round-robin of people all wanting to cast the demon out, or worse, everyone yelling at once. (Demons are not deaf. But they do love that kind of attention.) I don't care who leads, but if I am called to lead, everyone else *must* follow that lead and back me up. If someone else leads, it is my responsibility to pray, back him up, and only engage if called on to do so.

III. Stay focused.

It is not for us to dialogue with demons. Part of their strategy, because they are desperate to maintain their dwelling in the person, is to engage you in conversation. Do not fall for it. If you begin to speak to them, they will twist you, intrigue you, lie to you, and wear you out. Your *only* communication should be the steady and unbending demand for their expulsion. *Nothing else.*

Whatever you think you've learned from the last deliverance, put it on the back burner. This is a whole new situation. You are dealing with demons that are older than you can fathom. God has *not* required you to match wits with them. You are only to expel them, not with methods or what you learned before or from some book, but with the pure power of God alone. Make sure your team is not made up of people who have their own ideas based on books or "deliverance manuals." They will only cause division and chaos.

Recently, a well-meaning person who brought a woman with epilepsy cornered me to engage my help in casting demons out of her. I declined. He had already decided that epilepsy = possession. Such assumptions are dangerous and can result in terrible harm, and on rare occasions, even death. I cannot bide that. Not all epilepsy and sickness (by any means) are the result of possession. Multiple personality disorder is not the result of demons (though sometimes the person may be demonized.) Schizophrenia (healable by God) is not demons but a quantifiable medical brain condition. I have even met occultists who were saved and were not possessed! (They did, however, need deliverance from oppression and occult ties of the past.) I have also witnessed, for example, a good church-going lady who came to an outdoor rally I was speaking at, and she began to "preach" from Revelation right in the middle of my message—loudly, crazily, disrupting the whole evening—as demonized as anyone I've ever seen. We simply cannot afford to "assume" what we are dealing with. Assume *nothing* but that it is God's intention to deliver the demon bound and that we have been given the authority to do so. Perhaps terminology hangs us up too much. Demonization can be anything from oppressive headaches to full-blown takeover. Let's not get too hung up over words here.

Having read numerous "deliverance manuals" I can pretty confidently recommend that you don't bother with them. There *is* no "formula" deliverance.

IV. Know your authority.

You do not cast out the demons. It is Jesus Christ in you. They fear you not one whit. In fact, they could crush you without God's protection. Do not allow *one ounce* of arrogance, either in you or in your team when you walk into that room. Let it be only, "It is *Jesus* who commands you to leave. It is *His* Name, *His* Blood and *His* Power that demands that you leave." The minute you forget that it is only *His* authority they fear, you become like a uniformless, badge-less police officer in the middle of a gunfight trying to convince them to stop.

A few additional points:

- Do not fear either the devil or the demonic. Fear cuts those in need off from those who could set them free. It is the devil and demons who truly fear Jesus in *us*. Even a child who speaks the name of Jesus can make all Hell tremble and every demon flee.

- Do not become "interested" in knowing about the demonic realm. Pretty much most of what I have read is either useless, wrong, or dangerous—or all three. All you need in order to be able to accomplish the job is an intimate relationship with Jesus Christ, a solid knowledge of the Word of God, humility, and availability.

- *Do not* tackle a situation alone. Always work with a team, and have plenty of prayer covering besides.

- Treat deliverance as just one aspect of all Jesus has called us to do and to be.

There is little doubt that we are living in an age of unprecedented demonic influence, which is resulting in vast numbers of demonized people. Be ready for anything. And do not be afraid. This is part of the church's job, and we need to stop relegating it to a few because the majority are afraid and unprepared.

Encouraging Scriptures to Ponder

For God hath not given us the spirit of fear; but of power, and of love, and of a sound mind. (2 Timothy 1:7)

Therefore being justified by faith, we have peace with God through our Lord Jesus Christ. (Romans 5:1)

And Jesus came and spake unto them, saying, All power is given unto me in heaven and in earth. . . . Teaching them to observe all things whatsoever I have commanded you: and, lo, I am with you always, even unto the end of the world. Amen. (Matthew 28:18, 20)

According as his divine power hath given unto us all things that pertain unto life and godliness, through the knowledge of him that hath called us to glory and virtue: Whereby are given unto us exceeding great and precious promises: that by these ye might be partakers of the divine nature, having escaped the corruption that is in the world through lust. (2 Peter 1:3-4)

Ye are of God, little children, and have overcome them: because greater is he that is in you, than he that is in the world. (1 John 4:4)

For whatsoever is born of God overcometh the world: and this is the victory that overcometh the world, even our faith Who is he that overcometh the world, but he that believeth that Jesus is the Son of God? (1 John 5:4-5)

These shall make war with the Lamb, and the Lamb shall overcome them: for he is Lord of lords, and King of kings: and they that are with him are called, and chosen, and faithful. (Revelation 17:14)

Not by might, nor by power, but by my spirit, saith the Lord of hosts.(Zechariah 4:6)

Endnotes

Disclaimer

1. https://en.m.wikipedia.org/wiki/Ideological_bias_on_Wikipedia#:~:text=Sanger%20has%20cited%20a%20number,Joe%20Biden%20does%20not%20sufficiently.

Introduction

1. See chapter 19, under "Perspectives" for information about the McMartin case.

2. "Man Tells Court Sex With Boys Is Sacred Ritual" (Fox News for AP, August 4, 2006, updated January 13, 2015, https://www.foxnews.com/story/man-tells-court-sex-with-boys-is-sacred-ritual).

3. "Life Sentences Handed Down in Hosanna Church Case" (Associated Press, Jan. 18, 2008, https://www.religionnewsblog.com/22391/austin-bernard-hosanna-church).

4. Rick Nathanson, "Satanic Temple to Offer Abortion Services in New Mexico" (Feburary 6, 2023, https://www.abqjournal.com/news/local/article_6faf1580-0b5e-55db-a6b2-80a41e53841d.html).

Chapter 1: Preparing for War–1986

1. "State v. Distasio, 2007-Ohio-5454" (Court of Appeals, Ohio, https://www.supremecourt.ohio.gov/rod/docs/pdf/8/2007/2007-Ohio-5454.pdf).

2. Greg Reid's biography, *Nobody's Angel: A Story of Occult Bondage, Abuse and Redemption* (https://www.amazon.com/Nobodys-Angel-Occult-Bondage-Redemption/dp/B0875ZMQXW).

3. KVIA News, October, 1987.

Chapter 2: The History of Satanism and the Occult

1. Ray Yungen, *For Many Shall Come in My Name* (Roseburg, OR: Lighthouse Trails Publishing, 2nd ed. 2007), p. 180.

2. "Thule Society" (https://www.encyclopedia.com/science/encyclopedias-almanacs-transcripts-and-maps/thule-society).

3. "Lucis Trust" (https://en.m.wikipedia.org/wiki/Lucis_Trust).

4. Alice Bailey, *The Externalization of the Hierarchy* (New York, NY: Lucis Publishing, 1976), pp. 510, 514.

5. "Solve et Coagula: Part 1—Rowling's Alchemical Tattoo" (Mugglenet, May 23, 2020, https://www.mugglenet.com/2020/05/solve-et-coagula-part-1-rowlings-alchemical-tattoo).

6. "Root Races" (Theosophical Publishing House, Manila, https://www.theosophy.world/encyclopedia/root-races).

7. "The Disappearing Spoon Podcast" (Science History Institute, March 12, 2024, https://www.sciencehistory.org/stories/disappearing-pod/the-sex-cult-antichrist-who-rocketed-us-to-space-part-1/). Also see: https://occult-world.com/parsons-john-whitesides.

8. "Dianetics" (https://en.wikipedia.org/wiki/Dianetics).

9. Lawrence Wright, "Sympathy For the Devil" (*Rolling Stone* magazine, September 5, 1991, https://www.rollingstone.com/culture/culture-features/anton-levey-interview-1235074429). Also see: https://www.worldhistory.org/Walpurgis_Night.

10. See: https://forums.ledzeppelin.com/topic/11796-led-zeppelin-iii-do-what-thou-wilt.

11. William Ramsey, *Aleister Crowley: A Visual Study* (Occult Investigations, LLC; 1st edition, January 4, 2014), p. 100.

Chapter 3: Satanic and Occult Crimes

1. "Sacrificed on Spring Break: The Satanic Drug Cult Murder of Mark Kilroy" (Investigation Discovery, March 14, 2018, https://www.investiga-tiondiscovery.com/crimefeed/murder/sacrificed-on-spring-break--the-satanic-drug-cult-murder-of-mark).

2. Marcus Risen, "The Basin's Unsolved: Just a Normal Girl" (News West 9, June 6, 2023, https://www.newswest9.com/article/news/crime/the-ba-sins-unsolved/the-basins-unsolved-just-a-normal-girl/513-2ae40c30-c903-406d-a70a-792d4df9c052).

3. "Black Dahlia" (FBI, https://www.fbi.gov/history/famous-cases/the-black-dahlia).

4. A personal recall from the uncle of the victim.

5. "'Abhorrent': Harvard Manager Charged With Selling Human Body Parts, Including From Infants" (*Western Journal*, June 15, 2023, https://ijr.com/harvard-manager-charged-selling-human-body-parts).

6. Nolan Clay, "Slaughter's execution brings victims' family relief" (*The Oklahoman*, March 16, 2005, https://www.oklahoman.com/story/news/2005/03/16/slaughters-execution-brings-victims-family-re-lief/61950772007).

7. "Sacred Trees of the Celts and Druids" (Celtic Connection, https://wicca.com/celtic/sacred-trees.html).

8. Betsy McArthur, "Teacher Charged With Kidnapping" (*El Paso Times*, May 26, 1996).

9. Michael R. Sisak and Michael Balsamo, "New Details of Jeffrey Epstein's Death and the Frantic Aftermath Revealed in Records Obtained by AP" (June 1, 2023, https://apnews.com/article/jeffrey-epstein-jail-suicide-prison-death-8d194a756f2b429067f009a0c70f96c0).

10. "A Gift for the Prince, A Guide to Human Sacrifice" (Houston, TX: Vindex Press, Order of Nine Angles, 1994, http://www.satanism.50megs.com/library/prince.html).

11. See chapter one of Bob Kirkland's book, *Calvinism: None Dare Call It Heresy* to read about Calvin's involvement in over three dozen executions.

12. Read *Foxe's Book of Martyrs* to read about these papal persecutions and executions (some editions of Foxe's book have removed these; Lighthouse Trails has an edition that has not omitted them).

Chapter 4: Gathering the Facts

1. Rebekah Riess, "6 cows in Texas found dead and mutilated" (CNN, April 23, 2023, https://www.cnn.com/2023/04/23/us/texas-madison-county-cow-deaths/index.html).

Chapter 5: Media, Midland, and Two Talk Shows

1. "Dean Corll" (https://en.wikipedia.org/wiki/Dean_Corll).

2. From Philip Carlo, author of *Stolen Flower* on Best Talk in Town with Stephanie Edwards.

Chapter 6: The Devil Made Them Do It

1. Tom Strong, "Interest in Occult Transformed Teen Before Slaying Mother, Self" (AP News, January 12, 1988, https://web.archive.org/web/20210624201738/https://apnews.com/article/1b4b085e5578659714b3c1d204c0012d).

2. "When the Children Cry" Vito Bratta Mike Tramp, from the album, Pride, recorded by White Lion in 1987, Atlantic Records.

Chapter 10: Face to Face With the Enemy

1. Paul E. Vallely and Michael A. Aquino, "From PSYOP To Mind War: The Psychology of Victory By Colonel Paul E. Valley (Commander) With Major Michael A. Aquino (PSYOP Research & Analysis Team Leader)" (Headquarters, 7th Psychological Operations Group United States Army Reserve Presidio of San Francisco, California, 1980. https://archive.org/details/from-psyop-to-mind-war-the-psychology-of-victory).

2. Michael Aquino (November 8, XVII, https://ia601604.us.archive.org/16/items/LeftHandPath666/WewelsburgWorking.pdf).

3. Sister Beth Kimbrell, "Cakes of Light and the Buzz about Beeswing" Knights Templar Oasi, The Book of the Law III:23-25 (The Hermetic Library, https://hermetic.com/kimbell/essays/buzz-about-beeswing).

4. William Ramsey, *Aleister Crowley: A Visual Study*, op. cit., p. 100.

Chapter 11: The Enemy Within

1. Aleister Crowley, Book of the Law, 1:40.

Chapter 12: Bigger Hands at Work

1. File 18 Law Enforcement Intel Report, Fall 1989. On file with author.

2. From Wikipedia: "When she was questioned later, she added that she learned about occult techniques from her mistress in 'her own Country' (presumably Barbados), who taught her how to ward herself from evil powers and reveal the cause of witchcraft. Since such knowledge was not supposed to be harmful, Tituba again asserted to Parris that she was not a witch. Still, she admitted that she had participated in an occult ritual when she made the witch cake in an attempt to help Elizabeth Parris" (https://en.wikipedia.org/wiki/Tituba).

3. From Newsletter to Wiccan Community of Southern California by the High Priestess.

Chapter 13: Pinging the Web

1. Gordon Thomas, *Journey Into Madness: The True Story of Secret CIA Mind Control and Medical Abuse* (Bantam; First Edition, 1989), pp. 162-163.

2. David McGowan, *Programmed to Kill: The Politics of Serial Murder* (Lincoln, NE: iUniverse, 2004, https://ia802809.us.archive.org/17/items/FindersCult_201810/Finders%20Cult.pdf), chapter 6, "Finders Keepers."

3. World War II: Paperclip (Jewish Virtual Library, https://www.jewishvirtuallibrary.org/operation-paperclip).

4. *Franklin Cover-up*: https://www.amazon.com/Franklin-Cover-up-Satanism-Murder-Nebraska/dp/0963215809.

5. "'Havana Syndrome' Likely Caused by Directed Microwaves" (BBC, December 5, 2020, https://www.bbc.com/news/world-us-canada-55203844).

Chapter 14: Courts, Principals, and Principalities

1. Adriana M. Chávez , "2007: Mysterious Tunnels (*El Paso Times*, April 27, 2012, https://www.elpasotimes.com/story/news/history/blogs/tales-from-the-morgue/2012/04/27/2007-mysterious-tunnels/31509621).

Chapter 15: Some Don't Survive

1. Anton Szandor LeVey, *The Satanic Bible* (William Morrow Paperbacks, First Edition, 1969).

2. Ibid.

3. Ibid.

4. "The Devil Worshippers" (20/20, May 16, 1985, https://web.archive.org/web/20171206230821/https://www.youtube.com/watch?v=_UQuwxBgpAg).

5. Anton LaVey, "The Eleven Satanic Rules of the Earth" (1967, https://ia800607.us.archive.org/33/items/Satanism_201812/Anton%20LaVey%20-%20The%20Eleven%20Satanic%20Rules%20of%20the%20Earth.pdf), #11.

6. "Shane Stewart and Sally McNelly" (Unsolved Mysteries Wiki, https://unsolvedmysteries.fandom.com/wiki/Shane_Stewart_and_Sally_McNelly).

7. Robert and Gretchen Passantino, *When the Devil Dares Your Kids* (Eagle Publishing, 1992), p. 58.

8. Book review by Vicky Copeland (Cultwatch Response, Vol. 4 #1, 1992, http://smokyhole.org/wicca/cwr4-01.htm).

Chapter 16: A Tale of Two Towns

1. Terri Osborne, "Crime History: The Story of David Parker Ray, the 'Toy Box Killer'" (Investigation Discovery, September 30, 2016, https://www.investigationdiscovery.com/crimefeed/crime-history/crime-history-the-story-of-david-parker-ray-the-toy-box-killer).

Chapter 17: The *Real* "Satanic Panic" Story—Part 1

1. Malachi Martin, *Windswept House* (Broadway Books, a division of Random House, 1996), pp. 7-20.

2. "Proverbial Expressions" (https://sacred-texts.com/cla/bulf/bulf42.htm).

3. Info from debriefing a former Luciferian.

4. Katie Heaney, "The Memory War" (*The Cut,* January 6, 2021, https://www.thecut.com/article/false-memory-syndrome-controversy.html).

5. *Padika Magazine* (AKA: *The Journal of Paedophlia*) - June 1991; also see *Prosecuted but Not Silenced: Courtroom Reform for Sexually Abused Children,* written by Maralee McLean published by Morgan James Publishing in 2018. McLean discusses and quotes Underwager.

6. Ibid.

7. March 23, 1993, *Good Morning America.*

8. Shelby Leonard, "An Unquenchable Thirst" (*Baylor News,* October 25, 2013, https://baylorlariat.com/2013/10/25/an-unquenchable-thirst).

9. For more about Benjamin Rossen, see "Where Satan Goes Unseen" written by Beatrix Campbell in UK's Independent (https://www.independent.co.uk/voices/where-satan-goes-unseen-1433564.html).

Chapter 18: The *Real* "Satanic Panic" Story—Part 2

1. Mike Warnke's website: http://www.mikewarnke.org/about/faq.

2. Catherine Gould, P.hD, "Denying Ritual Abuse of Children" (S.MA.R.T., "Ritual Abuse Pages," from *The Journal of Psychohistory* 22 (3) 1995; posted with permission, https://ritualabuse.us/ritualabuse/articles/denying-ritual-abuse-of-children-catherine-gould/).

3. This was first-hand information given to me; the investigator was a personal friend of mine, and I cannot give more details in order to protect his identity.

Chapter 19: The *Real* "Satanic Panic" Story—Part 3

1. Harry Ironside, *The Epistle of Jude*, 1931.

2. "Teach us Your real secret, Master! How to become invisible, and oh! Beyond all, how to make gold, But how much gold will you give me for the secret of Infinite Riches? Then said the foremost and most foolish,: Master, it is nothing; but here is an hundred thousand pounds. This did I deign to accept, and whispered in his ear this secret, A Sucker is Born Every Minute": from Mike Hertenstein and Jon Trott's book, *Selling Satan* (Chicago, IL: Cornerstone Press, 1993), from the book's front matter.

3. Bob and Gretchen Passantino, Jon Stott, "Satan's Sideshow: The Real Story of Lauren Stratford" (http://www.logosresourcepages.org/Occult/lauren.htm).

4. Book review by Vicky Copeland, op. cit.

5. Mike Hertenstein, "Reality Is a Sometime Thing: A Strange Evening With Anton LaVey" (From *Selling Satan*, Cornerstone Press, Chicago, 1993), Appendix, p. 419.

6. "Lt Colonel Micheal Aquino on the *Oprah Winfrey Show* & His Involvement in the Church of Satan" (1988, https://rumble.com/v3a9tpr-1988-lt-colonel-micheal-aquino-on-the-oprah-winfrey-show-and-his-involvemen.html).

7. Lauren Stratford, *Stripped Naked* (Firebird Press; First Edition, 1993), pp. 9-10 (Preface).

8. She had contacted Lauren after years of being warned to have nothing to do with her as she was "dangerous." I spoke with her both before and after Lauren's passing to validate her testimony.

9. Letter on file.

10. Judith Reisman, from the endorsement pages of *Satan's Underground* (written by Johanna Michaelsen and Lauren Stratford, published first by Harvest House in 1988, then by Pelican Publishing company in 1991).

11. Walter Martin, "Satanism on the Rise" (Christian Research Institute, 1993; can read at: https://believersweb.org/Satanism-on-the-Rise).

12. Ibid.

13. Bob and Gretchen Passantino, "What About Halloween" (Christian Research Institute, 1995, https://xtianity.com/tfc/Halloween%20CRI.pdf).

14. Here is an example of this: https://johnwmorehead.blogspot.com/2006/07/imaginarium-cornerstone-and-days-of.html.

15. James Crawford Smith, "'The Crown': What Prince William Said About Controversial Diana Interviewer" (*Newsweek*, November 10, 2022, https://www.newsweek.com/crown-what-prince-william-said-controversial-diana-interviewer-martin-bashir-1757763).

16. See Ken's complete bio at: https://web.archive.org/web/20241109170520/https://childluresprevention.com/ken-wooden.

17. Endorsement by Ken Wooden inside Lauren's book, *Satan's Underground*.

18. Sarah Young, *Jesus Calling* (Nashville, TN: Thomas Nelson, 2004, 2011, 2016), Introduction, p. ix.

19. Ibid.

20. Ibid.

21. Read Warren B. Smith's book, *"Another Jesus" Calling: How Sarah Young's False Christ Is Deceiving the Church*. Available through Amazon or Lighthouse Trails Publishing.

22. *The Devil and the Deep Blue Sea* (*Christianity Today*, November 2024 to May 2025, https://www.christianitytoday.com/podcasts/devil-and-the-deep-blue-sea).

23. Robin D. Perrin And Les Parrott III, "Memories of Satanic Ritual Abuse (*Christianity Today*, June 21, 1993, https://www.christianitytoday.com/1993/06/memories-of-satanic-ritual-abuse).

Chapter 20: Occult Crimes and Sexual Abuse

1. B. Bradway, "Ritual Sexual Abuse" (Department of Justice Virtual Library, abstract at: https://www.ojp.gov/ncjrs/virtual-library/abstracts/ritual-sexual-abuse, originally from School Intervention Report, Volume: 7, Issue: 1, Fall 1993). May request full article by contacting DOJ; ask for item # NCJ 145785.

2. Adam Shaw, "Whistleblower Tells Congress That Govt Is Delivering Migrant Children to Human Traffickers" (*Fox News*, April 26, 2023, https://

www.foxnews.com/politics/whistleblower-tells-congress-that-govt-delivering-migrant-children-human-traffickers).

3. "Guyon Society" (https://en.wikipedia.org/wiki/Ren%C3%A9_Guyon_Society). See also: "A Pedophile's Pedigree," https://breakpoint.org/a-pedophiles-pedigree.

4. Xanthe Mallett, "Child sex abuse doesn't create paedophiles" (*The Conversation*, September 18, 2016, https://theconversation.com/child-sex-abuse-doesnt-create-paedophiles-60373).

5. Aleister Crowley, *Magick in Theory and Practice, XIII: Of the Banishings; and of the Purifications* (https://theonerds.net/aleister-crowley).

6. Richard Cavendish, *The Black Arts* (New York, NY: Penguin Group, 1967, Perigree Paperback edition, 1983 edition), p. 10.

7. "Solve et Coagula: Part 1—Rowling's Alchemical Tattoo," op. cit.

8. Katherine Donlevy, "Roman Polanski's Victim, Samantha Geimer, Claims Rape Was Never a Problem" (*New York Post,* April 16, 2023, https://nypost.com/2023/04/16/roman-polanskis-victim-samantha-geimer-claims-rape-was-never-a-problem).

9. Kate Arthur, "The Convicted Hollywood Pedophile Who Won't Go Away" (*Buzz Feed News*, October 27, 2017, https://www.buzzfeednews.com/article/kateaurthur/victor-salva-jeepers-creepers-pedophile). Also see an interview with Nathan Winters: https://www.youtube.com/watch?v=1M9ATFAYsEk.

10. "Disney Was Informant for the FBI" (*Tampa Bay Times*, May 7, 1993, https://www.tampabay.com/archive/1993/05/07/disney-was-informant-for-the-fbi).

11. *The Mountain Press,* October 25, 1995.

12. "Schwartzmiller Accused of Worst Child Molestation Case in History" (Creating Safer Havens, June 19, 2005, https://www.creatingsaferhavens.com/other-cases/schwartzmiller-accused-of-worst-child-molestation-case-in-history).

13. For more information on Lloyd Alexander, see https://www.homefacts.com/offender-detail/TX03221106/Lloyd-Gene-Alexander.html and https://www.casemine.com/judgement/us/5914ae28add7b04934746520.

Chapter 21: The Cries of the Children

1. Robin D. Perrin and Les Parrot III, "Memories of Satanic Ritual Abuse," op. cit.

2. "Defendant in McMartin Preschool Trials Is Acquitted" (History, November 13, 2009, https://www.history.com/this-day-in-history/January-18/the-mcmartin-preschool-trials).

The *Real* "Satanic Panic" Story

3. Three articles to read:
- "How do we know children rarely lie about abuse?" (https://www. stopitnow.org/advice-column-entry/how-do-we-know-children-rarely-lie-about-abuse.)
- "Myths/Facts Regarding Child Sexual Assault" (https://www.porter-countyin.gov/341/Myths-Facts-Regarding-Child-Sexual-Assau#:~:text-t=Children%20rarely%20lie%20about%20sexual,and%20what%20 fears%20are%20imagined).
- "Do Children Lie About Sexual Abuse? (https://cmsac.org/wp-content/uploads/2011/03/do-children-lie-about-sexual-abuse.pdf).

4. https://duckduckgo.com/?q=nembutal+ad&iar=images&i-ai=https%3A%2F%2Fconsumerist.com%2Fconsumermediallc.files. wordpress.com%2F2008%2F09%2F090908-004-nembutal494.jpg%253F-w%3D494%26h%3D674.

5. See: "Million Dollar Ride" (National Library of Medicine, May 2017, https://pmc.ncbi.nlm.nih.gov/articles/PMC5429053).

6. "McMartin Scientific Report" (https://ia802206.us.archive.org/6/items/the-gunderson-files/McMartin%20Scientific%20Report.pdf).

Chapter 23: Down in the Zero
1. Dave Quinn, "Corey Feldman Begs for Peers Who Witnessed Pedophilia in Hollywood to Come Forward" (*People* magazine, October 21, 2017, https://people.com/movies/corey-feldman-sexual-harrassment-abuses-in-hollywood).

2. https://www.jamaicaobserver.com/2013/07/31/not-too-ghoulish-gaga-singer-eats-fake-blood-off-womans-naked-body.

Chapter 24: A Light in the Darkness
1. October 30th, 2015, Fox News, Houston (https://web.archive.org/web/20151030221815/https://www.fox26houston.com/).

Chapter 25: Now What?
1. CyberTipline 2023 Report(https://www.missingkids.org/gethelpnow/cybertipline/cybertiplinedata).

Acknowledgements

It would take a small booklet to thank everyone who has been part of this book and the history of it. To Ben Kennedy, my friend and fellow worker in the difficult field of helping at-risk kids, who was there every step of the way. To Beth Stokes, who opened the door for me to be part of the pioneer Killeen Police Academy training and a lifelong friend: Thank you for believing in me to do a cop's work in a private investigator's outfit. To Chuck, Mary Jo, and Tony, the team I taught many conferences with and the best friends one could ask for. To Josh, who nixed the "puppies and pancakes" book until I finally finished this book after thirty-five years. (*Can I write it now?*) To Tim G., who shared many of these battles and remains a warrior for truth. To Randolph and Johanna, who held up my arms in battle and prayed me through every step of this agonizing book-writing process. To Tom Dunn, Steve and Darla, Warren and Joy, Angelo, Rick Howard, Tim S., Tim M., Lee, Gary and Judy, Greg Upke, and all those who knew me during the most challenging moments of these accounts and were there for me when I needed encouragement and prayer.

Detective Chuck Goode and his wife, Evelyn (both on left) still in the battle, standing with friends (the two on the right are Dr. Mary Jo Schneller and Calvary Chapel youth pastor Josh Munoz) at a human trafficking conference in 2024

The Color Pain

Boys Who Are Sexually Abused and the Men They Become

One in every six boys is sexually abused. That's just the ones who eventually tell their secret. *The Color of Pain* speaks to the professionals, pastors, and loved ones as well as to the boys and men who were abused. And who better to write a book like this than one of the victims who has lived the pain and later experienced the healing through Christ. *The Color of Pain* is a combination of some of the facts that most don't think about and some of the pain that most won't talk about. Available through major online book outlets (including Amazon and Barnes and Noble). Retail price: $10.95 | 114 pages.

Nobody's Angel

A Story of Satanic Abuse, Occult Bondage, and Redemption

The true story of former occult practitioner Gregory Reid. Born in Southern California, his childhood was a schizophrenic double life of wonderful, loving parents at home—and horrible satanic and sexual abuse outside of their care. Obsessed with the occult, victimized by pedophiles and on his way to crossing over to black magick, at the age of fifteen, he was pursued by Jesus through persistent encounters with Christians until one July night he ended up at a prayer meeting and surrendered his life to Jesus Christ. It was the beginning of new life, an end to the old, and the beginning of a decades-long search for answers to his tormented childhood. Available through Amazon and other online book outlets. Retail price: $13.50 | 103 pages.

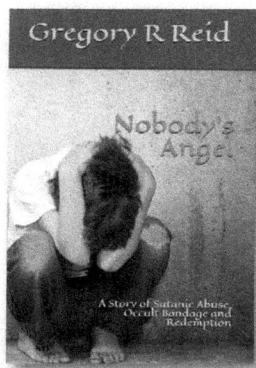

To order additional copies of:
The Real "Satanic Panic" Story
Send $15.00 per book plus shipping to:
YouthFire Publications
P.O. Box 307
Roseburg, Oregon 97470

Add the following for shipping costs,
($4.00/1-2 books; $6.00/3-5 books; $10.00/5-30 books)

You may also purchase the book from
amazon.com and other major online book outlets.

For bulk (wholesale) rates of 10 or more copies, contact: 866-876-3910.

You may contact the author at:

YouthFire Ministries
Box 370006
El Paso, TX. 79937

www.ingramcontent.com/pod-product-compliance
Lightning Source LLC
Chambersburg PA
CBHW072113270326
41931CB00010B/1543